George Matheson

The distinctive messages of the old religions

George Matheson

The distinctive messages of the old religions

ISBN/EAN: 9783337261511

Printed in Europe, USA, Canada, Australia, Japan

Cover: Foto ©Lupo / pixelio.de

More available books at **www.hansebooks.com**

THE
DISTINCTIVE MESSAGES OF THE OLD RELIGIONS

THE

DISTINCTIVE MESSAGES OF THE OLD RELIGIONS

BY THE

REV. GEORGE MATHESON
M.A., D.D., F.R.S.E.
MINISTER OF THE PARISH OF ST BERNARD'S, EDINBURGH

NEW YORK
ANSON D. F. RANDOLPH AND CO.
EDINBURGH AND LONDON
WILLIAM BLACKWOOD AND SONS
MDCCCXCIII

PREFACE.

I NEED not say that my design in this little book is not to describe the old religions, but to photograph their spirit. To describe any religion would require a volume twice the size of the present. But a photograph must be instantaneous or abortive. It is a generalised result; it only dates from the time when all the materials have been arranged in order. It does not *involve* work, it presupposes work. When you have completed the perusal of some elaborate encyclopædic article descriptive of a religious faith, the question which rises in the mind is this, Such being the facts, what then; what is its mental contribution to the life of the world? In our days this question has been dwarfed by another—the problem of development. In intellectual circles the whole inquiry has been how any one faith has passed into a different faith. Now,

I am a firm believer in development, and thoroughly alive to its value. But before a thing can *pass* it must *be*. It must originally have had a worth for itself alone and not for another. No object, no ideal, could have exercised for centuries a sway over thousands, which had no other cause than the contemplation of that final link by which it was to pass away. To the men of these centuries the power lay in the faith itself—in something which was not only potent but present. This I have called its distinctive message. By the distinctive message of a religion I mean, not an enumeration of its various points, but a selection of the one point in which it differs from all others. My design is therefore more limited than that of some volumes of equal size. I do not seek the permanent elements in religion with the Bishop of Ripon, nor the unconscious Christianity of Paganism with F. D. Maurice, nor the moral ideal of the nations with Miss Julia Wedgwood. I seek only to emphasise the dividing lines which constitute the boundary between each religion and all beside. In the concluding chapter I have tried to reunite these lines by finding a place for each in some part of the Christian message. I have given a sufficient number of references for a book which is not meant for a contribution to linguistic research, but simply as a mental study. This is not a matter in which the linguist has any advantage over the unprofessional, provided only that the details, so far as they are known, have become common property and are sufficient to warrant a conclusion. It is a doubt on this last point which has induced me to omit from the present generalisation the otherwise interesting religions of Assyria and Chaldea.

CONTENTS.

CHAP.		PAGE
I.	INTRODUCTION,	1
II.	THE COMMON ELEMENT IN RELIGIONS,	37
III.	THE MESSAGE OF CHINA,	61
IV.	THE MESSAGE OF INDIA,	93
V.	THE SUBJECT CONTINUED,	113
VI.	THE SUBJECT COMPLETED,	141
VII.	THE MESSAGE OF PERSIA,	162
VIII.	CONTINUATION,	178
IX.	THE MESSAGE OF GREECE,	193
X.	THE MESSAGE OF ROME,	215
XI.	THE SUBJECT CONTINUED,	231
XII.	THE MESSAGE OF THE TEUTON,	247
XIII.	THE MESSAGE OF EGYPT,	275
XIV.	THE MESSAGE OF JUDEA,	297
XV.	THE SUBJECT CONTINUED,	312
XVI.	CONCLUSION: CHRISTIANITY AND THE MESSAGES OF THE PAST,	327

THE DISTINCTIVE MESSAGES OF THE OLD RELIGIONS.

CHAPTER I.

INTRODUCTION.

THERE are two questions which are often confounded —What is the nature of religion? and, What is the origin of religion? We frequently hear it said that religion has its origin in certain feelings of the mind. We are told sometimes that it is the product of fear, sometimes that it is the fruit of superstition, sometimes that it originates in a sense of absolute dependence. However true such statements may be, they can in no case reach the root of the matter. They may tell us what religion is; they cannot tell us whence religion comes. If we should succeed in reducing the religious faculty to an experience of fear, or a feeling of primitive superstition, or a sense of absolute dependence, we shall not have gained one step in the solution of the great problem, whence and how. What we want to know is, how came this fear, whence arose this superstition, what wakened this sense of dependence? There is no reason why primitive man should have been more subject to these influences than cultured man; there is, *a priori*, every reason to the contrary. The experience of fear increases in proportion to the mind's development. The feeling of superstition, or presentiment of a violated law, demands that already in the heart of the man there should exist some knowledge of law. The sense of dependence is not a primitive instinct, but only reaches its flower when primitive instincts have been superseded. How comes it that these states of mind, which we should naturally expect to arise in the later stages of life, have found their crowning manifestation on the very threshold of human existence?

There is a question which I have often asked myself and which leads directly into the heart of this subject, What is the reason that in the primitive stages of life the individual man does not begin by deifying *himself?* He possesses a wonderful power of canonisation. There is scarcely an object in heaven or earth or the waters under the earth which he does not make divine. He deifies the stars; he deifies the hills; he deifies the rivers; he deifies even a block of wood and a piece of rag. His bestowal of divine honours is by no means regulated by the grandeur of the object. On the contrary, with the full perception of the visible universe, he begins by selecting for worship precisely those things which are not fitted to attract the eye, which, when they do attract the eye, are conspicuous by their want of beauty. These are facts patent and undeniable, but they are none the less suggestive, and they do not seem to me to have received adequate attention. For, the point to be considered is, that amidst this almost universal canonisation of the universe there is one object which the primitive man does not canonise—his own soul. He canonises the souls of others; he worships the spirits of his ancestors; but it never occurs to him to bow his head in reverence to that mysterious life which dwells within his own breast. Why is this? The life within him is the nearest object to him in all the universe, the only object in all the universe of which he has any real knowledge. One would naturally have expected that with the dawn of the tendency to worship, the earliest object of his adoration would have been precisely that mysterious life which manifested itself in contact with all other things, and without whose contact no other thing could be perceived. Why is it that the primitive man turns away from that which is nearest to him and bestows the gift of divinity originally upon those objects which are seemingly the most alien to his own nature—upon a petty piece of timber which his foot has accidentally struck, or a miserable bit of rag which has been lifted by the passing wind?

Now I believe it is possible to arrive at a solution of this question. If we want to know why the primitive man deifies everything but his own individual soul, we have only to ask whether he can discover in his own individual soul any imperfection which he cannot find in the objects around him. Is there any respect in which the things of surrounding nature seem to have an advantage over this individual life which beats within him? There is, I think, one. When the primitive man looks within himself, he becomes conscious of something of which he is not conscious when he looks at anything outside of him; he becomes aware of a limit to existence. In casting back his individual memory he is almost immediately arrested by a blank. He can retrace his steps some forty, fifty, or sixty years, and then he is stopped by a stone wall. There is a point beyond which he cannot go and at the back of which there is oblivion. In the recognition of that point and the oblivion beyond it the primitive man arrives for the first time at the definite conception of a beginning. He feels that there was a time when he was not, and that the existence of which he is now conscious has had a distinct origin. There must have been something to cause that origin. Two facts lie before him—the fact that he is now an individual being, and the fact that a few years ago he was individually nothing. Even to his primitive consciousness it is already clear that two such contrary states cannot have followed one another without the intervention of a third agency. If yesterday he was nothing and if to-day he is something, there must have intervened some mediating power to effect the transformation from the one state into the other. It is in the felt necessity for such a mediating power that the primitive man awakens for the first time to the conception of a cause in the universe.

It will be seen that the view I have here taken is essentially different from the view taken by Paley. Paley, as is well known, regards the primitive man as arriving at his notion of a universal cause by an observation of the objects of nature. He tells us that, if a savage found a watch, his immediate conclusion would be that there must have been a watchmaker. He intends to teach by analogy that, when the primitive man first beheld the mechanism of the universe, he would come at once to the inference that it must have had a creator. Now, of course we all understand that whenever an object is beheld as a piece of mechanism, it must at the same moment be beheld as requiring a maker. But the question is, Would either the watch or the universe or any part of the universe suggest to the primitive man the conception of a piece of mechanism? I believe that it would not. I believe that the primitive man would look upon all objects in movement in the same manner as a child looks upon all objects in movement. A child's delight in looking at a steam-boat lies precisely in the fact that to the child the steamboat is not a piece of mechanism, but an independent and self-acting agent, moved by its own power and impelled by its own will. A man has no such joy in the perception, just because a man has arrived at the notion that the appearance of self-agency is a delusion. The primitive man's first sight of nature is a sight which awakens wonder; but why does it awaken wonder? It is precisely because he seems to find in the universe something which he has found to be lacking in himself—*i.e.*, a principle of self-origination. He has arrived already at the conviction that he himself is not independent. He has reached that conviction by the blank in his own memory. He has found that his individual life has come into existence at a very recent date, and that therefore it must be dependent for its being on the existence of some other thing. What is that other thing? Where shall he seek it? Where can he seek it more naturally than in the objects which strike his eye? These objects arrest him in the first instance just by their seeming contrast to himself. He has arrived at the conviction that he is a poor, passive thing, that yesterday he was nothing, and that he owes the breath of to-day to the intervention of some other agency. When he opens his eyes upon the universe he sees in it a collection of objects which appear to be more privileged than himself. They do not suggest to him the notion of a beginning. They seem to stand out in contrast to his own limited existence. He finds that they have been already on the field before his coming and independently of his coming. Is it not natural that, instead of seeking an origin for them, he should seek in them an origin for himself? Is it not to be expected that, instead of saying "who made these?" he should begin by saying "have not these made *me*"? He has come to the universe not in search of a cause for the universe, but in search of a cause for the only limit he has hitherto found in nature—the limit to his own existence: is it not to be presumed that his earliest pursuit of such a cause will be amidst those objects of the material world which are not subject to the limits of his human consciousness?

I do not think, however, we are entitled to suppose that the primitive man will find in every object of the universe an equally probable source of his own origin. There is a fact to be accounted for in the history of religions—the fact that the earliest objects of worship are precisely those things which are not in themselves the grandest. We should have expected that the primitive man would have fixed his first reverence on the most exalted things. We should have thought that he would have looked up to the sun and moon and stars and yielded to them his earliest tribute of praise. On the contrary, his gaze is riveted to that which is not above his head but beneath his feet. Instead of looking up to the heavens he casts his eye downward upon the earth. He takes up the pebble from the beach, or the stone from the causeway, or the piece of cloth that has been wafted to his feet by the passing breeze, and he invests each or all of them with a magical power. Why is this? It is clearly an act performed in the full exercise of choice. It is not as if his senses had been originally defective and incapable of taking in distant objects. His perception of the heavenly bodies is as distinct and lucid as is his perception of the pebble or the piece of cloth. In selecting the one in preference to the other he is determined by some principle of judgment. What is that principle of judgment? Would we not expect that the sun and moon would present by their very activity more likeness to his own spiritual nature than would be seen in the sluggish inertness of the stone? Why, then, does he pass the former by and concentrate upon the latter his whole attention and his earliest reverence?

Now I take the reason to lie precisely in the fact that seems to constitute the ground for an opposite conclusion. I believe that the primitive man prefers the stone to the star just because he finds in the stone less likeness to himself than in the star. Remember the conclusion which he has reached with reference to his own spiritual nature. He has found it to be a poor, perishable thing, a thing which yesterday had no existence and which is dependent for its present life upon the agency of some other power. He comes to the sight of nature with a prejudice against himself. If he seeks in nature for a cause of himself, his hope to find it shall certainly rest in those objects which seem to him most foreign to his own being. What are those objects which seem most foreign to his own being? Clearly not the highest but the lowest things of the universe. The higher objects of nature exhibit to the eye the appearance of a continual change. The glory which the heavens declare is a perpetually shifting glory. The sun rises and sets, and even during the time of its abiding it reveals stages of fluctuating light. The stars which one moment are bright are in the next obscured by a passing cloud. In these appearances the primitive man beholds simply a repetition of his own image, and it is his own image which he wants to avoid. He wants to find some object in nature which shall not suggest the idea of a beginning. The higher objects of nature do suggest such an idea. They seem to rise and fall with circumstances. They convey to his mind the same sense of limitation which he has experienced in contemplating his own life. Where shall he meet with an opposite suggestion? Clearly he must seek it in the things of the lower sphere. When he turns from the star to the stone he seems to find all that he is in search of. Here is an object which, so far as he can observe, exhibits no fluctuation and is subject to no structural change. It does not rise or fall in its apparent magnitude; it does not vary in its intensity with the circling of the hours. It suggests to the mind of the beholder no beginning, no origination, no need of an outward cause. Its very inertness, its very passiveness, its very imperviousness to surrounding impressions, invest it with a semblance of eternity. Upon this, therefore, the eye of the primitive man fastens. It seems to him that he has found here the object best suited to meet and to explain his own sense of dependence. In the shifting feelings of his individual life he has reached the conclusion that his own being is short-lived. Here is an object which exhibits no shifting, which to all appearance is the same yesterday, to-day, and for ever. Is not this the eternal something which lies at the base of the other fleeting things? Is not this changeless substance the power on which depends the human spirits that are born and die, and the physical stars which rise and set? May he not rest here in his search for causes, and recognise in this abiding object the origin and the source of all things?

This I believe to be the explanation of the undoubted fact that the earliest manifestation of worship is what is called Fetichism—the worship of the lowest things. It is not denied that the primitive man seeks his first object of adoration not in the stars of heaven but in the fragments of wood and stone which he picks up from the earth. But in the view which I here have taken, I have departed essentially from the reason commonly assigned to this phenomenon. It is popularly said that the primitive man reverences the lower in preference to the higher objects because his own nature is as yet too lowly to be aspiring. He is supposed to be seeking things on a level with himself. To my mind, on the other hand, it is exactly the reverse. I believe that the primitive man in preferring the stone to the star is actuated by precisely the opposite desire. Instead of being attracted to the stone by its levelness with his own nature, he is drawn to it by its appearance of superiority to his own nature. He sees in it something which presents the aspect of a being above his own. He finds in his individual life the evidence of fluctuation and change; he finds in this inert piece of matter the evidence of steadfastness and immutability. Its very inertness marks it out to his mind not only from the world within but from the higher portion of the world without. Accordingly he gives it the pre-eminence. But in giving it the pre-eminence he is manifesting not the absence but the presence of aspiration. He comes to it not because his level is low, but because he is in search of a standard higher than himself, and one that shall be free from those limitations which he has found in his inmost nature. He has been taught to reverence above all things the attribute of longevity, eternity, everlastingness. He has been taught to reverence that attribute just because he has found it wanting in himself. He believes it to be wanting in himself by reason of the changes and fluctuations in his own thoughts and feelings. This belief is a delusion, but it is none the less present and strong. He flies for refuge to the things which seem free from change and not subject to fluctuation. He finds them not in the highest but in the lowliest forms, and he makes these forms his gods. He is unaware as yet that they owe the aspect of changelessness not to their perfection but to their imperfection, not to the presence of power but to the absence of life. His worship is based upon an erroneous premiss; yet it is the expression of an instinct that is true and real. The man has reached the knowledge of his individual nothingness, and he has made an honest attempt to pay some tribute to the source of his being.

I would not have it thought, however, that in

this attitude of the Fetich-worshipper we have reached any real recognition of the nature of religion. We have arrived at the *origin* of religion, but not at religion itself. Man has come to the knowledge of his own absolute dependence; but religion can only begin where absolute dependence ceases. The sense of individual nothingness has led him to the recognition of an outward cause; but what is to lead him into communion with that cause? Clearly it must be something above and beyond the feeling of absolute dependence, must in some sense be a counteraction of that feeling. Religion is not merely a getting; in its deepest essence it is a giving. It begins with the sense that it derives everything from another, but it must culminate in the persuasion that it has something to give back. It has its root in the feeling of dependence on the divine; it must reach its flower in the desire to rise to the divine. Before it can reach that flower the thing which has been first sown must die; the sense of absolute dependence must be broken. The primitive man can attain the knowledge of a first cause by the realising of his own nothingness, but he can only commune with that cause by arriving at the sense of liberty. Communion is a giving, and he who gives must feel himself to be free. The stage of passiveness must be superseded before religion can begin.

Now the defect of the Fetich-worshipper is his

state of passiveness. His sense of dependence is too absolute; before he can rise it must be broken. I am aware that I am here in direct contradiction to the popular view. The popular view regards the primitive man as having fallen into error by selecting an object of worship from things too far beneath him to be reverenced. Paradoxical as it may seem, I hold the error to lie in the opposite extreme. The object of worship selected by the primitive man is, to my mind, too far above him. The piece of wood or rag or stone to which he bows is a detrimental object of reverence precisely from the fact that it is reverenced by reason of its transcendentalism. He has chosen it because it is unlike himself, because it is removed from everything which his experience has ever realised. He recognises it as divine because it seems to be free from what he regards as the limits of the human spirit, because it reveals no spontaneity, no inward movement, no structural change. His earliest worship is directed to that which is most remote from his own humanity; his reverence for the divine is dictated by his repudiation of the human.

How, then, is this dream to be broken? How is the primitive man to be brought to the recognition of the truly religious life? There are two possible ways in which the delusion might be dispelled—either by the depression of the Fetich, or by the elevation of the spirit. If the Fetich-worshipper were permitted for a sufficiently long time to examine the object of his reverence, he would certainly come to see that it did not possess that attribute of changelessness in which he has clothed it. He would come to see that the pebble on the beach is as certain to be worn away as is the life of the individual soul. But it so happens that the Fetich-worshipper cannot get a sufficiently long time to make any such observation. The pebble on the beach will survive him, and, in spite of its constant diminution, it will during his earthly life never seem to get less. There is no hope, therefore, of breaking the illusion through the depression of the Fetich. But there is another and a higher method. What if, instead of depressing the Fetich, it were possible to raise the spirit? What if the primitive man could be brought to change his first conclusion? What if he should be led to alter his mind as to his own nothingness? He has fled to the Fetich as a refuge from that fleetingness and short-livedness which he has found within himself. What if he should find that after all he is not fleeting, not short-lived? He has arrived at his first notion by the discovery that his individual life had a beginning in the past; what if he should come to the discovery that a beginning in the past does not involve an end in the future? Would not the effect of such a revelation be to lift the spirit of the man out of its sense of dependence into a sense of exaltation, and to clothe with the attribute of divinity that which in days of yore had been the symbol of creature-life?

Now this is exactly what happens in the history of religion. The stage of Fetich-worship is broken not by the depression of the Fetich but by the elevation of the spirit, and the spirit is elevated by losing the sense of its own short-livedness. It loses its sense of short-livedness by reaching the conclusion that a beginning in the past does not involve an end in the future—in other words, by arriving at the conception of immortality. As long as the primitive man believes himself to be mortal, he worships the pebble and the rag. As long as he associates changefulness with death, he deifies that which appears to have no change. But if he should cease to associate changefulness with death, if he should come to believe that an object may be permanent which has yet a life free from monotony, the effect must inevitably be to withdraw his admiration from the things which he first worshipped, and to concentrate his thoughts upon a new and an opposite ideal.

The question, then, is, how is the primitive man to be brought to the belief that changefulness needs not be associated with fleetingness—in other words, how is he to arrive at the notion that the spirit of man, though it has a beginning in the past, may be without end in the future? Remember that the primitive man does not need to reach the *idea* of immortality; he has already reached that idea. Not only has he reached it, it has been the master-light of all his seeing. It would not be too much to say that it is the idea of immortality which has made the primitive man a Fetich-worshipper. We have seen in our previous analysis how he was first led to the search for a cause in nature by the recognition of his own individual nothingness. We have seen why he began by adoring the lowest and not the highest objects of the universe. We have seen that he invested with divinity the pebble in preference to the star, just because he fancied that he found in the pebble a greater permanence than in the star. But what does all this amount to? To nothing less than a search for immortality, a search for some principle in nature which shall prove an abiding principle. The idea of immortality, so far from being a superstructure in the religious temple, is itself the foundation-stone of that temple; it lies at the base of all worship and constitutes the condition of all faith. The idea of immortality is not only at the base of all religion; it is at the foundation of the human intellect itself. How has the Fetich-worshipper come to the conception of a cause? It is just by arriving at the notion that his own individual life has been too short-lived in the past to be *itself* a cause. He has been from the beginning impelled by the very sense of his nothingness to seek before all other things for an object in the universe which shall suggest abiding permanence, and he has come to the idea of causation because his earliest consciousness has been the conviction that the fleeting life of man depends on a life that is not fleeting.

It is not, then, the idea of immortality which the primitive man requires to reach. His error as a Fetich-worshipper does not lie in the absence of that idea. He has all along recognised the necessity for an immortal principle in nature; the mistake he has committed has been in finding that immortal principle in the wrong place. He has not sought it in the soul, but in the pebble, in the wood, in the rag. The transition which he has to pass through must be a transition not into the *idea* of immortality but into the *sphere* of immortality. He must learn to see in the soul what he has only seen in the pebble, the wood, the rag. He must lose his fear of the changeful. He must cease to believe that variety of experience is incompatible with continuance of existence. He must be brought to the conviction that the human spirit, with all the shiftings of its scenery, may be itself the most permanent thing in the universe, and that the changes in the life of man may themselves be prompted by the movement of a life which is the same yesterday, to-day, and for ever.

How is the primitive man to be brought to such

a conviction?—or rather, how has he *been* brought to it? The transition from the immortality of the Fetich to the immortality of the human soul became very soon an accomplished fact: if we find the first generation worshipping the piece of wood or stone, we find the second worshipping the spirits of their ancestors. What is it that has effected this transition? What is that experience in human life which has caused human life itself to assume an exalted position in the eyes of those who yesterday looked upon it as a debased and worthless thing? Mr Spencer would explain it by the phenomena of dreams; I think it would be more correct to say that it was produced by reflection on the waking *out of* dreams. It is quite true that to the primitive man the dead come back in the visions of the night, and, if none but the dead came back, it would be easy to see how he should mistake the visions for realities. But to the primitive man everything returns in sleep as well as the dead. The memory of the dead is not an isolated phenomenon of the hours of night; the whole past day comes back with all that ever was in it—its lights and its shadows, its suns and its systems, its men and its women. There is no account taken of the difference between the things which still exist and the things which in the interval have passed away; it is a *universal* memory. And this universality must even to the primitive mind deprive the memory of the dead of all significance. How can it have significance when it is only one phase of a vast landscape which has all equally and in every detail been reproduced by the hand of sleep? I cannot, therefore, accept the view that the memory of the dead in dreams had any large share in awakening the primitive mind to a sense or a hope of its own immortality. But I think that the phenomena of dreams do, from a totally different direction, suggest a solution of this difficult problem. It is not in the sphere of dreaming itself that I would look for an explanation, but in that other and more interesting phenomenon—the awakening out of dreams. When the primitive man reaches the stage of reflection, is not the study of this fact of all others best suited to raise him into the hope of his individual immortality? For, what *is* the fact that is here contemplated? It is the sensation of a continuous life which has preserved its continuity through a change of consciousness. I do not think that any other experience in the world is so fitted to convey to the primitive mind this impression—not even the experience of the awakening out of dreamless sleep. The awakening out of sleep would in itself suggest only a repetition of the first miracle, a repetition of that process by which the individual life was originally lifted out of nothingness. It could have no other effect than to impress the untutored mind with an additional and reiterated sense of its own impotence. But the transition from dreamland into waking consciousness is a very different thing. Here, the mind is itself an agent, an actor in its own changes. It is quite conscious that it has passed from one world into another world, and that in the course of that passage it has kept its continuity. It has been recipient of experiences not only varied but contrary, yet through all the contrariety it has remained the same. It has made a transition from one stage of existence into another and an entirely different stage of existence, and between them it can find no thread of connection. But it has awakened to the fact that it is itself the thread of connection. It has come to the consciousness that it has an identity quite independent of circumstances and quite irrespective of similar experiences. It has been taught the new and the desiderated truth that the individual life of man may keep an unbroken continuity amid the constant breaking of every outward association and amid the perpetual shifting of all extraneous things.

Now, when the primitive man arrives at this thought, he arrives at a new revelation. He learns for the first time to associate the idea of immortality with the life of an individual soul. Hitherto he has associated that idea only with things from which individuality is absent. He has given the palm for longevity to those objects of nature which display the greatest monotony, and therefore manifest the least individual power. But when there breaks upon him the reflection of what an individual soul really is, there comes inevitably a transference of his ideal. When he finds that the human spirit within him is capable of living in two totally different worlds and yet remaining the same, when he discovers that the life which he believed to be so fleeting is able to subsist in the midst of a transition the most complete and the most radical, the effect will assuredly be to invest that life in his imagination with the attribute of immortality. His human spirit will cease to be a poor contemptible thing by reason of its shifting scenery; that which was once its weakness shall be deemed its glory. The test of immortality shall be no longer the power of an object to remain unchanged: it will be the power of an object to abide in the presence of changes; and his own individual life, which has first manifested that power, shall receive his first association with the thought of everlasting being.

You will observe that when the primitive man has reached this stage he is no longer primitive. The detection of what is involved in the transition from dreamland into waking consciousness demands already that the man should have arrived at a period of reflection. Accordingly, I would place the recognition of the soul's immortality in the second and not in the first stage of the history of religion. As far back as the eye can reach, we are confronted by the spectacle of two forms of faith dwelling seemingly side by side—the worship of the inanimate Fetich, and the worship of departed souls. Yet, though seemingly side by side, it does not follow that they are really so. For, just as in the world of space things which in reality are far apart seem in the distance to be grouped close together, so, in the world of time, systems which appear to be contemporaneous forms of thought may be actually separated by many generations. The Fetich-worshipper and the worshipper of departed spirits cannot have had their origin in the same hour of the day. Both are in search of an immortal principle, yet they seek it by different roads and by roads which indicate a different plane of development. The Fetich-worshipper seeks the immortal principle amongst the things which are changeless and monotonous; the worshipper of departed spirits looks for it amidst the varied manifestations of life. The former is certainly the earlier, because it is the lower and inferior form. The latter could never have begun to be until the man began to think. Before he could reverence the spirits of the dead, he must begin to reverence the spirits of the living, must begin specially to reverence the only spirit which he directly knows—his own individual life. Why is it that he comes to invest the dead with a consciousness and a personality outside of the present world? It is because he himself has already become conscious of having lived in two worlds—the world called dreamland and the world called waking. When he becomes conscious of that fact in himself he transfers it to those around him, transfers it especially to the spirits of the departed. He says, "If two worlds are mine, may two worlds not also be theirs? If I have been able to keep my continuity through a transition so marked and so complete as that from dreamland into waking, may not those whom I call the dead have also preserved their continuity in a transition from the things of earth to the things beyond the earth." And when he has made this reflection the man changes the object of his reverence; he transfers it from the Fetich to the soul. He turns from the worship of bare matter to the worship of pure spirit. He had begun by reverencing nothing but the form; his tendency now is to reverence the spirit without the form. The souls of his ancestors are not originally conceived as clothed in an earthly garment. He thinks of them as shadowy, impalpable presences, for the most part invisible and inaudible, manifesting themselves through imperceptible avenues and influencing the mind by subtle agencies. The man in his first moment of reflection revolts entirely from the ideal of his primitive days. It would almost seem as if he designed to compensate the human soul for the dishonour he had done her. In his primitive age he had denied the divinity of spirit because he had found it subject to change; in his reflective age he denies the divinity of matter because he finds it unable to keep up with the changes of the spirit.

Have we now reached the completed idea of religion? No; there is one stage remaining to render it perfect. Hitherto the mind of man has vibrated between two extremes. The Fetich-worshipper has reverenced the body where it has least life; the worshipper of departed spirits has reverenced the life where it has least body. There is wanted something which shall unite the extremes. The reflective mind has revolted from the tendency of the primitive mind, but it has revolted too far. In its recoil from the inanimate wood and stone, it has deserted too much the clothing of the temporal form. The spirits of the departed before whom it bows are too ethereal, too shadowy. They are in want of flesh and blood to take away their vagueness; they wait for some earthly covering to invest them with the attributes of the human. Accordingly, there is wanted a principle of religion whereby that which has been unclothed shall be clothed upon. The bodily element is dead without the spirit, but the spirit is equally dead without the body. The stage of completed religion must be one in which there is recognised a union between body and soul, one in which the Fetich is lifted out of its meanness by being filled with the spirit of life, and in which the spirit of life is emancipated from its vagueness by being incorporated in the form of the fetich.

The whole subsequent history of religion is an accomplishment of this process — a narration of those steps by which the spiritual life finds increasingly its embodiment in outward things. Perhaps the first stage is the spiritualising of the Fetich itself. The man takes the piece of wood and the piece of stone and carves them into a human image. When he has done this we give him for the first time the name of idolater. And yet, nothing is more certain than that we have used the name in the wrong place and time. If it was applicable at all, it was to the earlier period. It is when the man reverences the unconscious Fetich believing it to be unconscious, that we ought really to call him an idolater. When he comes to form the Fetich into a likeness of himself, when he begins to carve the wood and stone into the image of the human, he has already in the deepest sense ceased to be an idolater. He is no more an idolater than the little girl is an idolater when she dresses and speaks to her doll; in fact the two cases are almost identical. The little girl speaks to her doll not *as* a doll but as something more. If she realised the fact that it was a doll, she could not speak to it. It is because she invests it with her own girlhood, with her own prospective womanhood, that she is alone able to make it an object of communion. So is it with the childhood of man. He begins to dress in his own likeness the forms which he sees around him, and then he proceeds to commune with the image he has made. But it is essential to the very existence of such an intercourse that he should have ceased to view these forms merely as what they are. It is essential that he should see them transfigured into his own likeness, lit up by his own intelligence, permeated by his own spirit. It is essential that he should think of them as responsive and capable of responding to the aspirations of his human heart through the possession of a kindred nature and the sharing of a common life.

I do not think, however, that the childhood of the human race can long continue to rest in the adoration of these lower forms. It seems to me that, when man has once arrived at the notion of the glorification of spirit, he will naturally be most attracted to those objects which require least transfiguration. We have seen how in the earliest age he was drawn to the lower rather than to the higher objects of nature from the fact that he found the latter too like himself. That fact will now have the exactly opposite tendency; it will attract instead of repelling. He has come to find that the capacity for change is not a mark of perishableness but of permanence. Accordingly, the things which he once avoided on account of their changefulness shall be precisely the things which he shall now most earnestly seek. The higher regions of nature shall be to him a more congenial sphere of worship than the monotonous materials from which he selected his Fetiches. He will go with most alacrity to the things most like himself, the things most allied to the movements of life. He will go to the sea, to the winds, to the rivers, to the stars,—to everything that exhibits motion and indicates continuance in change. His new Pantheon will be filled by the gods of the upper air, because in the gods of the upper air he shall find the objects nearest to his own being. He shall interpret their movements after the analogy of spirit, shall clothe them in the attributes of his human life, and shall reverence in them the vision of that profound mystery which he himself has found to be living within him.

It is a very barren subject of inquiry to ask whether at this stage of his religious history the man shall worship many gods or one. If I brought a company of children into a large room in which I had previously placed a variety of toys, what would be the effect of this variety? Would the children be attracted simultaneously to all, or would they fix their minds upon one and the same? Clearly, they would follow neither of these alternatives

They would neither be united in the admiration of the whole, nor would they be agreed in recognising the superior excellence of any single object; but each would fix his attention upon that particular thing which best suited his own ideal. One might be drawn to the image of a wooden horse, another to the imitation of a ship, a third to the similitude of a steam-engine. But the point for us to observe is that, whatever the object might be on which the attention of each child should be fastened, this object to that child would become, for the time, supreme. Whether it were horse or ship or steam-engine that first attracted its admiration, the object of attraction would, for the instant, be the only object in its universe. It would hold sway to the exclusion of all others. The period of its reign might be short-lived; it might last a few hours or it might expire in a few minutes; but during the time of its continuance it would rule alone and unrivalled. Every other form would vanish from the sphere of the child's observation. When it entered the room it would find many objects; but, the moment it had made its choice, it would see only one. It would regard the possessions of the other children with a species of contempt, and the other children themselves with a certain amount of pity. It would say of its own new-found idol, "There is none among the gods like unto thee."

Now all this is highly pertinent to the present

question. The children of the human race are exactly in the position of my hypothetical child. They are brought into a large room which has been already stored with a multitude of attractive things. These things are not equally attractive to all. Each child gravitates towards a different object—one to the sun, one to the moon, one to the stars, one to the rivers or winds or seas. But whatever the object of choice may be, it is, while it lasts, supreme. He who worships the winds worships them exclusively, sees in them the arbiters of all other things. It is another question altogether, how long that worship will last; the childhood of the race cannot, any more than the childhood of the individual, retain for a lengthened period one object in its admiration. To-morrow in all probability its allegiance will be transferred from the winds to the sun or to the river. The one point for us to observe is that during the time of its allegiance it recognises no other form but that which has first attracted it, admits into its worship no other object of adoration than that before which it has already bowed.

This is not Polytheism and it is not Monotheism; it is what Max Müller calls Henotheism.[1] It cannot be said to be either the recognition of many gods or the recognition of one; it is the recognition

---

[1] Lectures on the Origin and Growth of Religion as illustrated by the Religions of India, p. 285.

of one god at a time. The child-world does with
the objects of its religion what the child-life does
with the objects of its play — selects that which
suits it best, and keeps it until it is tired of it.
In this religious stage, therefore, there is an element
both of Polytheism and of Monotheism which is
yet different from either. I do not indeed think
it possible that Polytheism as an actual experience
ever existed. I do not believe that the human
mind at any stage of its being is really capable
of fixing its attention on more than one thing at
a time. I say *really;* apparently it is the reverse.
The transitions of human thought are so rapid, and
the combinations of human thought are so multiform,
that one is apt to be deceived. It often seems as
if the mind were contemplating two objects at
once, when in reality it is fixed upon a single object.
It is quite possible, for instance, to have in view
at one moment the different parts of a house. Yet
in this case the object of contemplation is really
one; the house constitutes a single image, and all
its different parts are comprehended at a glance as
things which make up this image. So is it, I
believe, with the systems called Polytheism. There
have been times when men have seemed to bow
down before a multitude of gods, and to recognise
the sovereignty of many heavenly rulers. Yet,
closely looked at, the rule of the many will be
found to melt into the government of the one

This so-called polytheism is in reality the recognition of one vast building—a house not made with hands, eternal in the heavens. The apparent diversity in the objects of worship is really nothing more than the diversity subsisting between the different parts of an earthly dwelling. Looked at singly, each part has a function of its own, and each part may be described in distinction from the others. But, viewed in connection with the whole, there is no plurality; there is in truth one structure and only one, and all the varieties in the formation of the separate angles are lost and overshadowed in the unity of the completed building.

I hold, then, that as a matter of fact Polytheism is impossible; that there never really existed or could exist a time in which the mind of man had its attention simultaneously fixed upon two objects of worship. The nearest approach to the worship of more gods than one is the stage called Henotheism, in which there is indeed recognised a plurality of heavenly objects, but in which the place of honour is occupied by each in turn. Even here, there is no real plurality. Each ruler may have a short reign, but, while it lasts, his reign is absolute. The attention of the worshipper is at no time fixed upon more than one god, and is at all times dominated by one. If now it be asked, What is that point of transition in which the one object of worship becomes a permanent object? I answer, it will be found at that stage in which the mind's attraction passes from a sensuous admiration into a principle of love. What is the difference between a child's devotion to its toy and a man's devotion to his friend; why is the one so much more short-lived than the other? The reason lies in the fact that the bond of attraction is in each case fastened to a different object. The child is attached to his toy through a cord that communicates with the eye; the man is attached to his friend through a bond that communicates with the heart. The transition from the many gods to the one God will be accomplished in that hour when a corresponding transition has been made from the attraction of the eye to the attraction of the mind. It is in my opinion a great mistake to imagine that man's sense of the divine unity was originally awakened by his sense of natural law. I believe that it came before the coming of science, before the knowledge of nature, before the perception of law. I believe that it was awakened not by the intellect but by the heart, not by the sense of material fixedness, but by the recognition within the soul of a permanent love. If the child's toy were adequate to the child's whole nature, the toy would hold over the child a perpetual sceptre. The reason why tomorrow it changes the object of to-day is the fact that the object of to-day is only sufficient for the

c

day; to-morrow the child's nature will be bigger and will need a larger toy. So is it in the world of religious history. The childhood of the race will have a new god each day as long as each god shall only suffice for each day. But whenever the race shall find an ideal whose attractiveness shall be coextensive with all the instincts of humanity, whenever it shall fix its heart upon a form whose beauty shall be unaffected by the changes in natural beauty, it shall at that moment enter into the recognition of an object of worship which shall not only be supreme but permanent in its duration.

It is, then, a barren question to inquire at what time the race of man passed from the recognition of the many gods into the recognition of the one. There was, I believe, no such time, no settled date at which the collective human species made a simultaneous transition from Henotheism into Monotheism. It depended entirely upon the progress of the individual mind. Those men who had received from their object of worship the deepest satisfaction of their nature would keep their object longest; those who had received from it the satisfaction of all their nature would keep their object *always*. In one community there might exist side by side the representatives both of the old faith and of the new —some who were still each day exchanging one image for another, and some who had fixed their hearts upon a foundation that could not be moved.

But while it is useless to seek a precise stage in history when the worship of the many passed into the worship of the one, there *is* a search for unity which is far more legitimate and far more satisfactory. Instead of trying to determine at what time the many gods were combined into the single Deity, it would be of infinitely more purpose to determine what made it possible at any time for such a combination to take place. Is it not transparent on the very surface that, if the many have become the one, it can only be because there is already within the many a principle of unity. When two are made one it is because the two are already harmonious: a true marriage has its beginning not in the tying of the nuptial cord, but in that unity of life which has existed implicitly in the lives of the separate individuals. Even so is it in the religions of the world. If to every race there has come a time when the worship of one God has supplanted the worship of many deities, it can only be because in the worship of these many deities there has existed from the beginning one common element, one underlying principle which has made them already a unity. The marriage is not the cause but the effect of their union, the last result and the outward expression of what has been all along latent within. What is this principle of union that exists already in the diversities of worship? It is a far more important question than the historical question of when Monotheism began to be. If Monotheism ever began to be, it was only by reason of a preceding and a pre-existent unity. Nay, if ever the time shall come when all men shall worship together one God, one faith, one baptism, it shall only be because in their separate faiths and in their separate baptisms there has been a connecting bond which has ensured their ultimate union. What is this bond; what is that common element which underlies religious diversity and makes it possible for religious diversity to pass away? The consideration of this subject demands a separate chapter.

CHAPTER II.

THE COMMON ELEMENT IN RELIGIONS.

THERE are few spectacles which have habitually appeared more sad than the variety of forms assumed by religious worship. To the eye of every missionary the number and the variations of human creeds have always seemed amongst the things most to be deplored in the world. The question is, Why? No man will say that the sight of variety is in itself more sad than the spectacle of monotony: every one must feel that it is the reverse. No one regards it as a blemish in the art of poetry that it embraces within its pale so many different forms of poetic thought. No one looks upon it as a blemish in the art of painting that it holds within its sceptre so many different ideals of the painter's power. Why should it be thought a blemish in the aspect of religion that it is found throughout the world in ever-varied shapes and in ever-changing garbs? In every other department of study the existence of variety is reckoned a triumph. Why should the sphere of religion be the only exception? Why should the multiplicity of religious beliefs and the diversity of religious schools be viewed by earnest minds as indications of the depravity of human nature and as signs of incipient development in the life of the soul?

Now I think it will be found that the reason of this difference lies in something deeper—lies, indeed, in the fact that religion is not habitually regarded either as a science or as an art. The scientific man seeks the presence of law beneath every form; the poetic man seeks the presence of beauty beneath every form; but the religious man tends originally to recognise only one form. Every nation looks upon its own mode of belief as an accidental privilege—something which has fallen from heaven as a special gift to itself. Accordingly, it feels constrained from the very outset to magnify that element in its faith which most separates it from other faiths. It not only glorifies the form—which is legitimate—but it feels bound to disparage every other form. It has received its own religion not by a law of human nature, but by a miracle which has set the law of human nature at defiance. It has been elevated above the worship of other lands as far as heaven is distant from the earth. The worship of other lands is therefore to it only a falsehood and a blasphemy. The variety in the religious opinions around it is a source of inexpressible sadness. Every divergence from its own form of faith is a divergence from the path of holiness. Its missionary zeal is prompted and inflamed by the sense of this surrounding destitution. It feels impelled to establish uniformity of worship, and to make itself the pattern of this uniformity. Yet even in its missionary efforts it does not hope to reach the hearts of men through a human channel. Its own faith has come to it by miracle; by miracle must it come to others also. The only chance for the establishment of religious unity lies through the suppression of humanity; for the human is the antithesis of the divine, and God is only reached by the annihilation of man.

Now, if this view be the true one, religion is the most unscientific, the most inartistic, the most inhuman thing in the world, and the longer the world lasts, the more unscientific and the more inhuman it must become. The tendency of all mental progress is to reduce phenomena under one law. Every advance of thought has in other departments been an advance in unity. If religion should elect to linger behind, its position must ultimately be one of absolute solitude. But *is* religion to linger behind? For some time back there have been signs of the contrary. In nothing has our age been more distinguished from previous ages than in the revolt from this first conception of the nature of faith. It is not in the loosening of its creeds and formulas that the nineteenth century is distinguished as a Broad-Church century. Creeds and formulas have been loosened before; the age of the Reformation was more pronouncedly an age of religious licence than ours. The peculiarity of the nineteenth century lies in this, that the loosening of its creeds and formulas is not a cause but an effect, not the inauguration of a movement but the result of a movement already inaugurated. It is not a negative but a positive tendency that has produced the liberalism of the nineteenth century. The minds of men have relaxed their interest in details only because they have found an interest in the existence of a general principle whose being was hitherto unsuspected. They have awakened to the recognition of the fact that in addition to *religions* there is a religion. They have come to believe that beneath the various forms there is something which is common, that, underlying the diversities of creed, there is already existing an element of unity. If reverence for the form has declined, it is only in order that there may be more room for the operation of the spirit. The movement towards the recognition of a common element in religion has been, strictly speaking, a purely modern one. It found its initial note in the latter half of last century. It was inaugurated by Lessing in his "education of the human race." It was taken up by Herder in his search for a common principle of universal evolution. It was carried on by those systems of German illuminism which during the first quarter of the nineteenth century made the field of speculation itself a region of romance. It was borne into our own country by the very increase of those mechanical appliances which are supposed to minister only to the outer man. The increased facilities for travel opened up lands which were before unknown, and in proportion as they became known, the points of difference between them and us were minimised. The spirit of liberalism in England has been exactly contemporaneous with her power of locomotion. It is popularly said that travel liberalises. The saying is true, but it is not true for the popularly given reason. It is not because the man of travel is brought into contact with many *diversities* that he becomes enlarged in his sympathies. It is rather because beneath these diversities he recognises for the first time a common bond of unity. It is because he wakens to the conviction that human nature is very much the same under all circumstances, and that, underlying the differences of customs and modes of life, there beats within the heart the same impulse and the same instinct. In short, it is because the man of travel arrives at a sense of the world's essential smallness, amid its wideness, that he ceases to believe in the exclusiveness of his own privilege or in the monopoly of his own creed.

Such has been the position of our country during the last half-century. It has obtained ever-increasingly a door of entrance into other lands, and the result has been to minimise its sense of their religious differences. It has found beneath these differences an underlying unity. Its search has been stimulated into a new direction. It has ceased to seek for the points of divergence between other faiths and its own; it has begun to study the points in which other faiths do not diverge from its own. It is trying to find in the sphere of religion what it has already found in every other sphere — an element of contact between separate forms. Just as it has discovered a principle of unity between the anatomy of the higher and the anatomy of the lower organisms, so it essays to find a principle of unity between the religion of the developed and the religion of the undeveloped races. If the effect of this tendency has been to abate the ardour of missionary enterprise, it has also been greatly to increase its facilities. The pioneers of a religion, the men who seek to carry their own form of faith into other lands, no longer need to depend on the influx of a force purely supernatural. They can henceforth be stimulated by the thought that in the minds of those whom they wish to proselytise there is already existing an element of concord with their own. They can be fortified by the knowledge that beneath all its diverse forms there is even now in operation one common religion, and that the diversities in the form are themselves only able to endure by reason of that principle of unity which abides ever the same.

What, then, is this principle of unity which underlies the different forms of religion? When we look on the surface of the surrounding faiths it almost seems as if there were no such bond. It cannot be said that there is any single doctrine of religion on which the worshippers of every creed are agreed. Even those beliefs which to modern development seem elementary have at no time commanded the simultaneous assent of the united world. The belief in a personal God has occupied little place in the religious philosophies of India. The doctrine of individual immortality has had no share in the development of Buddhism. The recognition of a moral government in the universe has been a comparatively late fact in the history of religion. If even in its most elementary aspects the study of human worship reveals little trace of unity, the diversities which it displays must be still more broadly marked when we pass from first principles to secondary details. On the whole, it may be fairly concluded, that wherever religious unity is to be found, it cannot be found in the acceptance of a common object of worship. It may be doubted if, even within the pale of any one religion, there is really recognised a common object of worship. We do not make an object common by giving it a single name. Millions of human beings are united in the recognition of Jesus Christ as the highest ideal in the universe; but it may be questioned if to any two individuals amongst them the ideal is exactly the same. The Christ of the middle ages is no more like the Christ of modern times than the Jupiter of ancient paganism is like the God of scientific evolution. A universally-sided character can never be universally seen in precisely the same light. The Christian claims for Christ such a character, and as the result of that claim he must be prepared to give up the hope of any unity which shall be based upon the sight of one outward form.

Is there any other direction in which we can look for religious unity? If we cannot find it in a common object of worship, is there any other region in which we may hope to discover it? There is; let us turn from the object of worship to the attitude of the worshipper. And to facilitate our search in this direction, let us take an analogous case, the case that of all others presents to my mind the nearest analogy—the sphere of the poet. No man will deny that there is in the world a thing called poetry. No man would ever dream of believing that the various specimens of rhythmic thought which meet the eye from all quarters constitute, each of them, a separate subject of study. We all feel that the points of separation between them are nothing in comparison to the point in which they are agreed. We feel, in short, that they are pervaded by one and the same spirit—a spirit of poetry. But if we ask what is this spirit of poetry, if we ask where lies the point of union which makes these separate verses the parts of a single science, the answer is not at first very easy. If we look on the surface here, we shall have very much the same experience which we had when looking on the surface of religion—a sense of diversity everywhere. Here also it may be said that the unity cannot lie in the subject-matter. It cannot be held that there is any one subject on which the attention of poets has been simultaneously concentrated. Every sphere of nature has been ransacked in search of materials for the poetic mind. The mountain and the valley, the grand and the commonplace, the strong and the gentle, the grave and the gay, have at one and the same moment been the theme of the sons of song. Nor can it be said that song itself has been the medium of union. Poetry needs not be rhyme, needs not be verse, needs not even be rhythm. Thomas Carlyle is the most unrhythmical of writers, communicates his thoughts in sentences that defy the possibility of scansion; yet Thomas Carlyle is worthy of a place amongst the greatest of the poets, worthy of a place amongst that band of poets whose form of diction has been specially rhythmical—the prophets of

Israel. In all these respects the idea of finding a point of union for poetic minds is shown to be abortive. And yet it remains true that, in spite of these variations of form, no one can fail to recognise that there *is* a point of union. Every one feels that there is a line of demarcation between poetry and prose, and that this line of demarcation is marked with equal distinctness whatever the form or the subject of the writing may be. What is this line of demarcation? What is it that enables a man instinctively and instantaneously to say of any composition, "This is poetry," "That is prose"? The feeling is patent to all; is it possible to translate the feeling into the terms of science?

I believe it is. I believe that it is possible to define in logical terms that line of boundary which separates the sphere of the poet from the sphere of the prose-writer. I think it will be found that the distinction between a poetic and a prosaic statement lies essentially in one principle—incarnation. The definition I would assign to poetry is the "incarnation of truth." The poet gives to every thought a body. He clothes one thing in the likeness of another thing. His mission is to find the analogies of nature. He is to the man of science what John the Baptist was to Christianity—a forerunner, a pioneer. If it is the province of the man of science to discover a common law, it is the province of the poet to discover a common likeness.

In every object of nature and in every thought of mind he sees, or dreams that he sees, the similarity to some other thing. He unclothes each form in order that he may clothe it anew, in order that he may behold it dressed in the similitude of something else. He gives to matter the garb of spirit, and to spirit the form of matter. If he looks upon the "gadding vine," he sees in its gadding the grief for Lycidas. If he beholds the dawning of the day, he interprets it as the rosy hand of morn unbarring the gates of light. If he hears a record of the miracle of Cana in Galilee, he explains the transformation after the analogy of life—

"The conscious water knew its Lord and blushed."

Not only does the poet clothe one object in the likeness of another; he clothes *himself* in the likeness of everything he depicts. Emerson says that if you want to paint a tree, it is not enough to describe the tree, you must *be* the tree. The poet must be everything of which his theme discourses; he must flow with the stream, bloom with the flower, glitter with the sunbeam, whisper with the zephyr, sparkle with the fountain. It is, in short, in the idea of incarnation that all poetry begins, continues, and ends. There may be the widest differences in subject, in form, in treatment, but in this one respect there must be a common soul. That which separates everywhere and always the poetic from the prosaic mind is the power to say, "Let the word be made flesh."

Now all this is not irrelevant; it has a strict bearing upon the question on which we are engaged. If there is any point where the secular blends with the sacred, it is in the sphere of the poet. Poetry and religion have always been regarded as the children of one family; whatever parentage be assigned to the one must be assigned to the other. I think it will be found that the community of origin is accompanied by a community of essence, and that what constitutes the poetic spirit amid all diversities of form is what constitutes the religious spirit amid all diversities of belief. In the religious world, as in the poetic world, the point of union between different schools is the idea of incarnation. The essence of religion is not the belief in a particular object of worship, but it is the belief that, whatever the object of worship may be, the worshipper himself is made in the image of that which he adores. This I believe to be the one element which lies at the root of all religion, which is common to all diversities of form, and indestructible by the suppression of these diversities. Everything else is but the body of worship; this is its soul. It is popularly thought that the old narrative of Genesis is peculiar in its doctrine that man is made in the image of God. This is a grand mistake. The Book of Genesis may be peculiar in the view which it has of God; it is not singular in holding that man is made in the image of God. No sacred writing, no religious ceremony, no theological dogma, no act of faith or prayer, could possibly be based upon any other foundation. The postulate of all religion, the condition preliminary to all worship, is the conviction that between the worshipped and the worshipper there exists from the very outset a bond of connection. You can only believe what you can conceive, and you can only conceive what is already in your nature. No man can figure in his imagination any object human or divine whose elements are not at the present moment within his own consciousness. The question is not between a God bearing our own image and a God bearing a different image; it is between a God bearing our own image and no God at all. There may be any amount of diversity in the superstructure, but the foundation is uniform. The religions of the earth constitute not a series of temples, but a single temple. The Father's house may have many mansions, but the house itself is one and indivisible. Every form of faith, every mode of worship, every approach of the human to the divine, rests upon one and the same foundation—the belief that the human is already in the image of the divine; other foundation than this can no man lay.

It is well to bear this in view, because it is one of the subjects on which there has been a great misconception. It is often thought that the belief in the identity of the human with the divine image is a belief which stamps the worshipper as belonging to a stage of primitive development. Accordingly, three forms of reverence have been proposed, each of which is regarded as a more developed mode of faith on the ground that it denies this identity. These three forms are — Deism, Pantheism, and Scientific Evolution. Each of these is supposed to mark a higher stage in the progress of thought, because each of them is supposed to emancipate the mind from the old doctrine that man is made in the image of God. Now, whether these be or be not higher stages of development I shall not here inquire; but one thing is certain, they are not higher on the ground alleged. Neither deism nor pantheism nor scientific evolution is really a departure from the old principle. They differ in their view of what constitutes the dominant Power in the universe; they are all based upon the belief that whatever that Power be, man is made in its image. The briefest possible examination will tend to make this clear.

Deism is the reaction against the idea of a God manifested in the flesh. It has had two great movements in history—the one in England, the other in India; the one directed against Christianity, the other against Brahmanism; the one rising in the eighteenth century and becoming extinguished in the flames of the French Revolution, the other originating in the nineteenth and continuing to the present day. But alike of the English and the Indian movements it must be said, that however true or however false they may be in themselves, they are both failures so far as their purpose is concerned. That purpose is to establish an object of worship upon a basis above the world, to unveil the statue of a God whose nature shall be free from all the limits of humanity. It is to present to the eyes of men the portrait of a Being dwelling not in tabernacles of clay but enthroned in the highest heavens — a Being omnipotent, omniscient, and eternal, full of all benevolence, rich in all wisdom, pervaded by all love. Yet, what is this conception but an incarnation, a God manifest in the flesh? It is the wildest delusion to imagine that a man escapes either Christianity or Brahmanism by running into deism. He has simply lifted his God on to a higher physical platform. The attributes which he reverences in the object of his worship are essentially human attributes; his God is still in his own image, though the image is placed in heaven. When you attribute to the object of your worship a sense of omnipotence, what else have you done than to assign Him a human limit? What is a sense of omnipotence but the consciousness that one has power to overcome any obstacle? When I say "I *can* do this," do I not express the fact that I feel a force within me which is capable of overcoming a force that I perceive without me? The very statement implies the idea of an effort on my part, and the idea of an effort is inseparable from the idea of a limit. To attribute to the object of your worship the power to say "I can," is to clothe your God in the likeness of a human environment. As long as you reverence that which is personal you can no more escape the idea of incarnation than you can escape your own shadow. It does not matter where you place the personality; you may lay it in the heavens above, or you may deposit it in the depths beneath. Assign it what locality you please, it is an incarnation still, and an incarnation equally. It is an incarnation because it is personal. It is a manifestation of the human not because it inhabits a human locality but because it is local anywhere. The moment I have said of my God, "Lo here," or "Lo there," I have given Him a special habitation, and the moment I have given Him a special habitation I have embodied Him in a material form. The effort of deism to transcend humanity has only ended in the old ideal of a God walking in the garden.

The second attempt to get rid of a God in the human image is Pantheism. It seeks to avoid the human image by imaging God everywhere. Instead of seeing Him in the likeness of a human form, it proposes to see Him in the aspect of the united universe. It looks upon Him not as a life circumscribed within a particular space, but as a life pervading all space and filling everything with its presence — an intelligence that sleeps in the plant, dreams in the animal, wakes in the man, vibrates in the wind, and throbs in the star. By this means pantheism hopes to emancipate the world from the original and primitive conception of a Ruler of the universe whose motives and whose attributes are analogous to the soul of man.

Yet a deeper reflection will convince us that this hope of the pantheist is also a dream. Remote as his conception seems from the idea of a God in the human image, it is really neither more nor less than a repetition of that thought in another form. Where does the pantheist get his conception of an all-pervading life? Is it not from the constitution of man himself? Has not man been called a microcosm of the universe? And why has man received this name? Is it not simply because he exhibits on a small scale the features of the collective whole? Man is a union of all the elements of the world. He unites within himself matter and spirit, personality and impersonality; the vegetable, the animal, and the rational. The idea of an all-pervading life is essentially a human conception, a conception derived from man's observation of his own inward nature. The existence which I call the soul is distinguished specially by this, that it seems to concentrate into a focus things which in space and time are vastly apart. It gathers into one picture stars and systems separated by millions of miles; it combines into one thought times and seasons between which ages roll. It is from this perception of unity in diversity that man has arrived at the notion of a life which shall include all other lives. It is because he feels within himself the influence of a power which makes the past present and the distant near, that he conceives in the universe the existence of an agency which shall be equally diffused through every form. The question is not whether this conception be or be not just; that is a matter for the apologist. The point for us to observe is that, whether it be true or false, the thought is distinctively human, derived from human nature and suggested by human analogy. Pantheism is no revolt from the primitive conception of the race. It is simply the reaffirmation, in a new form, of that ancient belief which from the beginning has regulated the rise of religions—the belief that man is made in the image of God.

The third attempt by which it has been sought to set aside the primitive conception is the modern doctrine of Scientific Evolution. It may seem strange that I should rank it amongst the systems of religion. But in truth it has been nearly always represented as a new form of reverence. The scientific evolutionist proposes to substitute the veneration of nature for the veneration of powers above nature, and he is quite willing to print "nature" with a capital letter. He is willing to recognise the fact that we are in the presence of a Force which is perfectly inscrutable, and to express his sense of its mystery by calling it the "Unknowable." All he insists on is the fact that it *is* unknowable, and therefore incapable of being imaged in a human form. He asks us to substitute the study of natural law for the study of things which are believed to be supernatural, and to occupy in the observation of physical phenomena that time which used to be spent in the investigation of unseen things.

Now we have no quarrel whatever with the printing of the word "nature" with a capital letter, nor do we see anything irreligious in transferring our veneration from the things which are unseen to the things which are visible. But we must point out here once more, that in putting the natural in the place of the human we have not, as we imagine, transcended the human. We are really on the lines of the same primitive conception which dictated the religious faith of our fathers. The transition from the belief in a Power above nature to the belief in a Power which is identical with nature may appear at first sight to be a revolt from the old conception of man in the image of God. But, in the light in which this view is presented by the doctrine of evolution, we get back everything which has been taken away. For, what is the doctrine of evolution? Is it not just the doctrine of the unity of species, just the belief that all things belong to one and the same order? If the scientific evolutionist removes the pre-eminence from man, he does not give the pre-eminence to anything else. His aim is rather a levelling up than a levelling down. He does not wish so much to deprive human nature of its dignity as to invest physical nature with the same dignity. He is not so eager to materialise spirit as to spiritualise matter. He does not seek to deny the presence of a life in man, but rather to establish the belief that the life which is present in man is present also in every object of creation. He says that matter itself has "the promise and potence of life." In that saying he has reaffirmed the old doctrine of the community of image between man and the Power which he serves. There is no longer a possibility of divergence. They both belong to one order; they are both identical in nature; they both follow one law of development. Extremes meet. The doctrine of evolution appears at first sight to be at the furthest remove from the old doctrine of man in the image of God; yet in reality it only affirms that belief in a new form. For the name "God" it substitutes the "Universe," but it invests this Universe with the attributes which men of old time applied to God. It invests it with the right to be venerated. It demands for it the self-surrender of the will. It claims for it the service of the hand and the obedience of the life; the alteration in its mode of worship lies chiefly in its change of name. But there is no change in its conception of the relation of man to the object of his veneration. If he was told by the men of old time that he was made in the image of God, he is told by the doctrine of evolution that he is made in the image of the Universe. He is asked to surrender himself to the latter on precisely the same ground on which he was asked to surrender himself to the former—the ground that he himself is in the likeness of that which he venerates. If he is required to submit himself to natural laws and to resign himself to the leading of nature, it is on the understanding that he himself is not only a product of these laws, but a part of that system of nature which demands the surrender of his will.

We arrive, then, at this conclusion: The common element in all religion is the idea of incarnation, the belief in the identity of nature between man and the object of his worship. The difference between one religion and another is a difference of ideal; but, the ideal once given, all religions unite in the belief that the worshipper has some point of analogy to that which he worships. It is not so much a doctrine of religion as a presupposition necessary to the very existence of religion. On the acceptance or the rejection of this belief depends the question whether man shall or shall not worship at all. All efforts at divine communion are based upon the recognition that there is a common ground on which the human can meet with the divine. It is the root of all prayer; it is the source of all sacrifice; it is the key to all devotion. Take this away, and you take away not any form of religion, but religion itself; not any article of faith, but the very possibility of faith. Communion with any being either in earth or heaven demands as a preliminary condition that there should exist between the communicants one element at least in common, one trait of identical experience. It is only on the ground of such an experience, and it is only so far as such an experience extends, that there can be any religion in the heart or any veneration in the life. Religious faith is the recognition of something above me, but I can only learn that it is above me through some phase of my nature on which I meet it as an equal.

If it be so, there follows one consideration which is of great interest to the missionary. It is of no use for the missionary to begin his crusade by vindicating the possibility of an incarnation: that is already common ground. When the disciple of Christ goes into India to conquer the disciple of Vishnu, he commonly begins by proclaiming the doctrine of a Word made flesh. He has no need to proclaim that doctrine; it has been proclaimed already. It lies at the root not only of the disciple of Vishnu's creed, but of all creeds. It is the basis of universal worship, and the ground on which all religions can already stand in brotherhood. The question between the disciple of Christ and the disciple of Vishnu is not whether the Word has been made flesh, but whether, after being made flesh, the Word is worth worshipping. The difference between Christ and Vishnu lies not in their incarnation but in their nature. If the worship of Vishnu presents a poor result in comparison with the worship of Christ, it is not because the one is in the flesh and the other out of it, but because the one is a rich and the other an empty ideal. The whole importance lies in the nature of that image after which man fashions himself. If the image be noble, the life will be noble; if the image be mean, the life will be mean. What the Christian missionary has to impart to other lands is not any doctrine about his ideal, but his ideal itself. India is narrower than Europe not by the absence of its belief in incarnation, but by the fact that it incarnates something whose nature is not enlarged. What we want beyond all other things in the modern missionary is the proclamation of a moral ideal, the setting up of an image which shall itself be noble and in whose likeness it shall be good to be made.

That is the reason why the preaching of the modern missionary should be above all things a moral preaching. His initial note must not be the Thirty-nine Articles but the Sermon on the Mount, not the insistence on a dogma but the revelation of a life. There are many who hold that the basis of Christianity is the belief in the doctrine of incarnation. So it is; but it is the basis not of Christianity alone, but of all religions and all possibilities of religion. What distinguishes Christianity is the largeness and the fulness of that which is incarnated; and the largeness and the fulness lie in its moral standard. In the holding up of that standard, in the presentation of that image in its unselfish majesty and its sacrificial power, the Christian missionary will attain his twofold object of revealing the distinctiveness of his own religion and preserving at the same time its brotherhood with other faiths.

CHAPTER III.

THE MESSAGE OF CHINA.

THE various attempts to trace the historical development of religions have for the most part been distinguished by the diversity of their starting-point. There has been no general agreement as to their order of precedence, as to which has gone before and which followed. No universal consent has established any religion in a position of superior antiquity. Each in turn has claimed the priority in time, and each in turn has found supporters and advocates of its claim. Some have placed China in the front as regards ancientness;[1] some have given the palm to India; some have bestowed the laurel on Persia; some have claimed the crown for Judea. My own opinion is that there are no facts to establish any

---

[1] There seems to be evidence for the statement that portions of Chinese territory were the seat of organised communities two thousand years before Christ. See Prichard's Researches, iv. 476-480; Gutzlaff, Chinese History, i. 75, English translation. Renouf makes China the oldest civilisation (Hibbert Lectures, 1879, p. 124).

of these claims, or, to speak more correctly, that there are equal facts for and against all of them. Every one of them has in it elements that point to a remote antiquity; every one of them has in it elements that indicate a comparatively late stage of the world's development. I believe that the relation of these religions to one another is not the relation between the steps of a ladder but the relation between the branches of a tree. They seem to me to be not successive but simultaneous, radiating at one moment from a single trunk. I have already indicated my conviction that the trunk itself *has* been produced by a process of historical sequence. I have pointed out in the introductory chapter what seem to me to be the successive steps of that development by which religion passed from a germ into an actual existence. But when religion has become an existence, there is no reason in the world why its progress should be only that of succession. No man holds that in the tree of human life the development of the plant must be completed before the development of the animal can begin. Is there any more reason for holding that in the tree of religious life two different phases of intellectual growth should not be contemporaneously existent? Is it not consistent with all analogy, that when once the common basis of religious life has been formed, the different branches of that life should break forth almost simultaneously, and should exhibit at one moment the graduated fruits of a higher and a lower culture?

Adopting, then, this standpoint, and waiving all questions of precedence, let us allow each branch to stand for itself. Instead of considering the place which one religion occupies in relation to another, let us try to find that feature in each religion which is distinctive, and that in each distinctive element which is of greatest significance. If by this course our work shall be less philosophical, it shall be less speculative and more on a level with experience. What we want to find is not a frame but a picture; not a theory into which we can get things to fit, but a portraiture of the things themselves. Let us look, then, at this branch of the religious tree which we call "China." The question for us is not, What is its nature? but, What is its distinctiveness? What is that which makes the branch "China" different from the branch "India" or "Persia" or "Egypt"? I may be reminded that this is a very wide question. I may be told that there are three distinct twigs in the branch "China," and that these are distinguished from each other by strong marks of opposition. It is quite true; but beneath the opposition there is something common to them all, something which makes each of them Chinese, and not Indian, Persian, or Egyptian. What is this distinctly national characteristic? It certainly does not lie in the branch itself. There is nothing peculiar in any

Chinese doctrine, nothing that may not be easily paralleled in the creeds of other lands. What, then, is that element which has given to the religion of China an aspect almost special, and has impressed upon its features the mark of something approaching very near to originality?

To resume the metaphor, let us look at the branch again. As we have said, there is nothing peculiar in its nature; but is there nothing peculiar in its attitude? Yes; if we examine it carefully we shall find that it differs from the surrounding branches in its direction. All the surrounding branches shoot forwards; the Chinese branch is bent backwards towards the tree. The peculiarity of this religion in all its forms is one and the same—its regressiveness. It would not be correct to say that it is a religion without desire, but, in the strict sense of the word, it is a religion without aspiration. The bird that sits on this branch is not tuneless, but it is wingless; it does not want song, but it wants the power of upward flight. The religions of surrounding nations are all movements towards the future; they seek rest by the wings of a dove that can lift them beyond the seen and temporal. The religion of China is also in search of rest, but it seeks it in the opposite quarter. It sees the home of its spirit not in the future but in the past; not in the attempt to fly away from the seen and temporal, but in the effort to reach the origin of the seen and temporal.

Its hope to find rest lies not in looking up to the heights of heaven, but in contemplating and in seeking the foundations of the earth.[1]

I have said that this description applies to the whole of China. I wish to emphasise the fact, because there is a popular notion that this nation exhibits rather a conflict of religions than one uniform faith. It is true that it does exhibit a conflict of religions, but my contention is that in spite of their diversity they are united by one common element which makes them distinctively Chinese. That common element is regressiveness; in all of them the branch is bent backwards. The truth of this will appear if we glance for a moment at the different forms of Chinese faith. I wish to avoid all technical language and to present above all things a lucid exposition. Accordingly, while I shall make use of only the old facts, I shall try to put them rather in an English than in a Chinese dress. I shall say, then, that, excluding the form of faith called Chinese Buddhism, which is not a native growth of the country, there remain three religious parties in China. The first and the furthest back are the worshippers of the ancestral dead, those who keep their reverence for the spirits of the departed. We have seen in the introductory chapter

---

[1] The whole character of the Chinese mind is in keeping with this tendency, being essentially prosaic. See Pauthier, Chine, p. 43: Paris, 1839.

that this form of belief is one of the earliest in the history of religions; and the fact that from the very beginning it has prevailed in China would seem to favour the notion of that nation's antiquity. It would do so, if there were no other explanation. But there is another explanation, and one which lies nearer to the door. Out of the multitude of possible objects of worship, why should the Chinaman have selected this? In the presence of sun and moon and stars, in the vicinity of mountains and lakes and rivers, in the contact with living kings and existing mighty men, why should he from the outset have fixed his veneration upon something which is neither visible nor present, but departed? It cannot be his reverence for things beyond the earth, for he does not reverence things beyond the earth. The very fact that he has fixed his mind not on celestial spirits but on the spirits of the departed dead, is significant; it shows that in some form his veneration must be connected with the earth. Why, then, with so many earthly things around him, has he put them all aside in order to bestow his reverence on something which is unseen, unheard, impalpable, incognisable by any human sense or through any worldly channel? Does not the reason lie in the nature of the Chinese mind itself? Is it not clear that to the Chinaman the spirits of the past are more venerated than the spirits of the present precisely because his own constitutional tendency is ever towards the past? We see individual minds of this nature; why not individual nations? The Chinaman's mental constitution is not the effect of his worship; his worship is the effect of his mental constitution. He reverences his ancestors more than his descendants because his mind is by nature retrospective and regressive. The branch of the religious tree is bent backwards because the heart of the man is bent backwards. I do not believe that to the educated Chinese the worship of ancestors is anything more than a commemorative anniversary, the observance of a festival of gratitude to the memory of the good and great who have passed away. But even as such, it is characteristic, significant of the national intellect. It shows that even in the earliest times, in that age of childhood in which a nation like an individual is generally prompted to press forward, the mind of the Chinaman was true to its future self, and, in strict accordance with its whole subsequent destiny, preferred the yesterday that was gone to the morrow that was coming.

The second form of religious reverence in China is the faith which was revived by Confucius, and which bears the name of its reviver. Put roundly, and expressed in English characters, the doctrine of Confucius may be said to be, the search for an ideal heaven through the rediscovery of a primitive earth.[1]

[1] Confucius himself declares that he cites the patterns left us by the ancients. See Pauthier, Chine, p. 134.

He proposes to lead men to a conception of the heavenly state by leading them back, by causing them to retrace their steps over the road by which they have travelled. The whole gist and marrow of the doctrine is regressiveness. The Chinaman looks out upon the existing aspect of society and he contemplates it with dissatisfaction. He has no hope whatever that his dissatisfaction will be removed by the advance of time; it is to the advance of time that he traces the corruption. Every increase of civilisation, every development of culture, every progress in the arts of life, presents to his mind the aspect of a decline. His perpetual cry is the prayer of the Jewish king, "Let the shadow go back ten degrees." It seems to him that what society wants to make it perfect is a process of divestiture. If man would see in earth a miniature of heaven, he must strip the earth of its adventitious ornaments. He must go back to a time when men dwelt in primitive simplicity. He must make a retrograde movement towards the dawn of civilisation, for in its dawn lies its glory. He must seek those beginnings of life in which communities were united not by the laws of the state but by the instincts of the life, not by bonds from without but by obligations from within. He proposes to revive the patriarchal age—to restore the glories of the family, to build the state in its image and to see God in that image. The father is to become again at once the king and the priest of the household;[1] he is to rule over all and he is to sacrifice for all. Wife and child and domestic servant are alike to be subject to his will; but he in turn is to be subject to their need. Sarah may protest if Abraham should desert her; Jacob may run away if Isaac should forget his fatherhood. It is to be a society founded on reciprocal rights. Ancestral seniority is to confer the right of rule, but juniority is to confer the right of being protected. If the father as sovereign is to wield the highest sceptre, as sovereign also he is to bear the weightiest burden. He is not merely to be the priest for himself but for his household. Every sin of any member of the family is to be the father's sin; *he* is to bear the burden, he is to meet the penalty, he is to offer the sacrifice; his responsibility is to be proportionate to his power.

Such is the ideal of family life which the follower of Confucius proposes to revive. And when he has revived it, his work is only half done; he has to build into its likeness the fabric of the body politic. He has to construct a state which shall be modelled after the similitude of the household, to rear an empire which shall be fashioned after the image of the family. Here again, as in the life of the family, the summit of power is the summit of sacrifice.

[1] Ever since the patriarchal period of China these two offices have been actually united in the Emperor. See Gutzlaff, Chinese History, i. 142, 143.

The emperor is the head of the state, and as such he has almost absolute control, but he is only the *king* because he is the *father* of his people. If he is the greatest man in the state, he is also the most burdened—strictly speaking, the only burdened man. If a sacrifice has to be presented to heaven, it is the emperor alone who presents it. It is not that the emperor alone is allowed to have his sins forgiven; it is rather that all sins are sins of the emperor. He alone is the sacrificer because only *he* has been the transgressor. The individual units of the nation are but the members of the imperial life,[1] and the imperial life is answerable for the multitude of individual sins. Such is the Confucian ideal of a kingdom—an ideal never realised, never attempted to be realised in practice, yet existing as an object of imaginary memory. And to crown the whole, the ideal of the kingdom of earth is to the mind of the Chinaman the ideal also of the kingdom of heaven. Other religions have looked forward to their millennium as something which is to be consummated in the golden future; to the follower of Confucius it is something which was realised in the remotest past. To find it he is not required to press forward but to look backward, not to seek the set-

[1] The emperor himself, viewed as an individual unit or private person, is of no more account than his people; he gets his value purely from his official character. Many emperors have in private not belonged to the school of Confucius. See article in 'Nouveau Journal Asiatique' (1854), iv. 292 *sq*.

ting but the rising sun. The kingdom of heaven has to him its ideal not in the advance of human development but in the original constitution of the most primitive human society. The Jew has his Garden of Eden, but it fades from his sight in the vision of a coming and a higher glory; the Chinaman has nothing to counterpoise the vision of his Eden, and he sees no glory but that which is passed away.

I shall point out in the sequel wherein consists at once the truth and the fallacy of this Confucian view, and shall endeavour to indicate the reason why a really high theory has proved utterly ineffectual to furnish to this people a source of aspiration. But in the meantime let me briefly pass to the one remaining party amongst the original beliefs of China. We have seen how in the worship of the ancestral dead the nation reverted to a memory instead of a hope. We have seen how in the idealising of a primitive society the Chinese mind again sought its anchor on the receding rather than on the approaching shore. We are now in the final phase to see another and yet a different form of the same tendency. The final phase is that strange creed which, at a period almost contemporary with Confucius, found its exponent in the mystic Lâotze.[1] And here once more regression is the order

[1] The system is called Tâoism, from a word *Tao*, whose etymology is uncertain, but which seems to indicate the surrender

of the day. If the ancestral worshipper proposed for imitation the men of a previous age, if the follower of Confucius sought his model in the imagination of a primitive society, the disciple of Lâo-tze virtually went further back still. He proposed in effect that man should retrace his steps into the life of the plant. He does not use the simile, but he clearly expresses the thought. He looks upon modern society—the society of his own age—as a departure from primitive simplicity. What makes it a departure from primitive simplicity is the accumulated product of human consciousness. Man has become too reflective, too calculating, too aiming. He has set himself against the stream of nature, and has tried to alter the course of that stream. Everything in the world but himself yields itself up to the order of nature. Man alone resists its order, and therefore man alone is unhappy. If he would cease to be unhappy, let him become what other things are—unconscious.[1] Let him yield himself again to that fixed order of nature which he is powerless to change. Let him go back to the life of the vegetable, which lives without knowing that it lives, and grows without considering its growth.

to a fixed order. For some definitions of the word, see Professor Douglas, 'Confucianism and Tâoism,' p. 189; also Watters, 'Lâo-tze, a Study in Chinese Philosophy,' p. 45.

[1] The admiration of the principle of unconsciousness in the system of Lâo-tze will be found expressed in 'Tao-te-King,' Julien's edition, Introduction, p. xiii.

Let him become spontaneous, uncalculating, aimless; let him cease to map out a plan for his earthly life or a means for his daily bread. His course is mapped out already in a fixed and unalterable way. He needs no ship nor helm nor oar, no sail nor chart nor compass. He has only to become sea-weed, and to drift, ignoring himself and everything around; the order of nature will do the rest.

I have thus tried in a few sentences to describe rather than to define the system of Lâo-tze. It will be seen on the very surface to present in some respects a marked and direct contrast to the contemporaneous view of Confucius, and in point of fact these two systems have been generally viewed as indicating contrary aspects of the Chinese mind. Confucius belongs to the outward order; Lâo-tze to the mystical and introvertive. Confucius is occupied with the problem of social wellbeing; Lâo-tze is concerned only with the peace of the individual. Confucius is inspired by the pride of empire; Lâo-tze is desirous above all things to sink into humility—not the humility of thinking lowly of one's self, but the humility of not thinking at all. Confucius requires in the members of the State an interest in the common welfare; Lâo-tze seeks a mystical resignation, in which all interest, common or individual, is forgotten. These are the points of contrast, and I do not attempt to deny them. But I say that these points of contrast are only two opposite tendencies of one national ideal—the spirit of regress. Just as the same sense of guilt may wake on the cheek of one man the blush of shame, and dim that of another with the pallor of fear, so has the national spirit of China expressed itself in one instance by an exhibition of materialism, and in another by a display of material crucifixion. The system of Confucius and the system of Lâo-tze are both modes of one spirit, and of that spirit which essentially belongs to China. They are both regressions toward the past; their difference lies simply in the fact that the one goes further back than the other. Confucius retraces his steps to the primitive age of man, and attempts to find there a model for the ages to come; Lâo-tze retraces his steps to an age more primitive still, and seeks in the life of the unconscious plant to bury the burden of human grief and care. The difference in their form is accidental; the one thing not accidental is their common motive of regressiveness. This is in all the forms of Chinese faith the essentially national feature, the one element which distinctively and for ever marks out this branch from all the surrounding branches of the religious tree. Neither ancestral worship, nor the doctrine of Confucius, nor the creed of Lâo-tze, presents anything that is new; each of them can be paralleled by things analogous in other climes. The element which is distinctive of China amongst the religions of antiquity is the fact that, whether in the worship of the departed, or in the search for a new kingdom, or in the pursuit of a mystical goal, the Chinaman is actuated by one and the same desire—the desire to regain the standpoint of an earlier day.

This, then, is the message of China to the religious world, "Go back." It is a strange, weird, unexpected message, altogether unlike what one looks for in such a sphere, and altogether unique amongst the voices of surrounding nations. "Speak to the children of Israel that they go forward" are the words which are inscribed on the threshold of the Jewish temple. They form the key-note to the whole history of that people. And they are the key-note of that music to which marches nearly all religious history. The impulse to go forward, to press toward the mark of a coming prize, to leave the acquisitions of the past behind in the pursuit of a higher goal, has been the almost unbroken aim of the religions of mankind. India presses forward to the future, and in all the forms of her faith seeks refuge from the present hour in a state to come. Persia presses forward to the future, and looks for a solution of the problem to the ripening circles of the suns. Even Egypt presses forward to the future; the motto of her pyramids is not so much the glory of antiquity as the power of everlastingness; she seeks to build something which shall endure. But here is a voice which seems dissonant amidst the other voices, a voice which says "Go back," where the others say "Go forward." It is remarkable by its very contrast; it arrests us by its discordance. Nor is it a voice which can be drowned by the others. In point of fact it has not been drowned. It has been powerful enough to arrest for centuries the development of one of the most extensive empires in the world. What is the secret of this power? That it has a secret is beyond question. It is not to be accounted for by anything on the surface. Climate will not explain it, for it looks behind the existing climate. Soil will not explain it, for it ignores the present soil. Priestcraft will not explain it, for the sceptre which it wields is precisely that sceptre which priestcraft would avoid—the empire of primitive culture over existing forms of civilisation. Where are we to look for the source of that strength which has been able to attract and to retain the minds of millions under allegiance to an ideal of the past?

In answering this question, let us first consider whether, in the history of religions, there be anything analogous to this tendency of the Chinese empire. I have said that it is something unique amidst surrounding nations. Is there anything like it amongst nations which are not surrounding? Is it a purely isolated phenomenon in the sphere of religious thought? I think it is not. I believe that we shall find the true analogue to the tendency of the Chinese mind if we extend our gaze into a wider circle. It does not, as we have said, present in this respect any point of contact with India or Persia or Egypt; but it does present a point of contact with something which is at once more modern and more universal—the religion of Christ. What is the secret of Christianity's moral power? Strange as it may seem, it is regressiveness. We commonly boast of it as a religion of progress; and so, doubtless, it is. But it is a progress which has been professedly reached by a process of retrogression. The initial command of Christianity is the command to go back. The Christian soldier receives at the outset the order to retreat. The distinctive motto of this faith is the preliminary necessity of regress, "Except ye be turned back and become as little children, ye shall not enter into the kingdom of heaven." In these words there is a thoroughly Chinese ring—a more distinctly Chinese ring than that which is supposed to reverberate in Christ's golden rule. Here, as in the faith of China, we have set before the mind the ideal of a great State or empire which is to represent in its nature the rule of the Highest—a kingdom of heaven. Here we have set before the mind the same possibility which besets the eye of the Chinaman—the possibility that this kingdom may be actually attained by the earth. But here too, in more striking resemblance still, the road to the attainment of the goal is declared to be a regressive road. It is declared that no amount of progress, no advance of civilisation, no addition of extraneous materials can of themselves hasten the coming of the kingdom. The first step must be not a learning but an unlearning, not a clothing but an unclothing, not an onward development but a backward march. What is wanted above all things and before all things is a new beginning,—an entrance for the second time into the stage of birth, the resuming of life in the form of a little child.

The key-note of Christianity is redemption — a buying back. It expresses the thought that what man wants for his amelioration is, first and foremost, a regressive movement, the power to become a new creature. And a moment's reflection must convince every one that Christianity has here struck a note of nature. The deepest want of human nature will be found to lie, not in the absence of some future good, but in the presence of some old experience, in the fact that we are still in contact with some element of the past. Wherein, for example, consists the powerlessness of mere morality to effect a reform of the life? Is it not precisely in the knowledge that, in order to be reformed, the life must first be renewed? You tell a drunkard of the miseries awaiting him in this and other worlds if he persists in his downward course; you point out the necessity for imposing a restraint on himself, and for cultivating above all things the virtue of abstinence. Why is it that the man to whom you speak, while perfectly conceding the truth of your every sentiment, is perfectly uninfluenced by any motive of reform? It is because he knows in his inmost heart that no reform of present action would really make him a new man. It is no use to tell him that the practice of sobriety would free him from future torments; he knows that it would only do so by bringing actual torments into the day and hour. Abstinence in itself is simply thirst, and thirst ungratified is torture. The root of the evil lies in the past, probably in the ancestral past. If the man could reverence his ancestors, he would have hope; but this is precisely what he cannot do. He has received from these ancestors an heirloom of misery. What he wants above all things is a new beginning, a rolling back of the shadow. Until he can cast back his eye upon a past without blemish, upon a heredity without taint, upon an ancestry without spot or flaw, he feels that every attempt at present reform is simply an effort to exchange one misery for another, to substitute for the inroads of passion on the body the ravages of passion on the soul.

Now this cry for a new beginning is precisely what Christianity professes to meet and satisfy. Its power over the moral life lies mainly in the fact that it claims to lead back that life to a fresh starting-point, or, to use its own words, "to pure fountains of living water." The strength of Christianity lies in its claim to reach the "fountains." It does not propose to purify any special part of the stream. It proposes to go back to the beginning, to the stream's source. It offers to alter the whole course of life's flow by making a new commencement, by pouring into human nature a fresh flood of heredity. Its watchword is, not inappropriately, "Salvation by *blood*." It proclaims to the world that it needs to be revivified, born again. It tells the race of men that their blood has become impure, tainted, corrupted; it tells them that no midway cure will have any effect in arresting the malady, that moral abstinence will at best only remedy the symptoms, not check the disease. It tells them that what they want is new blood, a fresh stream of vitality flowing from a new fountain and interrupting altogether the course of the old heredity. It proclaims this necessity, and it offers to supply it. And herein to the mind of the first Christian age lay the secret of its power. Its earliest crown was not its aspiration towards the future but its regress towards the past, its promise to roll back the shadows and let the soul begin anew. It was this which fascinated the mind of a Paul; it was this which made to him the difference between law and grace. Other systems might offer him incentives to moral reformation; other creeds might inspire him with motives to abstain from old vices; Christianity alone presented the hope of a buried past, the prospect of becoming a new creature by starting afresh and unencumbered, with the heart of a little child and with a heredity pure as heaven.

Now, such was in germ the religious message of the Chinese empire. Through all the absurdity of its details there rings this one note of truth—the necessity for a retraced past. In the heart of the Chinaman there was present a true instinct when he placed on the threshold of his temple the image of a new beginning. Every nation that has looked back to a paradise in the past has been prompted so to look back by an anticipation of the Christian impulse, by a sense of that great need which Christianity has claimed to supply. The Chinese empire has felt in her collective unity what every earnest individual man has felt in his single personality—that in order to advance there must be retreat, that in order to reach the goal there must be a return to the starting-point. This is her message to the world, this is her truth for all ages, and by this, even in her dilapidation and decay, she being dead yet speaketh.

Why, then, does she not speak effectually? Why has her message to the world been, after all, only in germ? Christianity, like the Chinese empire, has proclaimed to the world the necessity before all things of a regressive march, and Christianity by that proclamation has initiated its triumph. The religions of China have never triumphed; even in the stagnant East they have not held their own. Wherein lies the difference? It lies, after all, on the very surface. Christianity has proclaimed the necessity for a new beginning, but it has done so only for the sake of a new ending. It has declared that, in order to inherit the kingdom, the man must become a child; but it has made this declaration not for the sake of the child but for the sake of the man. Childhood is not the goal of Christianity. The retracing of the past is in itself no object; it is only the means to an object. If it proposes to go back to pure fountains of water, it is merely that through this purity it may inaugurate a new stream. Its paradise is not in the past but in the future; it retreats that it may advance. The regress is but a preliminary step, and it is taken with a view to higher progress. Hence Christianity has been, of all religions, the most progressive; of all faiths, that which has marched most abreast of the times. No form of worship has had so many environments, and no form of worship has so fitted itself to its environments. The reason is that it has proclaimed the emptying of the soul not for the sake of emptiness, but only with the view to a more satisfactory replenishment. It has proposed the removal of old prepossessions in order that the spirit of man may meet the world with a fresh eye and possess all things new.

How different is it with China! Here, as in the case of Christianity, there has been a regress towards the past, but here the regress has been for its own sake. The Christian goes back in order that he may come more forward; the Chinaman goes back that he may rest under primeval shadows. The Christian's paradise is always in the future; the Chinaman's always in the past. The Christian's regress is a means; the Chinaman's a goal. It is this which constitutes, from an intellectual point of view, the main and the crowning difference between the two religions; it is in this lies the secret of the one's progress and the other's decline. The religion of Christ and the religions of China have struck a common note of truth in seeking emancipation from the present by a regress into the past. But Christianity has alone perceived that the value of such a retreat is its preparation for a new outset. China has mistaken the means for the goal, has reverenced antiquity for its own sake. Nor is this the worst; she is seeking from antiquity what is not to be found there. The ideal of the Chinese religion is not a low ideal; it is on the whole lofty and grand. The error is rather intellectual than moral, rather in the judgment than in the soul. China has erred not in what she hopes for, but in where she expects to find it. Her picture of a kingdom is good and pure, but she has made a mistake in imagining that the past could realise such a picture. She has made a mistake in supposing that the goal she has figured to herself could ever be reached in going back, could ever be attained anywhere but in the ripeness of future development. She has placed her Eden in the primitive age, and she has been oblivious of the fact that, could she reach the gates of that primitive age, she would find only the flaming sword, without the cherubim.

To bring out this point, let us take the two great Chinese systems of which we have spoken — the system of Confucius and the system of Lâo-tze—and let us see how in each of them the conception is the reverse of primitive. The doctrine of Confucius is the idea of a kingdom which shall be based on the lines of the patriarchal age. In going back to the patriarchal age, Confucius is actuated by a very lofty motive. He wants to build up a State after the model of a family, to have the relations of political life rooted and grounded in reciprocal love. He divides the order of society into five great relations —father and son, husband and wife, elder brother and younger, master and servant, friend and friend. He seeks to adjust between these a bond of sympathy which shall at once be true and eternal, and which shall, moreover, typify in its pure perfection the life of the kingdom of heaven. He rightly judges that, in order to adjust such relations, he must seek a new beginning, must roll back that tide of existing corruptions which have been the product of years of misgovernment. But does he judge rightly in thinking that the new beginning is to be itself the goal? Assuredly not; it is here lies the error of his system and the mistake of his nation. It would seem that, of all things, the purity of family relationships belongs least to the primitive age.[1] It would seem as if it were one of those ideas which peculiarly require the fostering hand of a long development. Be this as it may, it is quite certain that it is not to be found in the Chinaman's patriarchal age. Perhaps the purest delineation of such an age ever given to the world is that exhibited in the Book of Genesis; and yet, with all its idyllic features, it is far from pure. It is a state of society for which one may well apologise, but which no Western mind would ever wish to reproduce. And why? I would answer, just because it *is* patriarchal. It is the reign of the father distinctively—that is to say, as distinguished from the reign of the mother. Wherever such a society prevails there is one uniform result; instead of monarchy being lost in fatherhood, fatherhood is lost in monarchy. The patriarchal relation has been an effort to obliterate the sense of power in the ties of home, but it has always ended in obliterating the ties of home in the sense of power; instead of the king becoming a father,

---

[1] Dr Lauder Lindsay adduces authorities to prove that the family relation itself is a comparatively late stage of animal evolution (Mind in the Lower Animals, i. 41, par. 12 and sq.)

the father has become a king. And the reason is plain. It is not the parent as such that is exalted; it is only one member of the parental relation. The father of the family is crowned to the exclusion and to the disparagement of the mother. The fact is significant; it shows that despotism, and not home-life, is the ruling motive. If Western civilisation has increasingly reached the ideal of a State modelled on family relations, it is because Western civilisation has started from a different ideal of the family itself. It is because it has learned to reverence not merely the paternal but the parental, not merely the headship over the household but the participation in a common life.

It is because it has started from the patriarchal ideal as the model of political excellence, that the Chinese empire has failed to realise the perfection for which it is seeking. The failure has been evidenced alike in its speculative and in its practical life. Its speculative life has been utterly dwarfed in its development. It seems to have started with a monotheistic idea of God, and Dr Legge maintains that this is the earliest conception in its whole religious history.[1] But whither has it departed? The first has in this instance not been the last. The idea of God has retired into the background, and its place has been taken by the idea of the

[1] Religions of China, p. 16.

kingdom of heaven.[1] The Chinaman has surrendered himself to the thought of a divine order, but he has ceased to think of a divine Orderer. He has nowhere denied it but he has everywhere ignored it, and the ignoring is more remarkable when it comes as the sequel of a previous recognition. Is not the inference plain? The Chinaman's idea of God has been corrupted by his own system. He has started with the notion of monarchy in the household, and therefore the idea of fatherhood has become to him a synonym for distance. He has transferred to heaven his ideal of the home-life, until heaven itself has ceased to be associated with anything which is near. God is only felt by His rule, and He rules from afar; He is Himself unseen, unfelt, unknown, and unknowable. It is the same result which is found afterwards in the history of Judea. The constant contemplation of a patriarchal God identified fatherhood with monarchy, until the idea of divine care was lost in the thought of divine majesty. The God of Judea, like the God of China, retired into the remote distance and ceased to be a recognised agent in the development of things below. The only difference was that, while the Jew filled up the gulf by the interposition of a hierarchy of angels, the Chinaman left the gulf unfilled, and

---

[1] It is only fair to state that the most modern development of Confucianism is to some extent regressive towards the primitive theistic standpoint.

denied to the spirit of man a vision of aught beyond the earth.[1]

And in practical life also the influence of the Chinese ideal has been equally cramping. It has had a peculiar effect in lowering the standard of woman. Not that the position of woman in China is more subordinate than in other parts of the East; in this respect the Chinese empire compares even favourably. But the point is, that from the hopes held out by Confucianism one would have expected a complete subversion of the Eastern subordination of woman. One would have expected that a creed whose leading principle was justice, whose leading article was reciprocity, whose leading aim was the establishment of a kingdom which should be based on the adjustment of the rights of man, would have found for womanhood a worthy and a ruling sphere. Proposing as it did to fashion the kingdom after the model of the family, we should have thought that in this kingdom the influence of the female would have had dominant sway. It has not been so, and why? Clearly because the Chinaman, in starting from the ideal of family life, has started from that ideal in its most primitive form. He has sought to find the per-

---

[1] On the impersonal character of the later object of Chinese worship, see M'Clatchie's "Paper on Chinese Theology" in the Journal of the Asiatic Society,' xvi. 397.

fection of family relationships in the type called patriarchal, and the result has been that on the very threshold of his development the idea of the parent has been swamped in the idea of the monarch. Power, masculine power, arbitrary power, has become from the very outset the symbol and the goal of the life of home, and instead of the kingdom being built up after the model of a household, the household has been constructed after the model of a kingdom. In such a society, by the very nature of the case, woman can have no ruling sphere. Her position is by necessity one of entire subordination. The empire belongs not to the parent but to the father, and the submission of the child is based not on love but on law. Hence Chinese society has been what the Chinese empire has been—a state destitute of feminine features,[1] hard, cold, rigid, motionless. It has exhibited no flexibility, no variety, no changes of expression, no capacity to be moved by the softer influences. It has been regulated, in theory indeed, upon principles of the strictest justice, but it has been the justice not of instituting equal rights, but of maintaining the rights of original possession.

[1] It would seem as if modern China had recognised this social want; she appears latterly to have made an attempt towards the establishment of virgin worship. See 'Nouveau Journal Asiatique,' p. 295.

If now we pass to the second of the great Chinese systems—the creed of Lâo-tze—we shall find that the national religion has again failed to realise itself by seeking from a primitive age what is not to be found there. The doctrine of Lâo-tze is in the abstract a very lofty one, more lofty than that of Confucius. It proposes to usher the human soul into peace by the destruction of self-consciousness, and in this respect it bears a striking resemblance to the great moral tenet of Christianity. Indeed, Lâo-tze is credited with having uttered a maxim similar to that of Christ in the declaration that the least shall be greatest. Yet just as Confucianism, in its effort after a kingdom of heaven, has failed where Christianity has succeeded, so the doctrine of Lâo-tze, in its effort after the destruction of self-consciousness, has also failed where Christianity has succeeded. That it has failed is a matter of historical certainty; the Chinaman is of all men the least typical of self-sacrifice. The question is, Why? And the answer is, Because Lâo-tze, like Confucius, has sought in a wrong quarter for the realisation of his dream. He has gone back to the most primitive type. He has proposed to destroy self-consciousness by reducing man to the state of a plant, by stemming the impulses of life and imposing the conditions of an absolute stillness. Christianity, like Lâo-tze, has proclaimed the necessity to salvation of an emptied self-consciousness, and the proclamation has been followed by a signal success. But why? Because Christianity has pointed out a source of self-forgetfulness exactly opposite to that indicated by Lâo-tze. Lâo-tze proposes to make man unconscious by giving him less life; Christianity, by giving him more. Lâo-tze would purchase individual peace by suppressing the emotions of the heart; Christianity would bring peace to the heart by giving it a new and an additional emotion. Lâo-tze teaches that to impart stillness to the spirit, it must cease to be; Christ teaches that it can only reach its stillness by *being* more abundantly. If China would attain the goal of Christianity, it must follow the method of Christianity; it must press forward after having gone backward. No man can attain spiritual unconsciousness by losing physical consciousness. Spiritual unconsciousness is not death but life, and it is to be reached only by the influx of a larger life. If the self-life is to be extinguished, it must be not by going in but by going out, by extending itself into the life of the universe and identifying its own interests with the interests of universal nature. Such a consummation can only be reached in the method opposite to Lâo-tze—can only be attained by forgetting the things which are behind, and pressing forward to the things which are before. It is by transcending the life of the plant, by surpassing the life of the animal, by leaving in the background even the life of the primitive man, and by entering into a life which shall be in sympathy with universal development, that humanity alone can hope to see the day when the dream of the Chinaman can be realised.

CHAPTER IV.

THE MESSAGE OF INDIA.

THE message of India! The expression seems almost self-contradictory. If there is one thing which India does not suggest, it is the proclamation of a single message. It seems to exhibit rather a clash of opposing voices striving for the mastery in the temple of truth. It has been said that the soil of Palestine unites within its compass the specimens of every kind of plant. It may be said, with still more accuracy, that the soil of India unites within its compass the specimens of every kind of soul. There is not a phase of religious thought which is not intensely represented here; there is not an aspect of philosophic speculation which does not find here a congenial home. Here dwell the worshippers of tradition—the men who place their reverence in the outward letter of Scripture. Here repose the mystics—the men who seek to lose themselves in a light inaccessible and full of glory. Here rest the followers of human reason—the men who claim to take their sole guidance from experience. Here live the materialists—the men who in the elements of sense would recognise the origin of all things. Here are the pioneers of reconciliation—the men who would find a place where matter and spirit could dwell side by side. Here, finally, are those in search of a personal divine love—the men who look neither to tradition, nor abstract mysticism, nor rationalism, nor materialism, nor even to an attempt at the reconciliation of all, but simply and solely to an unveiling of that face of God in whose vision and fruition the human spirit may find communion.[1]

Nor, if we turn from the inward to the outward life of the people, are we less impressed with the variety in their types and characters. The moment we have decided to assign a special quality to the Indian race, there starts up an exception to the rule so gigantic and so prominent as almost to nullify it. When we look on one side we say, "This is a nation of ascetics—of men who have abandoned all interest in the world and its concerns;" presently we are confronted, on the very surface of her earliest religious book, with the spectacle of a people in full employment and enjoyment of most of the arts of

---

[1] These tendencies respectively indicate the names of the six Indian schools—Mimansa, Vedanta, Nyaya, Vaiseshika, Sankhya, Yoga. The most interesting Western account I know is Victor Cousin, 'Cours de l'Histoire de la Philosophie,' 1827, vol. i. Also see Professor Monier Williams' 'Indian Wisdom,' pp. 48-154.

life.[1] When we turn in one direction we are impressed with the belief that we are in a land of dreamers; yet no nation in the world has ever exhibited such a one-sided tendency towards the practical, as appears in Buddhism. When we keep our eye on a single point we are impelled to say, "This is a religion of despair." And yet when we turn to the earliest records—to the very fountainhead of the Indian faith—our judgment is immediately reversed. Here, as we shall see in the sequel, all is hope; pessimism has no place within its borders, and everything is gilded by the morning sun. Amid such varieties of aspect and thought, one is tempted to ask if there is any principle of unity at all. Is it possible, in any sense, to regard these contrary manifestations as parts of a single whole? Is it possible to view such different products of the human mind as in reality the produce of one soil? Have we any right, in short, to speak of the "religion of India"? Has India one message to the world? Is there anywhere a connecting cord between her diverging faiths? Is there to be found, amid the apparent dissonance of her tendencies and her systems, one central, one comprehensive idea, which binds together her seeming elements of conflict, and blends her diverse colours in a rainbow's form?

[1] See Wilson's 'Rigveda,' vol. i., re-edited by F. E. Hall, vols. ii., iii., iv., edited by E. B. Cowell. London: 1850-1866.

I believe that there is. I think it will be found that the different phases of Indian thought are susceptible of union in one great idea, and that in this union lies her message to the world. That idea is human life. The message of India is the proclamation of the pilgrim's progress—the earliest announcement of the stages of that journey which has since been traversed by myriads of souls. Here, for the first time in history, we have a description of man's spiritual road—a description of the path over which the religious life is bound to travel if it would be a complete and rounded life. One corner of the earth is, as it were, selected to be a mirror and a miniature of the normal experience of each individual soul, and we are permitted to see within the compass of a single nation that process of religious evolution which has been the rule for all nations and for all men.

What, then, *are* the stages of the spiritual life? It is a question of individual experience. It requires for its answer no consultation of books or authorities; one has only to look within. The education of every completed life has passed through three stages. The opening or initial stage is one of hope. Its peculiarity consists in the fact that the spectator of life underrates its difficulties. The first impression of the youth in gazing upon this world is not, as we should expect, an impression of fear. He looks upon surrounding things with an eye almost of patronage. He is impressed with a sense of the world's comparative smallness—of its smallness in comparison with his own mighty power. He feels himself to be perfectly adequate, to be more than adequate, to the task before him. The goal towards which he is going shines with an illusory clearness; the sense of distance is lost, and to-morrow is already recognised as a portion of to-day. By-and-by there comes a change. The relative aspect of the world to himself is transformed; *it* becomes large and *he* becomes small. He begins to awake to the conviction that his first view of life *was* an illusion. He finds that what he had imagined to be only a mole-hill has become a mountain. The waters which in fancy he had held in the hollow of his hand expand into the dimensions of a vast ocean; the isles which in imagination he had taken up as a very little thing are found to be separated from each other by almost interminable tracts of sea. Originally his entire hope had rested in the realisation of his worldly dream; his only object now is to awake from that dream. The present system is illusory; if he would find reality, he must rise above that system into a light and a life which are now inaccessible. His daily course becomes a straining after the invisible, his daily occupation a search for things as yet not seen. The prize of peace lies for him behind the veil, and the more distant is the object from the day and hour, the more surely it becomes the hope of his rest. At last this second stage also passes away, and a third and final scene appears. The world, as a world, still seems an object of illusion; but it is no longer to the future that he looks for redemption from it. Instead of straining his eyes into the invisible, he begins to centre his gaze upon one corner—humanity. Instead of looking for peace to the advent of a new order of things, he begins to look for it here and now. He still believes that emancipation from care can only be reached by death; but he finds that death can itself be reached without leaving the world. He finds that it is possible to lose himself in the thought of others, to surrender his own personality by entering into the personality of his brotherman. He finds that he can get above the earth without going out of it, that he can be redeemed from the illusions of sense and time by being redeemed from the thought of self. He realises, in short, the truth that loss of life comes from loving it, and that the burden of individual care drops from the arms of him who has entered into the life of humanity.

Such in its completeness is the rhythm of all human life. It has been the message of India to foretell and foreshadow this rhythm. On a large national scale she represents to us for the first time these successive phases of the life of man. Let us unfold them one by one. Let us begin with the earliest phase known to us of Indian history. It is that which appears in the Mantras[1] or songs of her first sacred book—the 'Rig-Veda.' It is distinctively an age of hope. There is not a trace of pessimism nor a note of despair. The worshipper looks out upon this world with the eye and the heart of a child. He sees in it a theatre made for himself, and exactly suited to the part he is to play. He is altogether unappalled by the majesty of the surrounding scenery—although it is the same scenery which afterwards appals him. The objects before which he is in after-years to tremble are at the beginning the sources of his freedom and his power. He looks up to the forces of nature and worships them, but he worships them rather as allies than as despots. He makes them the object of his prayers, but his prayers themselves are acts of merchandise. He deals with the powers of nature as a man in business deals with his brother-craftsman. He offers them his adoration, and he expects in return their sustenance. He gives them his homage in order that he may receive from them those balmy influences of wind and weather which make life go smooth. His religious sacrifices are from beginning to end a commercial transaction;

---

[1] As I wish to avoid all technical details, I refer for the meaning of this word to Colebrooke, 'Miscellaneous Essays,' i. p. 308 ; Max Müller, 'Ancient Sanskrit Literature,' p. 343 ; and Goldstücker's 'Pânini,' p. 69.

they are not the emptying of himself but the lading of his ship; he gives something that he may get more. All this indicates an over-estimate of his own powers, an under-estimate of the powers of nature. It indicates that at this stage he is a totally different man from what he was afterwards to become. So far from shrinking before the universe, he is not even adequately impressed with its greatness; so far from feeling his own nothingness, he has an overweening sense of his necessity to the gods.[1] He stands like Jacob under the stars of heaven and strikes a bargain for his own profit, promises his piety and his offerings if he shall have bread to eat and raiment to put on.

I have said that at this stage the Indian worships the powers of nature. I do not mean that he worships them *as* powers of nature. He looks up to the dawn, to the meridian, to the setting, but he sees in them more than the eye sees. They are to him at this stage unconsciously what at an after-stage they became consciously—the forms of divine incarnations, the respective embodiments of distinct celestial beings. These natural powers, indeed, are nowhere equally worshipped at one time; each has its own day, each has its season for empire. Can we determine the order of their separate reigns?

---

[1] The spirit of Indian mythology is described by F. von Schlegel as one of boundless enthusiasm (Philosophy of History, p. 154. Lond., 1847).

Can we tell which of them took the precedence and which followed? Historically we cannot do so, for the simple reason that India has no history; her past, present, and future are all represented on a single chart, and we are called to determine their sequence on other grounds than testimony. These grounds must be internal. In the absence of historical annals, we are driven *within* ourselves to contemplate the order of human thought. But when we enter into this region, it seems to me that we begin to get light even on the path of history. If we take a simple survey of the Indian chart, and consider only the natural and normal movements of the universal human mind, I think we shall arrive at a tolerably fair and an approximately accurate reckoning of the sequence and arrangement of those steps by which the spirit of that great nation has climbed to its culminating worship.

I shall illustrate my meaning by comparison with a very early document, as old as many of the Vedas, and better known to the West than any of them — the first chapter of the Book of Genesis. Of course no one will imagine that I think there is any connection between them except that connection of human nature which it is my aim to establish. But what I wish to remark is this. The objects of creation selected in the first chapter of Genesis are in a very peculiar sense identical with those objects which are recognised in the Vedas as worthy of religious reverence. Now, in the Book of Genesis, these objects are presented to the view not collectively but *seriatim*. They are made to pass before us in a particular order. It has always seemed to me that it is not an order of creation, but an order of observation. I think the writer had in his view, not the sequence of God's working, but the sequence of man's perception. The six days of creation to my mind are meant to unfold those successive steps by which the eye of childhood rises to the appreciation of the visible universe. If this be the meaning, it would throw some light upon the sequence of the corresponding objects in the Vedas; for it would show that at a very early date such a mode of thought was native to the Eastern mind. But whether it be or be not a true exegesis, it is certainly a true delineation. It is a fact of experience that the child does arrive at the full conception of nature by a process very similar to that which is indicated in the order observed by the six days' creation. Let us look for a moment at that sequence.

When the infant opens its eyes upon this wondrous world, the first object which awakens its wonder is light. Light is to every individual man the "offspring of heaven first-born." It is the earliest object of perception which meets his gaze. I do not say it is his earliest sense of consciousness; that probably begins with inward pain. But it is the first thing which takes the child out of himself, which tells him that there is another world besides his own soul. You will observe, this earliest outward sensation is light itself, pure and simple. It is not yet light involving the idea of space. Everything at first is touching the eye; there is no sense of distance; there is nothing but glitter, and the glitter is not recognised as anything separate from the sight. This higher recognition only comes with the second day. When the child puts forth its hand to catch the light and finds that it eludes its grasp, it awakens for the first time to the sense of distance. Light ceases to be a mere glitter; it becomes a firmament — a brilliant and boundless expanse — overarching all things. As yet, these things which it overarches are undiscerned; the perception of the diffused light precedes the perception either of its own individual forms or of any other forms. But with the third day there comes this vision of individual things. There opens for the child a season in which the dry land appears with its variegated colours of vegetation, its fruits and flowers and trees. Everything begins to be seen "after its kind"—in its distinction from every other thing; and the eye which has been at first delighted only with the heavens, begins to revel in the growing forms of earth. Then there breaks upon the mind a new perception. The child wakens to the recognition that there is a connection between the earth and the heavens, that the sun rules the day and the moon rules the night. It is at this stage that it receives its impressions of the dread of physical darkness. That children dread the dark is proverbial; yet it is certainly not a primitive instinct—it is the result of reflection. It can only be reached when darkness ceases to be a mere fact and becomes a symbol—the symbol of some guiding hand withdrawn. Then for the first time begins to dawn the interest in life as distinguished from the interest in form. And the earliest interest in life centres in the animal world. The child seeks the first mirror of itself not in the face of its brother-child, but in the impulses and the movements of the lower creation; the horse and the dog excite its wonder ere ever it has learned to wonder at its own soul. The wonder at its own soul is the final stage of all; it is the sixth day. With the dawning of this day it begins to awaken into the sense of a human love, looks into a mother's face, and experiences that earliest impression of trust in another which is the portal into the Sabbath of rest.

Such is the order of man's childhood, and we have seen that it corresponds to the order of the Hebrew visions of creation. If we apply it to the Pantheon of India, we shall find that it will furnish at least a possible theory of the relative times of her different gods. Let us try to figure the process by which the Indian filled up that Pantheon. The Hindu child, like the Hebrew child, opened his eyes on the world of nature, and the first object which he saw was Light; he called it Agni. It was as yet to him what it is at first to every child—only a thing which glitters. It was discerned simply as a part of the eye, and was unconnected with any sense of distance. The Indian child, like all other children, would first learn its distance by the abortive effort to touch it. When it found the light to be something which eluded its grasp, it would awaken into its second stage of worship. That second stage was the adoration of Aditi — the boundless firmament. Agni had been only the glittering light; Aditi was the light enthroned in the heavens, the light diffused through immensity. Then to the Indian, as to the Jew, there came a third stage; the dry land appeared. The eye began to rest upon solid masses, and to transfer its reverence from the things of heaven to the things of earth. Singularly enough, the first earthly thing which received its reverence was plant-life. It is at the stage subsequent to the worship of the heavens that we find the Indian adoring the juice of a vegetable product under the name of Soma.[1] Then the fourth day breaks. The Indian has adored

---

[1] This juice is offered up as a libation, and the offering indicates a glimmering sense of something in man which needs expiation. (Rig-Véda, Langlois' edition, i. 38.)

heaven and he has adored earth; he is now to adore the meeting of heaven and earth. It is here that there come into view those forms and phenomena of nature which mark the transition from the celestial into the mundane. Here we find the worship of what Herbert calls

<blockquote>"The bridal of the earth and sky;"</blockquote>

and the union of heaven and earth is celebrated under the names of Dyaus and Prithivi. Here, in the united adoration of Varuna and Mitra, we have a reverential recognition of the truth that the evening and the morning make for the world one day. Here we have the reverence for things which in themselves seem slight and insignificant, but which receive a religious value as links between the heavenly and the earthly. We have the worship of Ushas or the dawn—the point where the golden sky begins to touch the hills. We have the worship of the Suryas—or beams which the sun bestows on the world. We have the worship of Indra—the heat which breaks the cloud and sends rain. We have the worship of the Maruts—those winds which bear to earth the messages of heaven. Finally, we have the worship of Pushan—the sun as the guide of humanity, the light, no longer merely in itself nor merely in its immensity, but in its journey round the world to fulfil the course of time.

The fifth morning breaks, and with it there comes a higher worship still. There rises a deeper interest in *life*. Hitherto the plant alone has been recognised as a legitimate offering to heaven; but with this fifth morning we begin to witness the phenomenon of animal sacrifice.[1] The gods begin to be adored under an unwonted form. As yet the Indian has only bowed before the powers of nature; here he is seen to bow before the majesty of life. His sense of the dignity of life takes the form of the worship of Brahmanaspati—the name given to a priest in the act of sacrifice. The priest is not worshipped as a man, nor in himself: in his private moments he may be esteemed a very poor creature; but in the act of sacrifice he is for the moment sublime. And the sublimity is clearly a reflection from the thing which he offers; it is the glory of his gift which to the mind of the Indian makes the priest worthy of reverence. The deification of the Brahmanaspati indicates beyond all doubt that the life of the animal creation is becoming to him an object of increasing interest. To the Indian, as to the Jew, one other stage remains: it is the recognition of the dignity of man. The sixth morning is the grandest of all; it is the adoration of Atman—

[1] The rules for sacrifice are contained in those parts of the Vedas called Brahmannas—evidently later than the earliest Mantras. For the meaning of the word see J. Muir, in 'Journal of Asiatic Society' for 1864, and introduction to M. Haug's edition of the 'Aitaruya Brahmana,' i. 4.

the self or soul. Here the Indian has reached a stage immeasurably beyond all the others. He had worshipped the heavens in the forms of the light and the firmament. He had worshipped the plant in the form of the Soma. He had worshipped the animal-sacrifice in the form of the Brahmanaspati. But here he has taken a step beyond the firmament, beyond the plant, beyond the animal; he has recognised the dignity of mind. He has uncovered his head to a new and higher principle—the principle of mental life. He has entered within the gates of a temple loftier and broader than the dome of the starry heavens, and has bowed before the ideal of the spirit of man.

Such appears to me to be at least a possible scheme on which to explain the order of the Indian Pantheon. It will doubtless be esteemed far-fetched and fanciful. Far-fetched it is not, if it be derived from so near a distance as human experience. Fanciful it certainly is; but the early system of the Indian Pantheon is itself fanciful, and demands fancy to account for it. It is the product of poetry and imagination, and by poetry and imagination must it be explained. Of course I do not mean to imply that the predominance of one object of worship involved the exclusion of the others, nor that there ever was a time in which one object was simultaneously predominant to all minds. It depended entirely upon that state of development at which the individual might have arrived ; one man might be worshipping Agni, while another was adoring Aditi. I have merely wished to express the fact that, if we were permitted to trace the development of any one complete Indian life, we would find it to portray those stages which are described on the opening page of the Hebrew records, and to be in all probability in either case connected with a natural law of human evolution.

But the main point on which I wish to insist in the exhibition of this opening phase of Indian religion, is its pre-eminent and almost unqualified hopefulness. There is not a trace of its future self, not a hint of the coming despair. The Indian, like the Hebrew seer, looks upon a world as yet unstained by a fall, a world whose prevailing note is joy, and which basks under the blessing of heaven. If the Hebrew evinces this by the constant averment, " God saw that it was good," the Indian not less strongly reveals it by distributing successively his tributes of reverence over every object of creation. And not the least remarkable feature of his worship is the fact that it includes even those objects of nature which might be supposed to suggest an opposite attitude. He is not afraid to take into his Pantheon the stormy winds. To the natural eye the winds suggest rather an irregularity than a harmony with the law of nature. They convey to the untutored mind the idea of a wilfulness which seeks to revolt from the established order, and to set up a kingdom of its own. The early Indian has an untutored mind, but he has not fallen into this error. He has refused to recognise in the seeming waywardness of the winds anything inconsistent with the universal harmony, and has insisted on giving them a place in the great temple of his worship. Nor has he scrupled to include the rains also. To an untutored eye the rain is a blot on the beautiful; for the time being it actually dims the face of the landscape, and might be supposed to be a force with a counteracting and impeding aim. Yet the primitive Indian has seen deeper. He has claimed for the rain an agency harmonious with the beneficence of all nature, and he has assigned a special divine work to that power which causes it to fall. All this in a primitive mind not guided by scientific knowledge is clearly due to an optimistic tendency. It results, and only can result, from a native and original hopefulness which starts upon the path of life with the foregone conclusion that all is well. It is true that here, as elsewhere, we have rites of sacrifice, and that wherever sacrifice exists there exists an evidence of not absolutely unclouded sunshine. Yet even the sacrifices of the Indian bear witness to the optimism of his early faith; for the object which he offers is itself deified, and the priest who surrenders it is himself invested with the attributes of divinity. The very hour of humiliation has been lifted into the Hindu Pantheon, and the act which naturally marks the sense of human degradation has been transformed by this early worship into an element of man's greatness.

The truth is, it would almost seem as if the first mission of India to the world was to proclaim the original hopefulness of the message of life. With all those geographical surroundings which naturally foster gloom, and which ultimately did foster gloom, the spirit of this race was at the outset light and airy, incapable of being depressed, and unable to be sombre. It became in this a revelation to the world of what the dawn of life by nature is, and by nature ought to be. Indeed, the conception of a pessimistic child is in itself a contradiction in terms. Childhood is the season of outlook, and where childhood is unimpeded the outlook is ever one of brightness. I say, where childhood is unimpeded. There *is* such a thing as a melancholy childhood; but where it exists it is always the result of some hereditary influence. India betrays no such influence; its morning is without clouds. If there is anything which would prompt me to assign to this faith an earlier origin than to others, it is just this original cloudlessness, this absence from the morning sky of all portents and of all shadows. It would seem to indicate that, in a deeper sense than the surrounding religions, the worship of India was the cradle of all worship. Nowhere is there so much freshness, even in the incipient stages of seemingly contemporaneous faiths. China, with all her hopes of empire, exhibits the traces of a life worn out by a long course of worldliness. Persia, in spite of her struggles and aspirations—nay, by the very struggle to realise her aspirations—gives evidence that her morning sky has long departed. Egypt, by her efforts from the very outset to pierce behind the veil of sense, bears testimony to the fact that the form of her faith is a comparatively late one, and one which could only come when the first age of life had been found illusory. But India is at the beginning a spontaneous child. She reveals in every movement the primitive instincts of the heart. She comes to the sight of nature without any trace of a theory, without any indication that she has received from others a creed to promulgate or a doctrine to defend. She paints only what she sees, and she paints it as if she had seen it for the first time. There are many things in the Vedas which do not suggest a primitive religion; there is a knowledge of the arts which implies a previous growth, and there is a subtlety of speculation which indicates a previous maturing. But the optimism of their first aspirings comes to us as at least one drop from the fountain, and the uncloudedness of their original view looks like the reflection of a dawn.

CHAPTER V.

THE SUBJECT CONTINUED.

I HAVE said that the message of Indian religion has been the revelation of life. I have pointed out that, as a matter of fact, the spiritual life of the individual man is unfolded in three stages. There is a stage of initial hopefulness, in which the world looks absolutely cloudless; there is a stage of disenchantment, in which the world reveals nothing but clouds, and in which the soul's only hope is to rise beyond it; and there is a stage of moral action, in which the soul surmounts once more its sense of care, not by rising above the world, but by finding within the world itself an object transcending materialism—the brotherhood of man.

I have in the previous chapter endeavoured to show how the earliest manifestation of Indian religion has revealed the earliest of these phases of life. We have seen how the first impressions of the Hindu mind were almost unqualifiedly joyful—how it looked out upon the forms of nature and saw in them only the mirror of its own freedom. We are now to let the curtain fall upon this opening scene, and when it shall rise again we shall be in the presence of a complete transformation. If the first stage of Indian religion is a sense of perfect freedom, the second is assuredly a sense of entire bondage. We have no historical clue by which to interpret the change; the interpretation lies behind the scenes. We have simply the successive representation of two contrasted pictures—the picture of national hope and the picture of national despair. In the absence of any outward clue we are driven inward. In the silence of historical annals we seek an explanation from the voice of human nature. We ask if there is anything in the constitution of the mind of man which can render intelligible this marked and contrasted transition, which can explain the substitution of a dark and sombre view of the universe for a view whose characteristic feature was sweetness and light?

More than one attempt has been made to furnish such an explanation, and some of the theories seem to me not wholly satisfactory. One very popular reason is the theory whose representative advocate is perhaps Mr Buckle. It seeks to account for the general depression of the Eastern mind by purely geographical influences. It tells us that in Europe man has power over nature, whereas in Asia nature has power over man.[1] It tells us that the Indian has been frightened by his vast mountains, appalled by his endless plains, dwarfed by his immense rivers; that his personality has been compelled to shrink into insignificance before the majesty of a natural creation exhibited ever on the largest scale, and that his life has trembled into nothingness in the presence of material forces which he is powerless to control and unable to comprehend. Now, I have already admitted that these geographical influences do exert a depressing influence, or, as I have expressed it, they "naturally foster gloom"; but I have used that expression advisedly, in order to guard against the notion that they can *create* gloom. When once the heart has been depressed, an environment such as that of India will certainly tend to retain and even to deepen its depression; but there is nothing in such surroundings which can *originate* the sinking of the heart. If a man enters upon such a scene with a disposition light and buoyant, he will find nothing in these elements to interfere with this lightness and buoyancy—probably much which shall minister to them. The vastness of the American continent has been made, in Longfellow's "Evangeline," to suggest to the individual mind the idea of melancholy. But such a suggestion belongs not to the morning of American history; it has proceeded

[1] See Buckle's 'History of English Civilisation,' vol. i., introductory pages.

from an age which is already weighted with care and oppressed with the burden and heat of the day. To the original settlers in New England, the vastness of the Transatlantic continent conveyed a very different impression; it stimulated into enthusiastic hope the hearts of the Pilgrim Fathers. But perhaps the most remarkable instance is that of India herself. We have seen that her morning was all brightness. Throughout that morning, even from the dawn, she dwelt in the same environment that subsequently evoked her spirit of gloom. She was surrounded by the same gigantic aspects of nature and the same vast scale of scenery; yet in these hours of morning she did not shrink before the spectacle, nor feel small in the presence of material greatness. How shall we account for this? It is true that many of her people had originally been transplanted from another soil; shall we say that her early hopefulness was only the expenditure of that former life, only the survival of a culture which the gloom of the new environment could not at once wear away? Such a theory is precluded by the facts. There would be some force in it if the period of India's youth had been of short duration; it might then, indeed, have seemed like the expiring gleam of a fire elsewhere lighted. But the period of India's youth is long, unwontedly long; it must be measured not by years but centuries. The proof lies in the fact that her earliest books reveal a civilisation that could not have sprung up in a night, and an acquaintance with the arts of life that demanded a lengthened past. The power, therefore, which conferred this primitive brightness on the Indian mind could not have been a foreign power; it must have been indigenous to the soil. It was capable of subsisting during a very long minority in the midst of these same geographical influences which are supposed to have produced its contrary; and the conclusion seems inevitably to follow, that the effect attributed to these influences has been due to some other cause.

The truth is, we habitually overrate the originative influence of nature upon mind. Nature is both a fountain and a mirror; but it is far more a mirror than a fountain. It does not *give* nearly so much as it gets. We talk in popular language of receiving our impressions from surrounding scenery; in reality, we first give our impressions to the scenery and then take them back again. Our moods of mind are rarely *created* by nature; they are almost always imparted to nature and restored to us anew. The visible creation dances to our piping and mourns to our lamenting; it laughs when we are joyful, it weeps when we are sad. If the Indian enters upon the scene with ideas of freedom in his heart, he will find these ideas mirrored in everything around him—expressed in the endless plains and typified in the gigantic mountains. If the Indian should come to the scene with a mind overwhelmed by a sense of its own impotence, he will find the impression confirmed by the very same aspects of nature; the boundless length of the plain will repeat to him the contrast of his own nothingness, and the towering strength of the mountain will remind him of his insignificance anew.

We must arrive, then, at the conclusion that the change in the Indian mind from gay to grave is not to be accounted for on geographical principles. A second attempt to account for it has been made from an opposite direction. It has been sought to explain it not from the world without but from the world within. We have been told that the shrinking of the Indian before the aspects of nature has been due to the natural inactivity of his intellect, to that want of mental energy which characterises the East in general and marks the Hindu race in particular. Now, no one would attempt to deny that from a Western point of view the Indian intellect is distinguished by its want of energy. But what do we mean by this? Simply that it is distinguished by its absence from that direction where in the West it is accustomed to blow. The manifestations of the Western mind are energetic in a *practical* direction; they exhibit themselves by their effects on the outer world. In India there is not this form of energy; but there is another and a more intense form. The mind here does not go out, but it does not therefore fall asleep; it goes in. It retires within itself and meditates upon the secret of its own nature. We are accustomed to think and speak of the Indian mind as an inert and sluggish thing. It is characteristically and emphatically the reverse. A man is not necessarily asleep because he is not outwardly moving. It is not too much to say that the mind of the West, with all its undoubted impulses towards the progress of humanity, has never exhibited such an intense amount of intellectual force as is to be found in the religious speculations of India. Nay, I will go further. It is not too much to say that the religious speculations of India have been the cradle of all Western speculations, and that wheresoever the European mind has risen into heights of philosophy, it has done so because the Brahman has been its pioneer There is no intellectual problem of the West which had not its earliest discussion in the East, and there is no modern solution of that problem which will not be found anticipated in Eastern lore. We must emphatically deny, therefore, that the Hindu mind is in any sense distinguished by the absence of force or energy.[1] If I were asked to mark its distinction from the European intellect, I should say that it is the

---

[1] Even those who admit that the second period of Indian history is a retrogression from the first, do not deny that it exhibits signs of mental progress—*e.g.*, Ritter, 'History of Ancient Philosophy,' i. 94.

difference between bearing and doing. The European energy is exerted in the construction of new masses; the Indian force is exhibited in the supporting of old ones. The weight of this world presses upon the mind of the Hindu. His main desire is to shake it off, to get free from it, to emancipate his inner self from the trammels of the outer day; and all the struggles of his life are directed towards this end. The fact of such an end is the disproof of anything abject or craven in his intellectual nature; and the struggle by which he seeks to compass it, subterranean and unseen as it is, exhibits a larger amount of actual power than can be witnessed in all the utilitarian movements of Western civilisation.

The question, then, still remains unanswered, How are we to account for the change of the Indian mind from optimism into despair? It cannot be explained by scenery, it cannot be referred to the inertness of the understanding; is there any other possible solution? There is; but it is one that lies not in the nature of India but in the nature of man. The searchers after causes have, in my opinion, looked too far in advance for an explanation of this problem. If they had looked into the glass of human nature, they would have found that India is here in no sense peculiar; it simply exhibits, in very pronounced and Eastern letters, the handwriting on the walls of all humanity. The transition of the Indian mind from gay to grave is itself a revelation of the message of life, an anticipative specimen of what every developed man and every developed nation does and must go through. What are the facts of the case? The beginning of all life is a search for individual happiness. By individual happiness I do not mean personal happiness; a joy which is not personal is a contradiction in terms. But the search for an individual joy is the pursuit of an object with a view to my own advantage, and to that alone. It is with this pursuit that all life begins. We start upon the course of our being with the firm conviction that each of us is an end to himself. We look upon the world as made specially for ourselves, and we expect with the utmost confidence that everything around us will minister to our pleasure. And in every case we experience a bitter disappointment. There are some instances in which the fortunes of life are unequally bestowed; but here the same lot falls impartially to all. / There is not a man in this world who has not come to the conviction that his first conception of existence was a dream, who has not arrived at the knowledge that things were not created to minister to his own individual happiness. And as his own individual happiness is at first the only kind of joy he knows, the advent of this knowledge comes to him as more than a pain—as a despair. As the conviction breaks upon him that the first hope was a delusion, and as the light of a higher hope has not yet dawned, the impression created by the discovery must be one of blank pessimism. It was so with India. She began with the belief that the universe existed for the sake of the individual; she reverenced the powers of nature as ministers to the wants of man. She valued Agni not so much because it was light as because it brought light to some particular path of life; she worshipped Indra not so much because it was itself a source of refreshment, as because it sent rain at some specially needed time to the crops of some special man. This was her first conception of the value of nature, and it proved a delusion. She found that whatever value Agni had, it was not this value; that whatever advantage lay in the worship of Indra, it was not this advantage. She found that to the individual man Agni often failed to send his light just at the moment when it was wanted; that Indra often refused to give the shower precisely at the time and place where it was specially desired. And in the breaking of that conviction there happened to India what befalls every man— an aggravated sense of the illusion life has given. Disappointed in her first expectation, she, like the rest of mankind, invested the whole world with the gloom of its transition moment. Her earliest hope had been a dream; she revenged herself by saying it was <u>all a dream</u>. The world in its length and breadth presented itself to her view as a scene of vanity and vexation of spirit, as an agglomeration of vain shadows, meaning nothing and tending nowhere. It stood before her as an illusion, a dream, an assemblage of phantasies, already detected as impostures, yet, by their vivid appearance of reality, impressing the mind with a sense of care. Henceforth the problem of India became one reiterated question—how to get free. How was she to emancipate herself from those deluding shadows? How was she to get rid of those illusory cares of the sense which clogged the wings of the spirit? How was she to be lifted from this grovelling in the dust into an atmosphere congenial to the life of the soul and harmonious with the instincts of the heart?

At this stage of her history it appeared to the Indian mind as if the only chance of emancipation were material disembodiment. To rise above the world seemed impossible, except by rising above the things of the world. How was this elevation to be effected? It is quite a common thing for men who are passing through this Indian experience, to attempt an emancipation from the things of time by contemplating the hour of death. But the men who do so are actuated by the notion that the things of time are now realities. The Indian mind had arrived at a contrary belief. It was not simply that she believed there was a time coming when these visible things would pass away; she did not believe them to exist now. There was no use to wait for death to find emancipation from them; they were at the present moment matters of mere imagination, and therefore there must be out of them some present mode of exit. What was that mode? The attempt to answer this question is the birth of Indian philosophy — a philosophy which directly or indirectly has dominated the whole course of human speculation. It is the transition from the hymns of the 'Rig-Veda' into the creed called Brahmanism — a creed which, dating almost from the dawn of history, has been unsurpassed in intellectual subtlety by all the subsequent efforts of the mind of man. Even at this remote date it does not appear an anachronism. It belongs as much to the nineteenth century after the Christian era as to the ninth century before it, and the student of modern times, in pondering its abstruse speculations, feels that he is breathing an atmosphere not alien to that which has come from the spirit of the German renaissance.

These efforts of the Indian mind to emancipate itself from the shadows of time will be found specially embodied in those philosophic works called the 'Upanishads,'[1] — a word which probably means "that which lies beneath the surface." Into any technical account of these speculations it is neither my inten-

---

[1] See Professor Max Müller's 'History of Ancient Sanskrit Literature (London, 1860); also John Muir's 'Original Sanskrit Texts,' vol. i.-iv. (London, 1858-1863).

tion nor my province to enter. I wish merely to photograph the leading features of the system, and to put them in a light which shall be intelligible to the English mind. I shall avoid all technical language, and shall endeavour, by an attempt at lucid exposition, to make clear a subject which the grotesqueness of mythological terms has invested with a mist beyond its natural mysticism.

Brahmanism, which we have characterised as the second stage in the life of India, is the effort through despair of the world to fly from the world. But the Brahman may say, like the Psalmist in a different sense, "Whither shall I flee from Thy presence?" The world is to him an assemblage of shadows—a dream; but for that very reason it seems to present no refuge. What advantage can he get by fleeing from one shadow to another? Must not all his efforts be only a flight from illusion to illusion? Yet, as he meditates on this dark prospect, there comes to him a startling thought. He says, This world is indeed a dream; but if so, must there not be a dreamer? Does not the very fact of illusion imply the presence of one who is subject to illusion? Conceding that all the phenomena of the universe are phenomena of a dream-sleep, who is the sleeper, and who is the dreamer? Whoever he is, he must lie beneath the shadows, must be independent of the shadows, and must therefore be an ultimate refuge from the shadows.

And the Brahman answers, The dreamer is God Almighty. If the world to him be an assemblage of shadows, it is not therefore an assemblage of sleepers. All the images of the universe, images as they are of the night, yet pass through the experience of a single soul—the Divine Soul. There are not two dreamers, but only one — the Absolute Spirit. The appearance of a multitude results from the fact that the one consciousness is presented in fragments. If a vase falls from a height, it will be broken into a hundred pieces; yet even in their brokenness these pieces will reveal not two vases but one. When the sun breaks upon various sheets of water, we have a better simile still of the Brahman's creed. A thousand suns are then presented to the eye, revealing not fragments, like the shattered vase, but the entire rounded image of the object. Yet all the time the plurality is an illusion. There are not a thousand suns, but only one—the original one in the heavens. The nine hundred and ninety-nine exist only in the eye—that is to say, exist only in the consciousness. The life that was a unity in the heavens, when it passes into the earth takes the form of diversity; the one becomes the many.[1]

Let us try to illustrate the point by yet another

---

[1] The pantheism of the Brahmanic creed will be well seen from a Upanishad of the fourth Veda, given by Colebrooke, 'Asiatic Researches,' viii. 475.

simile, which will bring the picture nearer than either of the two preceding. Let us imagine a fire lighted at the end of a room in which there are a hundred mirrors. Every one of these mirrors will reveal a separate fire. In this case there will be not merely, as with the sun on the sheets of water, a complete image of various objects, but these various objects will all be visible at one and the same moment. Nevertheless, here, as in the case of the images of sunlight, we are in the presence of only one reality—the originally lighted fire. The others are all illusions, and if we could imagine them gifted with intelligence, they would recognise themselves to be illusions. Each of them would say: "I am not the fire on the mirror, as you suppose; I am the fire at the end of the room. In myself I am nothing; my whole personality is the personality of this original fire. If you were to put out this fire, I would be nowhere, for I am nowhere even now except in so far as I reflect and image this primal light."

This metaphor seems to me to express exactly the doctrine of Brahmanism regarding God's relation to the world, with the single exception of the fact that in the doctrine of Brahmanism the mirror itself would be an illusion. The mirror here must be regarded as the dream—the canvas of fancy on which are painted the images of the night of time. You will observe that to the mind of the Indian the mirrors are the disturbing things. There are recognised by him three stages in the life of the Divine Spirit.[1] The first stage is that in which the fire burns alone in the room, without any object to reflect it; it is the period in which the Divine Spirit enjoys rest unbroken by a dream. When the Indian thinks of God in this light he calls Him Brahma. The second is that in which the divine rest is broken and the dream begins. It is the stage when the mirrors are introduced into the apartment, and when, by their deceitful reflection, the one fire appears to be the many. When the Indian thinks of God in this light he calls Him Vishnu. The third is that in which the dream vanishes again and the unbroken rest returns. It is the stage in which the mirrors are removed, in which the illusion of the many lights disappears, and the original fire resumes once more its solitary and undivided empire. When the Indian thinks of God in this light he calls Him Siva.

Now, it is to Siva that in the mind of the Brahman the main interest attaches. The word literally means the "destroyer." He belongs to the stage where the mirrors are annihilated, where the dream of life vanishes, and where the imaginary lights go back into the real and primal light. The worship of a destroyer seems a startling thing, appears to

---

[1] They are not stages of *development;* the third is only the first restored, after an imaginary interruption.

be something anomalous in the history of religion. It is not really so; it is the second stage in the message of life. Nearly every man experiences at one time what the Brahman has experienced and photographed. What is that destroyer whom the Brahman worships? It is the destroyer of shams, of illusions, of dreams. The destruction he craves is the destruction of things which to him have no existence except in imagination; in other words, it is the destroying of vain fancies. He wants to get his mind emancipated from illusions. He feels that the things of sense and time, shadows as they are, are yet shadows which eclipse from the sight the realities of being, and he longs for the rising of a sun which shall dispel even their semblance of existence.[1] This is what every life experiences in its second stage — the stage in which its primitive hope has faded into despair. The moment we find that life has failed to fulfil its early promises, we seek refuge in the belief that the things we desired were only shadows. Our greatest comfort lies in contemplating their unsubstantiality, and in looking to a state of things where they shall have no existence even in thought. At these times we all worship the destroyer; our view of eternity is itself that of a destroyer, of something

---

[1] The attitude of the Brahman towards the world is finely portrayed by Max Müller, 'Ancient Sanskrit Literature,' p. 18 and sequel.

that shall rend in tatters our webs of sophistry. Let no one imagine that this aspiration of the Brahman has nothing in common with Christianity. It presents, on the contrary, one of the main links by which a Christian missionary might connect the religion of the Cross with the religious life of India. When we sing in our churches every Sunday those words of Keble,

> "Till, in the ocean of Thy love,
> We lose ourselves in heaven above,"

are we breathing any other aspiration than that which, in somewhat fantastic form, is expressed in the creed of Brahmanism? When we chant in our worship the prayer of Toplady,

> "Rock of Ages, cleft for me,
> Let me hide myself in Thee,"

what else are we doing but re-echoing the old Indian desire to be liberated from our past and from our present by the entrance into a life which shall dissipate their shadows? This mysticism, as we call it, belongs to no special faith; it belongs to human nature. I do not say it belongs to human nature at every stage of its being; I believe that it is not the ripeness nor the fulness of the life of man. But it is assuredly the product of life's second period —its period of disenchantment. It comes ever with that time when the soul awakens to the sense that what it believed to be a substance was only a shadow. In the first discovery of the illusoriness of the things of time, the impulse of the human spirit is always to break away from time, and to seek a refuge in something which transcends the visible; its immediate voice is the cry of the Psalmist, "Oh that I had wings like a dove! for then would I fly away, and be at rest."

How, then, is this dream to be broken? How is the mind to be emancipated from the belief in these shadows? We often in the visions of the night recognise a dream to be a dream without being able to shake it off; we have an impression that we are not awake, and yet we cannot tell in what respect the waking consciousness ought to differ from the illusion which besets us. How is the Brahman to get rid of his illusion? He answers that in order to get rid of it he must cease to love it. That which in the view of Brahmanism tends to perpetuate the dream is the fact that the dream, in spite of its recognised illusoriness, is with the large mass of men an object of affection; they cling to the shadows even while they feel their shadowiness. Now, whatever we love tends to persist in the mind; even if torn away by violence, it returns to our thought with redoubled power. The Brahman had no hope whatever of getting emancipated from the dream by the mere fact of death. It was his opinion that if a man died with his heart fixed on the things of sense, the things of sense would come back to him again; in other words, that he would repeat his old life in a new form. This is the root of that doctrine which has been so fruitful of results in so many forms of faith —the transmigration of the soul. It is founded upon the Indian belief that there is a congruity between the body and the mind, a congruity which mere change of space cannot alter, and which death itself does not of necessity annul. If a man has left this world with a strong leaning towards animal impulses, he will in due time be born into this world again in a body corresponding to these animal impulses—perhaps even in an animal body. There is a principle of attraction between body and soul which stretches beyond the grave, and which tends to reincarnate the soul in an environment and in circumstances similar to its former self. The deeds which we do in the body are helping to mould the body, and the mould of the body shall determine the future home of the spirit. This retributive power of action, this tendency of bodily deeds to form a tabernacle for the man after death, is what the Indian called Karma. It answers more nearly to our modern idea of heredity than to any other conception. It is the reappearance in an after-age of seeds which have been sown by us in this, and its only difference from hereditary transmission consists in the fact that the seeds reappear not merely to the eye of posterity, but to the sight and to the experience of the man who sowed them.

In the religion of India, as in Christianity, a man has a judgment-seat after death; he must render an account of the things done in the body. But the account which the man renders in the religion of India consists not in bearing a penalty in some future state, but in getting back to the state from which death has outwardly severed him. His punishment lies in being obliged to retrace his steps into an environment corresponding in all essential respects to that which he formerly inhabited. If he leaves the world with the world in his heart, the world in his heart will bring him back again to scenes and situations which shall simply repeat the experience of bygone days, and clothe him anew in that form of vesture from which death ought to have set him free. The retributive power of Karma lies in the congruity between a man's body and a man's soul. The house in which the spirit dwells is a house not made with hands but with desires. The wish is not only the father of the thought, but the source of the embodiment; where a man's heart is, his tabernacle shall be also. The first and foremost thing is to remove and to improve the wish. If the soul would escape transmigration at the hour of death into a body and a life repeating the shadows of to-day, it must begin to-day by turning its thoughts from these shadows. It must set its affections already on the things above. It must tear up by the roots its propensity to live in the temporal, and must plant in its room a love for the unseen and eternal. Such a love will be more effectual than death in separating the man from his environment of clay. It will interpose a stronger barrier than the grave to the reappearance of his old conditions, and will usher him, even while on earth, into a life from which these conditions are excluded. The man who longs for eternity has parted already from the body of time.

In connection with this subject there is a point in the Indian religion which has often struck me as very peculiar: I allude to the institution of caste. Does it not seem a strange thing that the doctrine of caste should have found its origin and its most favoured home precisely in that region where men had decided to abandon the world? Would we not expect that a race which had awakened to a sense of the nothingness of time would have ignored above all things those petty distinctions of rank which tend to perpetuate temporal conditions? The superiority of man to man is supposed to have its origin in the desires of the flesh; why does a religion, whose leading aim is to obliterate these desires, place in the very foreground of its system a gradation of human ranks whose summit touches the heavens and whose base is on the ground?

. Such was the difficulty which often presented

itself to my own mind in contemplating the spirit of Brahmanism. On a deeper reflection, however, I came to the conclusion that even in its doctrine of caste, Brahmanism is not inconsistent with itself. It is true that in this doctrine it does recognise, in very pronounced terms, the superiority of man to man. But what is the ground of that superiority? It is the comparative amount of unworldliness. I do not say that this idea persisted through the history of caste, but I do believe that it existed at its origin, and was the immediate cause of its formation. Look at the four castes of India, and you will see, if I mistake not, that they are regulated by their relative degree of superiority to the things of time. At the top of the social ladder stands the priest. He stands there because in all ages priesthood has been the special type of sacrifice. That the priest has ever perfectly realised that type cannot be affirmed of any religion, least of all of the religion of India. But this does not by one iota alter the fact that the ideal of priesthood is sacrifice. The man who stands at the altar is by profession the representative of the highest form of self-surrender. He typifies the place and the hour in which humanity resigns its delight in all worldly things, and sets its affections on the things above. Therefore it is that the Brahman has placed him at the head of the social ladder. He has been made first in the world precisely because he is supposed to have given up the world altogether; it is the pre-eminence of social extinction. Then, a step lower down, stands the soldier. His is also by definition a sacrificial life. That in point of fact it has been often the reverse of sacrificial is indisputable; it has been frequently the most oppressive of all forces. Yet this is contrary to its ideal. The ideal of the soldier is that of a man who has lost his personality in the life of his country, who has given up his individual desires for a national motive, and who has become animated by one spirit which has displaced every private will—the spirit of patriotism. Therefore he stands in the second rank amongst the castes of India, yielding only to the priest in the order of his pre-eminence. Yet with him, as with the priest, the order of pre-eminence is a sacrificial order. He stands at the top of the ladder because he has less personality than those below, and he owes his superiority to the belief that he has made a more full surrender of his individual independence.

We take a step further down still, and we come to the third caste—that of the agriculturist or man of commerce. He is, from an Indian point of view, decidedly below either the priest or the soldier. His profession is by nature less sacrificial; it does not of necessity involve the giving up of himself for others. It is possible in such a life as his to make his own interest the sole motive of his living. Nevertheless, he does not stand at the foot of the ladder. With all his temptations to selfishness, he may still be unselfish. He may realise the fact that the life of commerce is, after all, not for the individual but for the community—that it is based upon the very idea of an interchange of wants, whereby a man gives to his brother what his brother needs, in return for receiving what he himself requires. In the very practice of agriculture he may recognise the symbol of a sacrificial life, in which the seed comes to the surface only because it has been buried, and he may be stimulated by that symbol to go and do likewise. Therefore it is that even for him there is reserved a place higher than the lowest—a place which touches, indeed, the borders of the worldly, but which yet lies intermediate between the secular and the sacred. He is a step below the heavens, yet a step above the earth.

The lowest place is reserved for the fourth order—that of the slave. The serf occupies in the religion of India the most subordinate position in sacred as well as in secular things. Yet I am by no means of opinion that he has been assigned this subordinate position in religion by reason of his lowly condition of life. It is not because he is a slave that he holds the lowest place amongst the privileges of the worshipper, but because, being a slave, he has not the opportunity of yielding up a voluntary sacrifice. It is not the fact of his dependence that places him on that step of the religious ladder which is nearest to the ground. Dependence, in the view of the Brahman, so far from being a thing to be despised, is a thing to be sought and venerated. The goal of all life, the ultimate aim of all existence, is that the individual should surrender himself to the sway of the Universal Will—that man should lose himself in God. But the difference between the surrender of the devotee to God and the surrender of the slave to his earthly master, is that in the one case the act is voluntary, in the other obligatory. The slave gives up his life to his master because he is compelled to do so; he is not under grace but under the law. It is this which puts him, in the view of the Brahman, lower than the priest, lower than the soldier, lower even than the merchant. He is not his own master. He is in the strictest sense a mere individual unit, impelled to act from motives of private interest. He is dominated every moment by the sense of fear. His action never passes beyond himself, never contemplates its effect on humanity. It is done purely as a source of self-preservation, and in the preservation of his individual self its purpose ends. Therefore to this fourth order of the body politic there is assigned the lowest place on the social ladder. He stands at the very base because his life does not transcend the earth, and his aspirations do not reach above the ground. He is a child of the soil, a creature of the dust, a denizen of the day and hour;

and therefore there is given to him a place on a level with the dust and an order commensurate with the hour.[1]

Such is, in my view, the mental origin of the idea of caste as exhibited in India. It is only as an origin that I propose it. It is certainly no longer the Indian motive for its own social order; that motive has long since become worldly. But originally it was not worldly. In that period of transition in which the Indian mind woke up from its dream that this earth was an elysium, it passed firmly and instantaneously to the opposite extreme. It came to regard this world not as a paradise but as a hindrance to paradise—as an illusion, a dream, a clog on the aspirations of the spirit. It was at this period of worldly pessimism that the idea of caste arose, and surely its rise must be interpreted in accordance with the age which produced it. Is it probable, is it conceivable, that at the very moment in which India proclaimed the despair of earthly life, she should have inaugurated a system intended to propagate earthly vanities? Is it likely that caste could have meant to her the superiority of one man to another at a time when she had reached a conviction of the nothingness of all

---

[1] The best account of these four orders of caste will be found in the first volume of Dr John Muir's 'Original Sanskrit Texts on the Origin and Progress of the Religion and Institutions of India, collected, translated into English, and illustrated by Notes.'

human things? Is it not far more probable that the idea of caste was itself an expression of this sense of human nothingness, and that the degrees by which she regulated the ladder of earthly greatness were degrees in the power to sacrifice and superiorities in the strength of self-surrender?

CHAPTER VI.

THE SUBJECT COMPLETED.

Has the Indian message of life now reached its consummation? It has proclaimed in its second stage that the world, which originally seemed a scene of perfection, is a scene unfitted to man — a scene which man ought to get rid of. Is this the last word on the subject? Does life rise into moral heights in proportion as it rises beyond the seen and temporal? India herself must furnish the answer, and her answer is an emphatic negative. Perhaps the votaries of Brahmanism are at once the most religious and the most immoral of all sects. They are pervaded with a sense of the nothingness of time, and their whole idea is directed to rising above this nothingness. But this negative relation towards the world is far from being favourable to morality. It may have the advantage of leading a man not to fret, but it leads him at the same time not to act. If time is but a vision of the night, if the forms of earth are but the images in a dream, there is nothing good any more than bad in the world; there is simply illusion. To abstain from righteous living is to abstain from vanity; to engage in unrighteous living is to do something which is not real, and if not real, then not really harmful. Accordingly the creed of Brahmanism is consistent with itself in its very inconsistency. It tells men to be sacrificial, and to realise their own nothingness. It tells them to look with contempt upon the things of space and the events of time. Yet it bases its precept upon the fact that they *are* things of space, and that they *are* events of time. The contempt is thus poured not only on acts of vice, but on all acts whatsoever. Every work, whether virtuous or vicious, is but a gesture in a dream. The virtuous act can do no good, and the vicious act can do no harm; they are both unrealities. Is it inconsistent in the Brahman to hold lightly the requirements of conscience? Is it strange that, with a creed which reduces everything to indifference, his own life should exhibit side by side the depths of self-surrender and the heights of self-indulgence? Is it peculiar that at one and the same moment we should find him prostrating himself in abject reverence before the altar, and putting forth his hand to defraud his brother man?[1]

---

[1] The moral tendency of Brahmanism is finely described by Professor Wilson, 'Essays and Lectures, chiefly on the Religion of the Hindoos,' ii. 75. Edit. London.

The Message of India.

We have not, then, reached the final word of the Indian message. There is a stage yet to come in the development of Indian life, because there is a stage yet to come in the development of universal life. There is a time in the life of every man in which the primitive vision of this world's glory vanishes, and in which the cry of the human spirit is only to get free. It is the period of man's asceticism, the period in which his whole desire is to be emancipated from the present order of things, and to be ushered into a life in which time shall be no more. It is a period highly favourable to what is popularly called religion, but highly unfavourable to what is universally known as morality. The world is dwarfed to the view, but for that very reason its interests dwindle. If there vanishes the temptation to do wrong, there goes out with it also the incentive to do right. If the world is contemplated merely as a thing which passes away, we shall have as little respect for the virtues as for the lusts of it. Accordingly, for the universal life of man, as for the particular life of India, there is wanted a completing stage. He has realised the fact that the world is a scene of care, and he has sought to get rid of care by getting rid of the world. This is equivalent to ending the pains of life by an act of suicide. Is there any other mode of getting rid of the pains of life? There is, and it is one which has been tried by all nations. It is the method of life's afternoon, as distinguished from either its morning or its midday. In its morning its individual hopes are high, and it sees a world whose streets are paved with gold. In its mid-day its individual cares are deep, and it beholds a world only worthy to vanish away. But with its afternoon there comes a thought different from either the one or the other, unlike the morning and unlike the mid-day. There breaks upon it the conviction that there is a possibility of escaping individual care without leaving the world, without leaving care itself. Is it not possible to get rid of my burden by taking on another's burden, to drop the weight of the individual life by lifting the weight of the universe? Such is the question that sooner or later is asked by every developed man; such was the question that was now about to be asked by India. She had tried the wings of a dove by which to fly away from the world, but she had found that this power of flight had not exalted her. Was there no other escape for herself than by flying away? Might she not stand in the midst of the world and be unworldly, in the midst of care and be free? Was there not a method of life remaining by which the spirit of man might enter into rest here and now, and in the very heart of the busy crowd might experience that peace which passeth understanding?

The answer to this question was the birth of one of the greatest religious systems which have ever dominated the mind of man—a system which at the present moment numbers amongst its votaries a large proportion of the earth's population,[1] and which ranks in moral intensity second to Christianity alone. I allude of course to Buddhism—the third great movement of the Indian mind, and one of the mightiest movements in the mind of the world. Let us try to mark distinctly the precise point of contrast between the old faith and the new, between the creed called Brahmanism and this new conception of the life of man. On one point they were agreed: both recognised the fact that this world was a state of nothingness. Where they differed was in the conclusion they derived from this position. Brahmanism said, "This world is a state of nothingness, therefore look up; turn away your eyes towards the things which are unseen and eternal." Buddhism said, "This world is a state of nothingness, therefore look down; when you are oppressed with a sense of your individual woe, try to contemplate the fact that this woe is not yours alone, but something which belongs to life as life. In your hour of sorrow and care, instead of turning away from the world, endeavour to contemplate the world more closely. Look beneath the surface, and you will find that the sorrows and cares which you experience are but fragments of a vast weight of suffering which

[1] On this point see Professor Max Müller's 'Chips from a German Workshop,' i. 214.

is pressing with equal intensity on the whole mass of humanity. In contemplating that fact, you will find a more complete solace than ever was experienced by the Brahman in his attempt to fly from the scene. You will learn that *in* the scene and not beyond it is the true secret of rest. Your own burden will fall in the very act of lifting your brother's. In the realisation that the weight is universal, it will cease to be particular. In the sense that you are bearing a common load, you will forget everything that is individual or uncommon, and in the midst of a world of war you will feel a great calm."

You will observe that the main distinction here between Brahmanism and Buddhism lies in the difference between a levelling up and a levelling down. Brahmanism is essentially a levelling up; it teaches emancipation from the cares of the world by rising into another world. Buddhism is distinctively a levelling down. It is conceived in the interest of the democracy. It proposes a remedy for universal man, and therefore it places that remedy within the reach of the lowest. It objects to the Brahmanical method, because that method appeals only to the transcendental few. It feels that when you tell a man to lose himself in God, you tell him to do something which demands a long spiritual training, and presupposes a preliminary education in the divine life. It perceives that such a precept will inevitably end in the privilege of a caste, and that the prize for self-surrender will be won by the more refined professions. Buddhism aspires to be the religion of the people; it seeks a remedy for man as man. It tries to find a refuge for those wants which are at the foot of the social ladder, and which, because they are at the foot of the social ladder, belong equally to all men. Accordingly, the refuge which Buddhism proposes is a refuge which can be sought and found alike by the lowest and the highest. It involves no metaphysical knowledge, it requires no transcendental flights, it prescribes no unnatural asceticism. It does not ask an abandonment of the present world, or the thought of it; it demands rather a deeper entrance into the thought of it. It tells the man of toil to look at his own toil as exemplified in another, the man of sorrow to contemplate his sorrow in the face of his brother-man. It tells him that by ceasing to view his cross as exclusively a private possession, it will cease to be a private possession at all. It tells him that what he wants to give him rest is not a diminished but an increased sense of the pain of life, and that if he only widen his horizon far enough to embrace the fact that grief is universal, he will enter into personal peace and learn the secret of emancipation from care.[1]

[1] For a full exposition of these views, see Hardy, 'Manual of Buddhism,' p. 496.

The system in modern times would be pronounced one of secularism. It would be called the gospel of humanity to distinguish it from any theological gospel. Without denying either God or immortality, it persistently ignores both. It ignores them not on the ground of any rational difficulties, but simply and solely on the ground of their own practical inutility, of their powerlessness to effect the redemption of mankind. And yet I am far from thinking that in the historical circumstances which prompted the rise of Buddhism, it is adequately described by the word secularism. That it ignored God and immortality is true, but what God, and what immortality? It was a God who was believed to stand to the world in a relation of antagonism, an immortality which was thought to consist in the annihilation of material life. The God of Brahmanism was not coextensive with the universe; He did not embrace in His being the works and ways of time. The immortality of Brahmanism was a life which could only exist by the destruction of earthly life; it had no place in the secret of its pavilion for the perpetuation of temporal interests. Against this partial Deity, against this limited immortality, Buddhism raised its voice in protest. In that protest lies its value; its so-called secularism is the secret of its power. It would have been a very different matter if Buddhism had arisen to expel God from the world; it would then have been entitled to be styled atheism. But we must never forget that the God of Brahmanism was already expelled from the world, and that in the creed of the Brahman the earth as such was already without a helper. When Buddhism appeared, it appeared to vindicate a neglected element. It stood up to advocate the cause of something which had been overlooked in the scheme of creation—the temporal life of man. It was willing to leave to the ancient Deity His original possessions in a transcendental heaven, but it asked to be allowed the possession of a field which had never been included within His dominions. It demanded the right to redeem the world *through* the world. It declared that there had been sufficient sacrifice to God, that the time was come for a sacrifice to man—a sacrifice which should be effected not by the hands of any consecrated priest, but by the hand of every man stretched out in aid of his brother. It maintained the doctrine of a universal priesthood, bound to accomplish a universal redemption by the lifting up of a universal burden.[1]

The truth is, the triumph of Buddhism lies in its protest against asceticism. That which gave it power over Brahmanism was its unascetic tendency. The view is frequently held that it has

[1] Buddha's own personal power lies in the belief that he has voluntarily submitted to sacrifice in order to be in sympathy with humanity (Hardy, Manual of Buddhism, p. 98).

derived its influence from the same root as monasticism; it has in fact derived its influence from exactly the opposite root. Monasticism was the shrinking of men into a place of refuge from the conflict of life and the burden of the day; it was essentially a retirement from the world. Buddhism was, on the contrary, a withdrawal from that retirement; it was an effort of the human mind to get rid of its isolation from common things, and to mingle once more in the pursuits and interest of the crowd. The relation of the two systems is not one of resemblance but of contrast. Monasticism has owed its power to the worldly nature of the age which has preceded it, to the weariness of minds that have been living long in the pursuit of earthly vanities. Buddhism has owed its power to the *un*worldly nature of the age which has preceded it, to the fact that men have been long immured in a life of transcendentalism, and are eager to join again in the concourse of the busy crowd.

It is the sacrificial character of Buddhism which has blinded the general reader to the view of its unascetic nature. It has been taken for granted that a life which is sacrificial must of necessity be a life which is separated from the world. The truth is precisely the reverse, and one of the great missions of Buddhism has been to teach us the reverse. The life most full of sacrifice is not that of the cloister but of the city. The heaviest burden which man has to bear is not the burden imposed by solitude, but the burden laid on him by society. It may be truly said that the most solitary moments in the life of man are precisely those moments in which he is least ascetic. He never realises the weight of his own personality to such a profound degree as when he is moving in contact with the masses of mankind. It is true, the weightedness is no longer for self but for others; yet the most selfish solicitude is not half so sacrificial. Buddhism professes to conquer individual pain, but it professes to conquer it by imparting to the individual the sense of a universal pain. It has been said that the aim of Buddhism is the extinction of desire; this is a mistake. The aim of Buddhism is the extinction only of _individual_ desire, and it proposes to extinguish it by a higher and a wider desire. Buddhism, in short, offers to the world a new remedy for individual pain—a remedy which in its nature is homœopathic, and which cures by an application resembling the old disease. That remedy is love —itself a sensation of pain, and itself a source of sacrifice. By the entrance into the love of humanity, Buddhism suggests the possibility of entering into a life which shall be sacrificial because it is not ascetic, and which shall give to the individual man a greater power to bear, precisely because it shall free him from the contemplation of his own burden.

There is another point in which I differ somewhat from the popular estimation of Buddhism. It is universally said to be a pessimistic system. In a certain sense this is true; but in what sense? In the same sense in which Mohammedanism may be said to be a sensuous religion. No man could deny that Mohammedanism allows a latitude to morals which would not be suffered by Christianity. Yet the man who would therefore state that the aim of Mohammedanism was to found a religion which should minister to the lusts of human nature, would be stating an untruth. Mohammedanism was intended to be, and actually succeeded in being, a reform in morals. It came to curtail the licences and the excesses of mankind. It stopped short of a thorough reform, and arrested itself before it had reached the total extermination of licence; but what it left unexpunged cannot be laid to its charge. It belongs to that old *régime* which the religion of the Prophet came to circumvent, and it ought to be viewed rather as the survival of a past culture than as a result of the new system. The legitimate fruit of Mohammedanism was the excess which it succeeded in diminishing; it is only indirectly answerable for the abuses which it has been too weak to abolish.

Now, precisely analogous to this is the position of Buddhism. Still less than the religion of Mohammed is it an original system. It was the child of Brahmanism, and therefore it was the heir to an estate of misery. Brahmanism was essentially the religion of despair. It had no hope whatever for the present world, and it made no effort to redeem it; its only hope was to be redeemed *from* it. The future to which it looked forward was a personal annihilation —a state in which the soul should be freed not only from every remembrance of the earth, but from every earthly form and human embodiment. As the child of such a mother, Buddhism came by nature into an inheritance of pessimism. Yet it must be confessed that she did not accept that inheritance without modification. Her whole aim was to improve it. Her leading purpose was the reverse of pessimistic; it was the attempt to find a break in the cloud of Brahmanism. Buddhism started on her path with the determination to discover in the world itself a ground for hope. I do not know what views she had about the state beyond the world. Her ideal was a paradise called Nirvana. Whether in the future state it meant annihilation or merely rest, I cannot say; the most eminent Eastern scholars are still on this point divided.[1] But the point for us to observe is that, in the original view of the Buddhist, the attainment of Nirvana was not limited to a future state; it might be reached here and now.

---

[1] See, for example, on the one side Max Müller, 'Buddhaghosha's Parables,' xxxix.-xlv.; on the other Gogerly, 'Journal of the Royal Asiatic Society,' Ceylon Branch, 1867-1870, Part i. p. 130.

In Buddhism, as in Christianity, there comes a message of peace on earth and goodwill to men—of peace on earth *because* of goodwill to men. There comes a message to the individual soul that, by fixing its thoughts upon the universal sorrow, its own troubles will melt away. This is the prospect of a present heaven,[1] of a life of rest which is to be reached in the earthly sphere, and to be reached through the very struggles which the earthly sphere involves. A religion which could formulate such a doctrine may be secular indeed, but cannot be wholly pessimistic. It must have in it something beyond pessimism, something which recognises a silver lining in the cloud, and which, through the present gloom, discerns the coming day.

I arrive, then, at this conclusion: There is in Buddhism an element of pessimism and an element of optimism; but the element of pessimism is derived, the element of optimism is original. The former is the fruit of her parentage; it is received by inheritance from Brahmanism. The latter is the result of her own native energy, and is the attempt to modify the natural conditions of her life. Now, in estimating the influence of Buddhism, it will be necessary to take into account both these elements

---

[1] Rhys-Davids indeed says that no Buddhist *now* expects Nirvana on earth (article "Buddhism" in 'Encyc. Britan.,' ninth edition); it may be so, but modern Buddhism makes up for this by its more definite view of the future.

—the pessimism which she has derived from her parent, and the optimism which she has received from her own nature. The influence of Buddhism has been great, yet I think I shall be generally borne out in the assertion that it has been disappointing. It has fallen short of the claims set up by the religion. These claims were universal; it aimed at nothing less than the emancipation of mankind, the redemption of all sorts and conditions of men. Has its influence been universal? has its effect been adequate to its claim? Assuredly not. It may have embraced numerically a larger number of votaries than any other religion, but numbers are in this sphere not the test of success. It may have proved the light of Asia, but to the eyes of Europe it has presented the aspect of a very dim twilight. The question is, Why? It is a religion with a beautiful theory, a theory very nearly identical with that of Christianity; why has Christianity succeeded where Buddhism has failed? It is because there is something in Buddhism which has prevented the realising of its own theory. And I think it will be found that this retarding element has been precisely the point adverted to—the blending of pessimism and optimism in its constitution. I think it will be found that the progress of Buddhism has been doubly impeded, and impeded from opposite sides. It has been arrested on the one hand by the natural pessimistic tendency which it derived from its ancestral descent; it has been arrested on the other by that native optimistic tendency which belonged essentially to its own nature, and by which it strove to ameliorate the misery which it had been taught to seek in man.

We begin with the former—the pessimistic impulse which it derived from Brahmanism. This original pessimism is, in my opinion, one great source of its failure to realise its own theory. What is that theory? It is the doctrine that, by fixing the love of the heart on universal man, the burdens of the individual heart will fall. Very good; but on what ground are we to fix the love of the heart on universal man? The Buddhist answers, On the ground of human misery. He tells us that the motive for our love to man is to be a sense of pity—an impression of the utter helplessness, and the perfect degradedness, and the supreme hopelessness of the life of the human community. Now the question is, Can such a motive be the basis of love? Is it possible that the practical benevolence of the heart can ever take its rise in a simple sense of pity unaccompanied by a gleam of hope? I think not. In point of fact there is no instance of a missionary effort which has not its root in a sense of the inherent possibilities of the objects to whom it is to minister. The lower animals occupy a very degraded position in comparison with man, yet no one ever dreamed of organising a mission for their improvement. Why? Simply because it is felt from the outset that such a scheme would be impossible. If the case of humanity were deemed from the beginning as hopeless a case as it appears in Brahmanism, it is safe to say that there would be the utter absence of any stimulus sufficiently strong to accomplish the elevation of human nature. And it is just here that, as it seems to me, the main distinction lies between Buddhism and Christianity. If Christianity has produced an impression on human nature which Buddhism has failed to produce, it is because Christianity has an idea of the possibilities of man which Buddhism has failed to realise. The religion of Christ has started with a perception of human guilt and sin, but for that very reason it has started with an impression of man's inherent greatness. There can be neither guilt nor sin where there is no responsibility, and there can be no responsibility where there is not power. The Christian conception of man is therefore in its root not the conception of a degraded being. He is contemplated from the beginning as one who occupies a sphere which is infinitely below him, and it is here that his degradation is supposed to lie. He is living beneath himself; he is dwelling in a far country; he is subsisting upon food which was only meant for swine. The call which Christianity gives to man is not a call which is dictated by mere pity; it comes ultimately from a sense of human possibility. It is stimulated by the belief that this being, who is crushed down by labour and heavy-ladenness, was yet made for rest, and has the capacity to attain rest. Therefore it is that Christian work for man has been so much more successful than Buddhist work for man. It has started from a different basis—a basis of hope. It has been prompted by no mere sense of compassion, but by an impression that the object is worth working for, and that the work will repay our pains. It has been begun and continued in the consciousness that the life for which we labour is essentially divine, and that the latent divinity within it shall sooner or later make it great.

But, as we have said, there is another side to the subject. If Buddhism is pessimistic by descent, it is optimistic by nature, and to this native optimism, as well as to its derived pessimism, has much of its failure been due. Buddhism has no hope for the life of the universe, but it has great hope for the life of the individual, and it is the hope, and not the despair, which impels it. Its primary motive is individual rest. It prescribes work for the sake of Nirvana. It advises each man to take upon himself the burdens of the universe, just in order that his own burden may fall. It tells him that, by lifting the universal load, his own weight shall disappear; that when the sorrows of others have cast their shadows over him, *his* sorrows shall be buried in the sea. This is all very well and all very true; but it is one thing to reach it as an experience, it is another and a very different thing to start with it as a theory. Every self-sacrificing man shall find the reward of his sacrifice in the death of individual pain; but if he makes that reward the motive of his sacrifice, will it not lose its sacrificial character? Buddhism, strange as it may seem, is in one aspect a selfish creed, as selfish as any system of pleasure-seeking. That which it seeks is not pleasure, but only an absence of pain; none the less is it sought for the sake of individual advantage. It aspires to lift the burdens of life in order that, in lifting the burdens of another, each man may rest from his own labours. This may be very prudent and very far-seeing; it is certainly very optimistic. But is it in any real sense sacrificial? Is it an impulse of spontaneous love, originating in devotion to humanity, and impelled by no other force than its intrinsic power? Is it not, on the contrary, a process of studied calculation, in which benevolence is contemplated with the view to a personal end, and in which the service of man is proposed in the interest of a selfish calm?

Let me put the matter in a nutshell. In an early Christian document I find these words written of the founder of another religion, "Who for the joy that was set before Him endured the cross, despising the shame." Here is a profession of open optimism. But let us observe carefully its difference from the Buddhist optimism. Christianity declares that she is impelled towards her mission of benevolence by a prospective joy. But what joy? It is the joy of hoping and believing that her mission will be successful, that her labour will be crowned, that the humanity for which she toils will ultimately be redeemed. Is that the Buddhist optimism? It is the reverse of that. The Buddhist has no hope for the redemption of the race; that is not the joy which is set before *him*. The joy which is set before *him* is the prospect of emancipation from *personal* care. The hope which impels him towards benevolence is the hope that, in pursuit of the universal burden, the sense of individual want shall be forgotten, and the soul of the individual man shall enter into Nirvana. Christianity is hopeful; Buddhism is hopeful also, but it is not hopeful likewise. The hope of Christianity is the prospect of a redeemed world; the hope of Buddhism is the search for a Stoic's calm through the sense that the world is incapable of being redeemed. And the reward of each has been proportionate to its aim. Christianity has spread its light over a sea of wave and storm, and its light has mingled with the wave and subsisted through the storm. Buddhism has poured its beams over a windless, waveless ocean, and its beams have lost their movement and entered into the ocean's repose. Buddhism has had its message for the world—a noble, a divine message in relation to the Brahmanic past. But its message has long since been delivered, and its mission has long since been fulfilled. It has no voice for the progressive life of the West, no movement with the waves of the modern sea. It has sought a Stoic's calm, and a Stoic's calm has been its goal. It remains still as a monument of noble effort and a record of high aspiration; but its record extends not beyond the range of ancient times, and even at its loftiest zenith it subsists only as the "Light of Asia."

CHAPTER VII.

THE MESSAGE OF PERSIA.

PARSISM, or the religion of Persia, is the second attempt of the ancient world to explain the great problem of human suffering. All religions of the world, whether ancient or modern, have had their rise in an effort to explain that problem. Even the unspeculative mind of China was induced to construct a religion by a sense of the social difficulties which prevailed in the natural state of man. But China did not encounter the problem; when brought face to face with it she ran away. Her whole system is based upon the presentiment that the evils of social life have their origin in social development, and that the only way to get rid of these evils is to go back to a primitive type having its roots in the far past. China, accordingly, does not attempt to grapple intellectually with the difficulties that surround the path of man. She is content to leave these difficulties unsolved. Her whole effort is to avoid them, to get into a state of life where they do not exist; and she believes that she will compass this aim by retracing her steps into a region of primitive simplicity over which the forms of subsequent civilisation exert no power.

It is to India that we must look for the first deliberate effort to face the problem of human suffering. We have seen how, in India, the awakening to that problem was somewhat slow. We have seen how her earliest view of life was rose-coloured, and therefore false. We have seen how she started with the belief that this world is a pleasure-ground, a place where men are put to sport and play. And we have seen how this belief was broken into fragments by the stern facts of experience. India woke from her delusion to an even exaggerated view of the misery of life. She passed from an unqualified optimism into an unrelieved pessimism, an antagonism to things as they are. Unlike the Chinese empire, she did not fly back from the shadow that she had conjured; she prepared to meet it, to face it — if possible, to account for it. She felt, and rightly felt, that when an evil is explained, one half of its sting has vanished. Accordingly India set herself to explain this evil. She accomplished her object in a manner satisfactory to herself, and by a method short and easy. She had found the optimism of life to be a delusion; she decided that its pessimism was also a delusion. She came to the conclusion that earthly life, as such, did not exist—

that everything in this world below was but part of a dream. This life which man calls human was in reality the dream of God. The divine Spirit had passed into a state of sleeping consciousness, in which the images and forms were unreal, and in which the most tangible experiences were but shadows of the night. This world was a vain show, an appearance, an illusion. The only reality was that which dwelt behind it, and that which dwelt behind it was the Almighty. The dream implied a dreamer, but the dreamer could only be reached by the annihilation of the dream. Things were not what they seemed, and he who would attain their reality must awake to the conviction of their imaginary character.

Let us consider, in passing, the extreme fascination of this idea. It was not merely fascinating as an intellectual speculation; I believe its main attractiveness lay in its influence over the moral nature. There are times in which we of modern days feel the same attractiveness, experience almost a wish that it might be true. As we look abroad upon the sin and sorrow of the world, as we contemplate the apparent inequalities in the destinies of men, as we survey the misery and squalor and penury which dwell side by side with prodigal wealth and lavish luxury, we ask a thousand times for a vindication of the justice of God. At such seasons the thought sometimes enters the mind, What if it is all a dream? What if we should awake and find that the things we wept over, prayed over, agonised over, had never any existence outside our own imagining? What if those experiences of life which suggested a doubt of the justice of God should be themselves illusions, apparitions of the fancy, nightmares of the sleep? Would not the very thought of such a possibility convey to the mind a sense of present calm, and suggest at least a method by which, in the days to come, the plans of Omnipotence might be vindicated?

Such I believe to have been the moral strength of Brahmanism. Its mere fantasticness would have been against its continuance, its pronounced speculativeness would have been adverse to its popularity; but its suggestion to the trembling heart was the secret of its power. It held out to the hour of trouble the idea that the trouble was an illusion. It told Job that his sufferings were inflicted by his own imagination, and that the Being whom he blamed for them had never once extended an aggressive hand. In stimulating such a belief, Brahmanism did something for the moral life; it helped it to rest under the shadow in the conviction that the shadow was no part of the divine. Nevertheless it was impossible in the light of reason that such a view could long maintain itself. It was inevitable that a time should come in which men would enter on a deeper questioning. Whence this dream, and whence its sadness? Is not the sorrow of a dream as real as the sorrow of a waking hour—as real in feeling, though imaginary in its cause? Are not the pains of the sleeping consciousness quite as genuine in their nature, and sometimes as hurtful in their effects, as the pains of the outer life? And is not the universe as responsible for the former as for the latter? Is it not specially responsible for the former on the Brahmanical supposition that this dream is the dream of the Absolute Spirit? If it originates in the nature of God, must there not in the universe be some barrier to the nature of God? Must there not be something radically wrong—wrong at the core, wrong in the essence of things? That which interferes with man may be only a relative evil; but surely that which interferes with God must be evil absolute and eternal.

Such was the question which at last was asked by a religion that originally belonged to the same family as the men who compiled the Vedas.[1] At what time it separated itself from that family I cannot tell—whether it remained behind in some old dwelling after the other inmates had left, or whether it itself went out to seek a dwelling more commodious than theirs. Be this as it may, we do

---

[1] In proof of this see Max Müller's "Last Results of the Persian Researches," as reported in Bunsen's 'Philosophy of Universal History,' i. 112; also Spiegel, 'Avesta,' 1-5: Leipzig, 1852.

know that ultimately this religion, which we now call Parsism, assumed, under the name of a distinguished prophet, an attitude of antagonism to the old Brahmanic faith. That prophet was Zoroaster. Carlyle has said that great men have short biographies; Zoroaster has no biography at all. He comes to us like a shadow, and like a shadow he goes. There has gathered round his name a series of sacred writings whose latest echoes have come down to us in a collected form under the title of the 'Avesta.'[1] But the figure round whom they gather is a veiled figure. God is said to have concealed from the Hebrews the body of Moses; He has concealed from all men the bodily life of Zoroaster. Who was the man? What was his ancestry? Where was his birthplace? When was his era?[2] Did he live in the thirteenth century of the old world, or did he live in its sixth century, or did he ever live at all? All these questions have been asked and have been variously answered. That Zoroaster did live at some time is almost certain; that he flourished somewhat contemporaneously with Buddha is highly probable; beyond this nothing can be known of the man as a personality. We are made to feel

[1] Translated with commentary by Professor De Harlez. Second ed., Paris, 1881.

[2] See a list of the conflicting testimonies with respect to his age in Dr John Wilson, 'The Pársí Religion,' pp. 398-400: Bombay, 1843.

that he fills a gap in history, but he fills it invisibly. We are sometimes conscious that there is a presence in the room even where there is no sight and no sound. Some such sensation we experience in contemplating the presence of Zoroaster. We see him not, we hear him not, yet we feel that he occupies a space which naturally would be vacant, and therefore we know that he is there.

What is the filling of this space which is occupied by Zoroaster? What is the nature of that message which he is supposed to have given to the world, and which appears in the writings that have circled round his name? As I have indicated, it strikes a note which was neglected by the Indian Pantheon.[1] That neglected note was the reality of an obstructive element in nature. The Indian religion, in all its phases, denied this obstructive element. Brahmanism took a gloomy view of the world, but she held her own view to be a delusion. Human life was in her eye a sad and imperfect thing, but human life was at the same time to her an unreality. It was a dream, an illusion, a vision of the night, a phantom in the brain of a higher life—the Absolute Spirit itself. All the sorrows of existence were but stirrings in the sleep of the

---

[1] The antagonism appears in the fact that many of the gods of India are the devils of Parsism. See Professor K. Geldner, article "Zoroaster," 'Encyclopædia Britannica,' ninth edition.

Almighty, partial interruptions of that rest which the Divine Life had enjoyed from of old. Zoroaster asked, Whence this interruption? He said, "If there be in the universe something which can interrupt the stream of the Divine Life, that something must be itself not only outside of the Divine, but equal to it in power. That which can oppose God must be not only alien to God, but possessed of an alien strength. If this life be a dream of the Absolute Life, whence comes the dream? Shall you say that the stream of the Divine vitality is inadequate to supply the whole course of its way? Is it possible that God in Himself should faint or grow weary? And if He does faint and grow weary, must there not be some other than Himself? Must there not be in the universe some element obstructive to the Divine — an element which is strong enough to oppose the Absolute Will, and powerful enough to paralyse its operations?"

This in effect was the question of Zoroaster. He felt, and rightly felt, that it is no explanation of the feeling of suffering to say that it is a sensation in a dream—that the problem will always remain, Whence arose this dream? He felt that Brahmanism had stopped short of the ultimate inquiry, that she really escaped no difficulties which her system was designed to escape. Accordingly Zoroaster stood forth in the midst of the universe, and declared that there was something wrong in it. He proclaimed in stentorian tones that there was a crack in the machine, and a crack from the beginning. This is the first note of his message to the world. I shall show in the next chapter that it involves other and deeper notes, and shall endeavour to estimate the value of that thought which he revealed. But meantime I wish to mark the fact that this message of Zoroaster is the first deliberate and systematic testimony given by the Aryan religious consciousness to the existence of sin.[1] Commonplace as it sounds to the modern ear, it was to the ancient ear very nearly a paradox. It struck a chord which, almost in its subject and altogether in its intensity, was new. Hitherto the ancient world had been directed either by the terrible, the beautiful, or the speculative. Men had worshipped from fear; they had worshipped from admiration; they had worshipped from philosophic instinct. They were now to be directed to a new source of adoration—the testimony of conscience. In Zoroaster the Aryan race opened its eyes upon the great problem of morality—the fact of sin. In a more pronounced sense than even Judaism, Parsism emphasised the power of moral evil. With the Jew there is always in the background a conviction, half latent and half ex-

---

[1] Professor Wilson has pointed out that, although there are a few exceptions, the large majority of the Vedic prayers are for purely temporal blessings, and that the moral consciousness is mostly in abeyance (Lectures, pp. 9, 10. Oxford, 1840).

pressed, that sin, with all its horrors, has still been made the servant of God, been compelled against its will to minister to the divine purposes. But in Parsism no such accommodation is either implied or permitted. Sin stands out not only as the enemy of God, as it does in Judaism, but as a frustrator of the plan of God. A Jew would never have admitted that anything could frustrate God's plan; to him the wrath of the wicked itself was made to praise God. But to the follower of Zoroaster every evil deed was for ever outside the gates of the divine kingdom. The acts of human sin could never be made stones in the temple of holiness. The development of goodness could only be promoted by goodness; there was no possibility of things evil being made to work together for a higher goal. The stream which flowed from the fountain of wickedness was a stream which never mingled with the waters of the pure sea; it held on its desolating way independent and alone.

For it is the doctrine of Zoroaster that this universe is not the work of a single being; it is the work of two. It has come from the hands both of a Principle of good and of a Principle of evil. This world has been made by two agents, Ormuzd and Ahriman. Ormuzd is the principle of good. He is embodied in the light, which is at once His garment and His symbol. He is the source of all beauty, the fountain of all purity, the origin of all morality;

from Him cometh down every good and every perfect gift. Ahriman is the principle of evil. His embodiment is the darkness, and this also both clothes and symbolises him. He is the source of all deformity, the fountain of all vileness, the origin of every violation of moral law; from him ascend those foul vapours which disturb the atmosphere of the world. Between these two agencies the life of the universe is divided. There are angels of light, and there are angels of darkness—the one obeying the will of Ormuzd, the other following the behests of Ahriman. The creatures beneath the angelic line are not separated by so hard-and-fast a division. Some have more of Ormuzd in them, some have more of Ahriman—all have something of both. This world, therefore, instead of being a dream, is a stern, waking battle-field, in which two competitors contend for empire. It is in all its parts a struggle between light and darkness, in which light strives to expel darkness, and darkness labours to exclude light. The struggle reaches its climax in man. Man is the microcosm of the universe. In him the forces that elsewhere play on a large scale at once diminish their scale and increase their intensity. Here Ormuzd and Ahriman meet in their deadliest conflict. Man, like everything else, has in him something of both; but, because he is man, he has more of both than all other things. The struggle in him is therefore at the fiercest. One part of his nature is overshadowed by the darkness, the other is basking in the light. His soul is the battle-field between two competitors, and night and day the struggle is maintained with alternating success and with unvaried fury.

What is man's own part in this conflict I shall consider in the next chapter. In the meantime I want to ask, What position does this doctrine hold in the development of the religious consciousness? That it is unscientific is beyond a doubt. That this world is the work of two principles is an idea which was too crude even for Brahmanism, and which is incompatible with the modern standpoints of evolution; though, singularly enough, something very like it has been promulgated in our day by one of the greatest English thinkers—Mr J. S. Mill.[1] Waiving, however, this point, and conceding the unscientific character of the system, the question remains, What is its moral bearing? At first sight it might seem to indicate a religious decline. When we hear of a God whose power is limited by another power, our earliest impression is that we stand in the presence of a low spiritual life. But if we look deeper, and specially if we consider the historical circumstances of Parsism, we shall, in this case at least, come to an opposite conclusion. We have been taught from childhood to praise the choice of Solomon—to admire that state of mind which could

[1] See his posthumous essay on Theism.

prefer the treasures of wisdom to the treasures of wealth. But now imagine that this narrative had been presented to us in another form. Let us suppose that before the eyes of Solomon there had floated the alternative of a choice not between wisdom and wealth in the abstract, but between wisdom and wealth in the nature of God. Let us conceive that in some critical hour it had been revealed to him that the constitution of this universe could no longer be deemed compatible with the existence both of perfect power and of perfect love, and that it would be necessary for him to give up from his creed either the one or the other. Let us suppose that in these circumstances Solomon had decided to hold by the ideal of perfect love, whatever else might go; what would our impression be of such a choice? Would it not be that the man had displayed a wonderful amount of moral insight? Should we not deem that, in preferring morality to physical strength, he had, for an Eastern, reached a remarkable height of development, and a height which was altogether above the ordinary level of his nation—a nation which habitually measured a man's moral purity precisely by the ratio of his outward and physical prosperity?

Now, the case of Zoroaster is exactly parallel to this. He lived in an age when men had come to realise the difficulties of human life and the arduousness of the struggle for existence. The problem of divine Providence had pressed upon his soul. It had become clear to him that, with his present amount of knowledge, he must adopt one or other of two alternatives: he must either hold that the Author of the universe was imperfectly good, or that He was imperfectly powerful. It was the choice of Solomon repeated, but repeated in the nature of God. Zoroaster was asked not to choose between morality and wealth for himself, but between morality and wealth for his Creator. Without hesitation he chose morality. He had every Eastern incentive to do the contrary. He was the member of an empire whose tastes and aims were physical—an empire which had set before itself the ideal of outward conquest as the highest goal of kinghood, and which was prosecuting that ideal with unflinching pertinacity. Would it have been surprising if a man trained in such a school should have preferred the physical to the mental, and should have deemed that attribute most divine which expressed most of sensuous power? And when, in his hour of crisis, in which he was called to choose between God's omnipotence and His holiness, he made his choice in favour of the latter, what can we think of such a decision? What but that the man who made it was far advanced in the spiritual life above the measure of his contemporaries? Is not his choice a declaration that to him the grandest thing about God is not that which men have hitherto worshipped—that the thing which he deems most divine is not the thunder and the earthquake and the fire of sensuous majesty, but the still, small voice which preaches purity of heart? He has before him the alternatives of a God of limited might and a God of limited love, and without hesitation he takes the former. Does he not thereby declare that for him the worshipful element of the universe is not sense but soul, not height but heart, not depth but desire, not power but purity?

And if he did exaggerate the power of evil, if he did invest the awful fact of sin with an importance too great even for itself, let us remember his provocation. Zoroaster was a protestant—a man who protested against an existing state of things. The first protestants always exaggerate; they have no choice but to do so. The very fact that they are the earliest on the field of battle causes them to strike more vehemently. Luther went too far in justification by faith; Calvin went too far with the divine decrees; Knox went too far in his opposition to images; and Zoroaster went too far in his estimate of the power of sin. He attributed its influence to the agency of a Force which was strong enough to compete with God, and in that he doubtless erred. But into that error he was provoked by a still greater error on the other side. The Brahman had said that moral evil was a dream, that the sins and sorrows of life were but the fantastic and illusory images of the sleeping brain. Zoroaster was roused into the opposite extreme. He declared them to be not only real but eternal realities, part and parcel of the constitution of the universe. His vindication for such a statement is the fact of his protestantism. He was the first in the history of Aryan religions who was called to make a stand in favour of the claims of conscience. He made that stand against heavy odds—against intellectual abstractions which had buried the instincts of the heart, against nature-worship which had exalted power over morality, against an ideal of heroism which had substituted the strength of the body for the beauty of the soul. If, in gainsaying this practice of long antiquity, he said too much and went too far, his excess was itself the result of his moral bias, and the exaggeration of his doctrine was the prophecy of a larger life.

CHAPTER VIII.

CONTINUATION.

We have now arrived at a paradox. We have seen how the foregoing religious systems arose out of an effort to grapple with some burden of life. Parsism also arose from an effort to grapple with life's burdens. But Parsism, unlike the foregoing religions, ended by adding a new burden. Like Buddhism, it approached the problem of this world with a view to emancipate the human mind from the weight of its sufferings. Yet the conclusion to which it came was very different from that of Buddhism. Buddhism proposed that the individual should emancipate himself by taking up the cares of the race. Parsism discovered that the deepest sufferings of life came from a burden which originated in the individual alone — a burden which in its nature was untransferable, which a man might pity and sympathise with, but could not lift from the shoulders of his brother. That burden was sin. To the mind of Zoroaster moral evil was the root of all evil, and moral evil belonged to the individual man. In assigning this as the cause of human suffering, he deepened the weight already pressing on humanity. One would have thought that the effect would have been to crush still more utterly the development of the human mind. In the preceding Aryan races, that development had already been almost entirely suppressed. The will of man had sunk into lethargy beneath the weight of a mystery which it could neither shake off nor explain, and the waters of human life had become a Dead Sea. The impartation of an additional burden might seem to have only completed the process, and to have effected the final extinction of that spirit whose powers had been already prostrated.

Yet, strange to say, the effect was the reverse, and it is just here that the paradox arises. Parsism, in adding to the existing burdens the new burden of sin, seemed to have put the final stone upon the sepulchre of man. In reality it began the process of his resurrection. For the first time in the history of Aryanism, the human mind, in the religion of Zoroaster, breaks forth into spontaneity. The sleep of ages appears to pass away, and there begins an age of vital and of waking activity. India had no history, because one day was the same as another, and every event was but an illusion. In Persia, history in the Aryan world may be said to have begun. Here the lethargy of ages is broken, and man breaks forth into the activity of outward life. In Persia we see the anticipation of Rome. We see a nation aiming at wideness of dominion, not so much by crushing as by incorporating. We see an empire struggling towards a headship which shall in some sense represent the relation of the human head to the human members. The sovereignty of the Persian king is the sovereignty of a feudal superior. He does not seek to reign alone, he only desires to reign supreme. He allows the existence of empires within the empire, of kings and governors who shall have power within their own sphere if only they shall acknowledge their common subjection to himself. It is a Roman ideal of imperialism, because it is a Roman ideal of the rights of man. The Persian has awakened to a sense of freedom, and it colours even his politics. He moves through history with a free step, and builds his institutions on the foundations of personal liberty.

But the paradox is still more marked when we turn from the political to the spiritual region. The creed of Zoroaster, with its revelation of human sin, might have been expected to have crushed the soul. On the contrary, it removed the thing which crushed it. The proclamation of the additional burden made man free. The cause of the paradox we shall presently consider; in the meantime we have to note the fact. When the Aryan race recognised its

The Message of Persia.

bondage to sin, it woke for the first time to a sense of freedom.[1] There dawned within the spirit of man the conviction that he was a responsible being. There rose within him the thought that he was not a machine, not a product of necessity, not the result of an inexorable law. He began to feel that he was answerable for his actions. He ceased to think of the universe as dependent entirely on one Supreme Will; he came to the belief that man is a fellow-worker with God. He felt that in the battle between Ormuzd and Ahriman the human creature was not a mere possession to be striven for. The soul of man was itself an agent in the strife; it could help either the one side or the other. Every human act, every human thought, every human confession, every human aspiring, was a weight thrown into the scale, and made for either good or evil. Whether it should make for good or evil depended on the will of man, and for that will he was responsible. Every day and hour man was under the judgment-seat of God. There was a recording angel who was writing down the result of his every deed in a book whose letters were indelible.[2] At the hour of death from out that book there would be made a reckoning of his actions and an estimate of the sum of them. When he

---

[1] The doctrine of human freedom is clearly expressed in the Avesta, Yasna, 31, 11.

[2] See Avesta, Vendidad, 19-27.

passed from this mortal scene he would have to cross the Accountant's Bridge—a structure which metaphorically represented the transition from time into eternity. Here at last would be determined the moral import of his life, and according to its import its reward would be. If the sum of good had outweighed the sum of evil, he would pass into the bright land of Ormuzd. If the sum of evil had outweighed the sum of good, he would travel into the dark shades of Ahriman. If the balance of good weighed equally against the balance of evil, he would be consigned into a state intermediate between sorrow and joy, waiting for that consummation — the final judgment-day which shall decide the fate of all things.

These are the facts; what is the interpretation of them? How are we to account for the circumstance that the Aryan race first came to its sense of responsible freedom when it realised its burden of sin? There is nothing accidental in the conjunction. It is the inevitable result of a great principle. As a matter of fact, man's sense of power is always contemporaneous with his sense of moral humiliation. He only comes to the recognition of his dignity when he comes to the realisation of his depravity. Nowhere does the fable of the Phœnix rising out of its own ashes find so perfect an illustration as in the spirit of man. The first idea which he receives of his greatness in the scale of being is directly derived from his experience of moral blame. The point is so suggestive, and at first sight so paradoxical, as to merit a few moments' consideration.

If it be asked where man gets his sense of freedom, the natural tendency is to answer, " From the powers of his mind." And yet so far is this from being true, that the contrary is the truth. It is not too much to say that it is from the exercise of his intellectual powers that man first learns the sense of his bondage. At the beginning of his life he is conscious neither of freedom nor of necessity; he lives as a plant lives. He arrives at the knowledge of his prison-house only by putting forth his hands. It is when he begins to exert his powers that for the first time he learns their feebleness. The freedom of the Indian mythology was but the freedom of a child, the spontaneity that exists only because it has never experienced the sense of contradiction. It was the infant putting forth its hand to catch the moon. When the infant found it could not catch the moon, it became a Brahman—gave up the universe as an impossible speculation. The Indian mind in its later stage was the child of abortive effort, the product of a despair which had arisen from the sense of intellectual incompetency. In the search for universal knowledge man learns that he is a slave.

Nor is the problem of human freedom much nearer to solution when the intellectual powers of man turned from the contemplation of nature to the contemplation of suffering. This was the transition actually made in the passage from Brahmanism to Buddhism. Man, having failed to make the intellect a source of absolute knowledge, tried to make it a source of absolute calm. The effort was not altogether unsuccessful. Buddhism, as we have seen, has become the Dead Sea of man. But even in reaching this calm, Buddhism did not reach the sense of freedom. She helped a section of mankind to be resigned to inevitable law, but she left the law inevitable still. The triumph of the human intellect in Buddhism was simply the triumph of discovering that the law *was* inexorable. It was the resignation of the soul to a supposed fact—the fact of human bondage. Man was deemed to have reached the pinnacle of wisdom in the discovery of the truth and in the submission to the knowledge that nothing is to be expected from life; the mind's charter of peace was the sense that it could not be free.

The human intellect, therefore, has failed to give to the mind of man the idea of its own liberty. Is there any other source from which such a revelation can arise? There is, and, strange to say, it is found in the realising of a new burden—the burden of sin. It is in the experience of moral want, and in the humiliation incident to that experience, that man reaches the sense of freedom. What the intellectual powers could not do is done by another power—that state of mind which we call conscience. What is the testimony of conscience? It is the announcement that we have done wrong. But what is implied in that announcement? Strange as it may seem, it contains a double implication; it proclaims at once the degradation and the glory of man. On the one hand, it involves a feeling of humiliation; but on what ground? On the ground that we are worthy of blame. What is blame? It is the sense that we could have done better. The testimony of conscience is not merely the testimony that I am not in a good state; that could be said of a withering tree. But what conscience tells me is not simply that I am in a withering condition, but that I have myself to thank for it. It tells me that, if I had done otherwise, things would have been otherwise, and in that message it says that I am free. It proclaims that the law under which I suffer is not a law of necessity—that I had power, if I willed, to shake it off and to walk forth in freedom. I am not discussing the rightness or the wrongness of that testimony; it is always open to the man of science to say, as he often does say, that it is a delusion. But even the man of science will not deny that, whether real or delusive, it is there. Whatever be the value of its testimony, conscience does testify that man is free; the sting of remorse itself is simply a revelation that the human soul has done its deeds under no mechanical necessity, but under the influence of a power which it was always within its province to control.

Now, it is here that the strength of Parsism lies. It has received one burden more than every other Aryan faith; but that one burden more is the moral conviction of sin. The result is that the additional weight has become a wing, and the element which threatened to bring Parsism to the very dust of humiliation has become the means of its rising above all surrounding religions. [It is not difficult to trace the process by which, from its waking sense of human corruption, this faith has climbed into the vision of an all but perfect day. In the conviction of sin it reached the feeling of blame. In the feeling of blame it reached the idea of responsibility. In the idea of responsibility it reached the belief in freedom. In the belief in freedom it reached the knowledge that there existed within the universe a power called Will. In the recognition of that power it learned, for the first time, that there is a force which is not material, but antecedent to matter and independent of its mutations—a force which mechanical combinations did not create, and which the dissolution of mechanical combinations needs not destroy. Finally, from a vision of this independent existence it reached the belief in a personal immortality—an immortality in which the individual should at once be preserved and sublimated, lifted from the dust of earth, and intensified by the life of heaven.]

Thus, as from a germ-cell, there rose out of conscience a revelation of all things—freedom, personality, God, immortal life. Parsism, by its definite recognition of the existence of a moral world, came to a definite recognition of a world of religious thought. But let us understand that, in order to realise the power of conscience, it was necessary to realise the power of sin. It is because Parsism is the religion of struggle that it is the religion of morality and immortality. Conscience only begins where disturbance begins; here as elsewhere, it is the cloud that reveals the sunshine. As long as my nature flows on in a stream of uninterrupted good, I am unconscious even of the stream. In order to become conscious I must be arrested in my flow. Something must intervene to break the uniformness of the rhythm of life. The beauty of virtue first asserts itself when I have tried to violate it; the box of ointment gets its fragrance by being broken. Parsism climbed further than all Aryan faiths, because it struggled more than all—nay, because first among these faiths it experienced the sense of struggle. It was the child of moral conflict, and out of its moral conflict came its revelation of God.

If now it be asked what, according to Parsism, is to be the outcome of this conflict, the answer is by no means directly at the door. It is popularly said to be an optimistic creed. Measured by Brahmanism and Buddhism, it is certainly optimistic; these were the religions of despair, this is to some extent a religion of hope. The children of light are not for ever to remain in darkness; Ormuzd is to get the victory over Ahriman. But who are to be the children of light? How many are ultimately to be included in the great salvation? Is it in the last result to comprehend all men, or is it to be limited to a part? What is to be the fate of the rejected part? Are they to exist in eternal misery, or are they to be submerged in a sea of annihilation? These are questions on which the commentators of Zoroaster are divided. Probably in this respect there is the same ground for divided opinion as exists in Christianity. In the one as in the other there are various interpretations of the same words. In the one as in the other there are passages of the sacred books which seem to make for either side. In the one as in the other there are opposite castes of mind—those who by nature are swayed by the dictates of law, and those who by disposition are dominated by the sentiment of love.

We shall waive, then, the question whether, according to the doctrine of Parsism, there is or is not prognosticated a final restoration of all things. But even when we leave this question in the background, there is an element in this religion which makes us pause before investing it with the attributes of optimism. Even though this faith had declared without ambiguity that all the sons of men were ultimately to share in the triumph of goodness, I would not feel justified in saying that Parsism was an optimistic religion. What is optimism? It is not merely the belief that all things shall at last be well; it is the belief that all things shall at last be found to have conspired to the universal wellbeing. It is not enough for me, when I am passing through the shadow of grief, to be told that a time is approaching in which the shadow shall pass away and the full light shall come. That may be very satisfactory, but it is an animal satisfaction after all; it is the gratification of being freed from pain. What I want in my deepest nature is more than that; I want to have the pain vindicated. I want to have the dark past not only expunged but explained — to some extent expunged in *being* explained. It is all very well that the years of shadow have come to a close; but they *have* been years. From the standpoint of the natural eye they have involved a loss of time, a waste of being, a dissipation of energy. If I am to call my life optimistic, I must be made to feel that the shadow was a part of the light. I must be convinced that the seeming waste was no waste, that the apparent void was full of possibilities, and that the desert potentially contained within it the blossoming of the rose.

Now, it is in this respect that Parsism fails. Irrespective altogether of the question whether it does or does not cherish a universal hope for man, it regards the sorrows of life as real sorrows — as absolute blots and blemishes in the constitution of nature. A human soul awaking in another world might, according to this system, be impelled to say, "Ormuzd has made it all right now." But even such a soul, under such circumstances, would not be impelled to say, "Ormuzd has been making it right all along." There can be no joy of retrospect in the creed of Zoroaster. Parsism may enable its worshippers to exult in the knowledge that what was once dark has become day, but it can never enable them to rejoice in the vision that the darkness was but a shadow of the day. The darkness came from Ahriman and remains with Ahriman; it has neither part nor lot in the final consummation. It has had nothing to do with the development of the kingdom of God; it has simply retarded that development. Whatever happiness the soul has reached has been reached in spite of it, in the face of it. The soul's joy must be the joy of an escaped bird; it can have no place for retrospect except a place of horror. It may revel in its acquired good, but it cannot say that all things have worked together for that good. Only the half of things have worked together—the things of Ormuzd; the working of Ahriman has been all for bad, and, even in the final reckoning of accounts, can have served no purpose in contributing to the sum of happiness.

And, with peculiar emphasis is this defect of

Parsism accentuated in its doctrine of sin. Zoroaster calls upon all men to be saved, and opens up to many men the way of salvation. But even those who have reached that way must be impressed that there is something wanting. It is not enough that a man should be redeemed, not enough that he should be loosed from his shackles and told that he is free. What about that life which he has lived *within* the shackles? What about the deeds done in that dark past from which he has been liberated? It is all very well that he himself has been emancipated from the sinking ship; but the ship is sinking still, and it is sinking through his blame. Can anything be done to undo the past deeds of the man? Parsism answers, and on its principles can only answer, "No." There is no atonement in this religion, no redress of former wrongs, no times for the restitution of all things. The sweetest note of Christianity is its promise of a cancelled past, its message to the weary soul that the evil deeds it has done shall be made to work out a beneficent end. The joy of a Paul was not only that all things had been made new, but that old things had passed away. He felt that if he had planted tares in the past, it was not enough for him to know that he had now ceased to plant them. He must be told, if he would be happy, that the tares he had sown would themselves be made conducive to the production of a riper wheat.

That is what Parsism could not tell him, could not tell any man. It could promise to Moses a salvation from his ark of bulrushes; it could predict for Joseph a liberation from his Egyptian dungeon; but it could not tell Moses that he had been magnified *through* his peril, nor Joseph that the dungeon itself had made him free. To the furthest horizon of its vision Parsism remains dualistic still. Even on that view of its most sanguine disciples, which looks forward to a salvation of universal man, the dualism continues unbroken and unmodified; for the past is itself unredeemed, and the errors of yesterday are written in everlasting colours. The glory of Parsism has been to exhibit the natural gulf between the pure and the unholy; it has been reserved for a loftier faith to construct a bridge between them.

CHAPTER IX.

THE MESSAGE OF GREECE.

HE who would photograph the spirit of religions must distinguish carefully between what is spontaneous and what is reflective. The former is a worship; the latter is a philosophy. The religion of a nation is its impulse towards an ideal; it is therefore in all its forms essentially a sacred movement. But the philosophic culture of a nation is a secular and a secularising process; even where it relates to a religious subject, it breathes the air of the common day. Nor can it be strictly said that the philosophy of any nation is a product purely national; it is always, to a great extent, the result of conscious appropriation from the best minds of many lands. Men like Thales and Parmenides, like Aristotle and Plato, like Epicurus and Zeno, cannot be said to be simply the offspring of their age and clime. We are very significantly told that before they wrote they travelled. Their writing was therefore a conscious and deliberate effort to emancipate themselves from what was purely local and national, and to reach a basis of thought the ground of whose recommendation to the world should be the fact that it was itself grounded on a universal soil.

Accordingly I shall, in the course of the present studies, deal with the philosophic sects of Greece as I have dealt with the philosophic sects of India; I shall pass them by. I shall confine this study of Greek religion to an examination of its earliest message—that message which preceded all intellectual culture, and was revealed to the spontaneous instincts of the heart. The period of its nature-worship is really the distinctive period of Greek religion; all its other times and modes are the result, more or less, of foreign influence. What, then, is this earliest message of the Hellenic faith? Is there anything peculiar about it, anything which marks it out from other forms and gives it the right to a distinct place among the religions of the world? It is popularly called a system of Polytheism; but there is nothing new in that. It is essentially a reverence for the things of nature; but neither in this is there anything new. If it is to be assigned a distinctive place in theology, it must be on other grounds than these—on grounds which make its Polytheism unique and its nature-worship singular. Does there exist in this faith such an element of peculiarity?

I think there does. I believe it will be found that there is one respect in which the religious worship of the Greek differs essentially from the religious worship of all other nations, whether Aryan or Semitic. If I were asked to express epigrammatically the difference between this religion and the forms of faith already considered, I might put it thus: The message of China is to teach the glories of yesterday. The message of India is to trace the development of the day. The message of Persia is to exhibit the struggle between the day and the night. The message of Greece is to reveal the intensity of the *hour*. When we have reached this last point, we have touched hitherto untrodden ground. China led us back to the past; India drove us forward to the future; Greece keeps us chained within the present. Here for the first time man looks upon the passing scene, and contemplates it not as passing but as permanent. Here for the first time man casts his eye upon the world as it actually exists, and sets himself to justify— nay, to reverence—things as they are. Other faiths had sought their object in the *glorification* of things; the faith of Greece seeks its object in that which is manifested to the common eye. India descended from the heavens to the earth; Greece ascends from the earth to the heavens. On earth she is always more at home. Her earliest and her latest philosophy starts from the reverence of things prosaic. Her earliest came from the men of Ionia.[1] Instead of looking up like the Indian to the shining heavens, they adored the water, the air, and the fire; they found food for their religious contemplation in the most common and the most commonplace things. Her latest was the Stoics, the men of prosaic mould —whose motto was common-sense, whose creed was sobriety and self-restraint, whose practice was to check the flight of the emotions, and whose ideal was bounded by the horizon of material things.[2]

Now, these tendencies were inherited tendencies; they came from the primitive religious instinct. The religion of Greece was essentially and distinctively the worship of the hour, the investiture with reverence of the things amongst which she lived and moved. Her object was to realise the joy of perception, as distinguished from the joy of retrospect and the joy of prospect. China had lived in the former; Persia had lived in the latter; Greece sought to occupy the middle ground. In order to occupy that ground unmolested, she put a wall on either side; she strove to shut out at once the memory of the past and the foresight of the future. She aimed to enclose herself within the bars of the present, and to find there her

---

[1] Döllinger regards the Ionic school as materialistic. 'The Gentile and the Jew in the Courts of the Temple of Christ,' London, 1862, i. 250 sq.; see also Cousin, 'Histoire Générale de la Philosophie,' Paris, 1867, i. 110.

[2] See Döllinger, ibid., i. 349.

perfect satisfaction. Hers has been called an optimistic creed, yet, in strict accuracy, I doubt if the name is applicable. Optimism is bound to take a survey of the universe on every side, to compare its present with its past, and its future with its present. Greece does not do that; she keeps rigidly within the environment of the hour. In those early days which constitute her distinctive days, she has no space either for memory or for anticipation. She does not look back to reflect on the years that are gone; the past is to her a sealed book. As little does she look forward to contemplate the years that are coming. The Greek has no bright prospect in the sky of the future. His only chance of keeping his optimism is to shut his eyes on that future. Beyond this life all to him is dark. Of the existence beyond the grave he has the most gloomy presentiments. It is to him a half-life, a state of partial consciousness, an assemblage of unsubstantial shadows. Every time he thinks of it he is made sad.[1] As he is determined not to be sad, he refuses to think of it. He imprisons himself within the moment; he crowns the world as it exists now and here. He uncovers his head to the joy of the scene before him, and

---

[1] Achilles says in Homer's 'Odyssey' (book xi. line 488) that he would rather serve on earth than reign among the dead. Contrast the subsequent view in Plato's 'Phædo'; this, however, is no longer the pure product of the Greek mind.

declines to worship aught but his native land. The object of the Greek's adoration is Greece— Greece as it presented itself to his youthful imagination, and as it appeared on the surface to his outer eye. Like the Chinaman, he may be said to have his heaven and his earth in the land of his nativity; but, unlike the Chinaman, he sees them in the present hour. His worship is the worship not of yesterday but of to-day; it is the reverence for things as they are.

Accordingly, in Greece every object receives a crown, and receives a crown precisely as it ministers to the national mind. The things of nature are adored not because they are natural but because they are Grecian, and they are adored in those special colours with which the Greek soil has invested them. There is a strong analogy between the faith of the Greek and the faith of the Jew— an analogy all the more strongly marked because it manifests itself amid things otherwise contrasted.[1] The Jew recognised a divine presence in everything that related to his country; he made no distinction between events important and events trivial; all alike were the voice of God. The Greek also recognised a divine presence in his national life, and to him, as to the Jew, that pres-

---

[1] The points of contrast will be found very well indicated in an article entitled "Greek Mythology and the Bible," by Julia Wedgwood, 'Contemporary Review,' March 1892.

ence filled all things. The difference lay not in the fact but in the ideal. The national life of Judea was not the same as the national life of Greece. Judea was the life of history; Greece was the life of perception. Accordingly, while the God of Judea was seen in events, the God of Greece was beheld in objects. And as the Jew attributed to his God the most opposite events, the Greek imputed to his divinity the most diverse objects. In one sense the Greek is in this respect more remarkable than the Jew. While to the son of Israel all acts were ultimately divine acts, the larger part of them were acts of penalty. But to the son of Greece there was no place for penalty. In giving to every object a divine significance, he gave it that significance absolutely, unqualifiedly. He filled his universe with God, not as an avenger, or a vindicator, or a rectifier, but as a presence and a power, for its own sake precious and in its own light beautiful. I have used the word "God" instead of "the gods," in order to mark the fact that the presence was universal. The Greek adored separate divinities, but he saw them everywhere. There was not a space of his world unoccupied by the divine. It was not enough that there should be a Spirit of the grove; it was not even enough that there should be a Spirit of the tree; there must be a Spirit for every leaf of the tree. The result is that the Greek enfolds in his Pantheon the most contrary species of things — forms the most diverse, ideas the most opposite. Goethe says that we weave for God the garment by which we see Him. The Greek wove no garment for God; he simply cut out patches from the garments of his fellow-men, and put them together unmethodically and heterogeneously; he deified the things around him just because they *were* around him.

Accordingly, his religion presents a strange medley. It attributes divinity to objects the most diverse and sometimes the most opposite. He looked out upon the manifestation of nature's physical power, and he called it Zeus—the origin of all things. He looked in upon the manifestation of mental power, and he called it Athene—the principle of wisdom. He contemplated the ideal of manhood in its strength and beauty, and he called it Apollo; he surveyed the ideal of womanhood in its chasteness and purity, and he called it Artemis. He gazed upon the turbulent and wayward forces of the world, and in his admiration of the power that kept them right, he gave that power a name—Poseidon, the god of the sea. But he beheld other forces which were wayward, not from their strength but from their stupidity. He felt that the sheep in the meadow needed a protector as much as the waves of the ocean, and therefore he gave the shepherds also a god—Pan. He surveyed the field of war, and he deemed it worthy of a presiding divinity—Mars was his god of battle. But when he turned inward to the domestic hearth, he was equally impressed with the divineness of a contrary scene, and he signified his reverence for the life of the family altar by placing it under the patronage of Hestia. He bowed before the serious aspects of nature; he deified the power that forged the thunderbolt. But he had equally a place of reverence for the pleasure-hour; he had his god of wine as well as of fire. He had a seat in his Pantheon for the god who directs the prosaic courts of law; but he had an equal throne for the god who stimulates the poetic flights of eloquence. He recognised a presiding divinity over the incipient movements of life, and crowned Demëtër as the fosterer of the grain. Yet, singularly enough, he had a temple also dedicated to the movelessness of death; and he was not afraid to assign a divinity to those very precincts of the grave which he himself so utterly loathed.[1]

The reader will be impressed with the fact that we have here a very remarkable and a very unique kind of optimism. In its usual form optimism says, "We believe that it will be all right in the long-run, though it is dark now." The Greek religion says, "We know nothing about the long-run; but it is all right now." The long-run was to the Greek an invisible

[1] Whoever wishes to study the subsequent symbolism grafted upon these divinities may consult Sir G. W. Cox, 'Mythology of the Aryan Nations.'

quantity, and he had no sympathy with the invisible.[1] The limit to his sympathy was the boundary-line between the seen and the unseen. Parsism looked forward to a time when the struggle with material things would be lulled to rest; the joy of Greece was the perception of the struggle itself. He had no place for hope; he lived in present experience, and that which made life to him glad was just the sense of its conflict. And the reason is plain. The Greek was by nature an athlete. His Isthmian games were only the expression of his deepest nature. Competition was his very atmosphere. He was a born wrestler, a man who felt from the very beginning that his destiny was to strive. Is it surprising that he should have deified in nature that in which he seemed to find a resemblance to himself? Is it wonderful that he should have projected his own ideal into the earth and sea and sky of his native land? At all events, he did project it. He saw in the world around him a reflex of that world which he felt within him. He recognised in nature the same elements of struggle which he found in himself, and he consecrated nature on this ground. He worshipped things as they were —as they exhibited themselves in the daily struggle for survival. And because his ideal of excellence was the power to strive, he bowed his head to things

---

[1] The Eleatic and Platonic schools are of course exceptions; but these are attempts to graft Eastern thought on a Western soil. Epicurus, on the other hand, has an echo of the native ring.

of opposite quality. Strife demands opposition; it demands a sense of difficulty on the part of the combatant. The Greek reverenced the powers of nature and the powers of mind more from their aspect of imperfection than from their semblance of completeness; he loved them because they seemed to make their way through opposing clouds and retarding storms. It is by this that I explain the strange combinations of thought that meet in his worship, the number of dissimilar things that dwell side by side in his temple. He puts them side by side, that out of their contrast there may come conflict, and that out of their conflict there may arise the ideal which he loves. Let me try to illustrate this.

One of the most prominent objects of worship in ancient Greece is Apollo. In later times he is the sun-god, but this was a light into which he grew.[1] Apollo became the sun as a reward for work done on the earthly plane. That work was the service of man. He is from the beginning the representative of ideal humanity, the embodiment of all that is pure and noble in the human spirit. He is to the mind of Greece what the names of the canonised are to the mind of Medievalism—a symbol of the saintly life. It is this purifying power which is sought to be indicated when he is

[1] In the Homeric poems Apollo is viewed as quite distinct from the sun-god; see, for example, the opening of the 'Iliad.'

called the god of medicine—the restorer and preserver of that physical health which has so much to do with the health of the soul. Apollo stands for the perfect man, the man unspotted by the world. But then, side by side with this picture, there is another and a different one, and the two are made to blend together. Apollo is the saintly man, but he is at the same time the gay man. He is unspotted by the world, but he is also at the very heart of the world. Pure himself, he holds in his hand everything that is supposed to be a temptation against purity. He has the hot blood of youth in his veins; his mildness is not the result of a cool temperament, but dwells beside a river of rushing passion. He is always represented with a bow and with a lyre. It is intended to mark the fact that he is the embodiment at once of the martial and the musical. He is the leader of men in the ranks of war, and he is the delight of men in the ranks of peace. He supplies at once the sources of physical strength and the means of social enjoyment. These are elements not commonly associated with the saintly life; they are supposed to furnish incentives to temptation, seductions from the path of that life. Why, then, are they associated here? Is not the reason plain? Is it not clear that the Greek put these temptations into the hand of Apollo just because they *were* temptations, just because they supplied an opportunity for that struggle in which the Greek above all things delighted? When he invests the pure man with the bow and with the lyre, it is because he wants purity to be not an empty thing, not the result of mere mental vacancy or of simple inanity, but the product of a deliberate choice and the fruit of a determinate struggle. The Greek has been here true to himself, true to his country, true to his national ideal. He has given Apollo the wreath of purity because he has won that wreath by conquest. He has worshipped his unspottedness because it has been an unspottedness where spots might have been—a whiteness which has remained uncontaminated amidst conditions and amidst environments in which the incurring of contamination seemed almost a necessary thing.

Again. If Apollo was the Greek's ideal of manhood, Artemis was his ideal of womanhood. In fixing upon Artemis as his type of womanhood, the Greek has done honour to himself. Artemis is the representative of chastity. Out of all the possible excellences which are associated with the name of woman, he has selected this one as the most glorious and the most desirable one. He has passed by his own natural predilection for the beautiful; he has subordinated his instinctive tendency to give prominence to the symmetry of form; he has made selection of a quality which is of all qualities the least distinctive of his race, and has thereby indicated an aspiration beyond his own environment. When the Greek crowned woman with the wreath of divinity, he encircled her head with that laurel which he deemed the most precious, and which doubtless *was* to him the most precious, because amongst the actual women of his land it was the most rare. He proclaimed the divineness of chastity, because chastity was as yet the most transcendental thing, the thing most removed from positive experience. But here again we are confronted by a remarkable combination. Artemis is the representative of chaste womanhood, but she is not the representative of ascetic womanhood. If she is crowned as the goddess of chastity, she is also crowned as the goddess of the chase. To her belongs the pleasure of the hunting-field — the exercise of limb and the strength of arm. She incarnates in herself all that is manly in sport, all that is vigorous in pastime. She incorporates in her nature the attributes of the other sex along with the distinctive qualities of her own. She is beautiful in feature but not gentle in expression, graceful in form but not feminine in mould; she is the woman in the man. And here again, can one fail to recognise the deep meaning that underlies the picture? Why has the Greek made the goddess of chastity the goddess of the chase? Clearly that through the chase he may give more value to the chastity. He wants the chasteness of Artemis, like the pureness of Apollo, not to be the result of an empty heart nor the product of a shallow life, but to be the expression of a nature which has known both sides of the question, and which adheres to virtue because it has made a deliberate choice. He wants it to be an abstinence which springs not from the fact that she has been immured in cloistered cell or hid from the temptations of the passing hour, but from the depth of a conviction that has come from worldly experience, and arrived at its determination by weighing the alternatives on either side. The Greek has been led to deify two natures in one person through his own admiration for struggle, through his consciousness that virtue is only beautiful when it stands out in contrast with that which would seduce it.

I shall give yet another illustration, because it is one which is deep and far-reaching. Let us take that god whom the Greeks called Hephaistos, and the Romans Vulcan. He is the god of fire, the maker of war-instruments, the man who forges the thunderbolts for Jove. Yet this herculean labour has to be performed by an imperfect body. Vulcan is both lame and deformed, and his movements are naturally slow; he is represented in himself as an object of laughter to the gods. The problem is why such a conception should have been deified and worshipped by man, specially why such a conception should have been deified and worshipped by the Greek. In later times the Greek did not scruple to invest the objects of his worship with human passions and mental weaknesses, and this has always seemed a marvel. But to my mind the earlier fact is far more marvellous—that the Greek should have reverenced a being whom he had invested with bodily defects. Let us remember what was to him the highest manifestation of life's glory; it was the exhibition of the beautiful in nature, in art, in man. Beauty was to the Greek the Alpha and the Omega, the beginning and the end of all perfection. There was no flaw to him like a flaw against symmetry; there was no error to him like an error against taste. One would have expected that wherever he had an object of worship, and whatever might be the endowments of that object, he would at least have invested it with an ample measure of beauty. Very startling therefore is it when we find him reverencing a being in whom there is no form nor comeliness, bowing down before a presence in whose outward aspect are the marks of an image more marred than the sons of men. How are we to account for this? How are we to explain the fact that the beauty-loving Greek has deserted his own ideal of beauty—that the man who habitually reverences above all things the symmetry of form, should have yielded his adoration to that which is distinguished for its want of symmetry?

The reason again is plain. It is because the Greek in his deepest nature is an athlete. He values a possession in proportion as that possession has been won. Even beauty would not be valuable to him if it were the rule and not the exception. It is the fact that, in the struggle for existence, some forms have been able to maintain not only their existence but their symmetry, which makes the possession of that symmetry to him a joy; the beautiful itself is only accepted as a road to the strong. In this light Vulcan's position becomes clear. There has fallen to him a herculean work to do; he has to forge those bolts of fire which shall execute the mandates of the universe. What more natural than that the Greek should make it more herculean still, should exaggerate the difficulty, to lend more glory to the strength? Accordingly he has done so. He has made the god of fire and of the thunderbolt a god with bodily defects; he has invested him with lameness and with the elements of physical imperfection. He has so invested him that he may magnify the execution of his task, that he may exhibit in more strong relief the greatness of his actually exerted power. Some worshippers would have reverenced the object of their worship in proportion as it found all things easy; the Greek bestows his reverence on the opposite ground. To him the glory of life, even of divine life, is its struggle. The powers of nature are reverenced by him because they are athletic powers—forces which act and react upon each other, and which keep their place by conflict. Whatever emphasises the conflict, whatever intensifies the obstacle, is prized and appropriated as a means to the ultimate effect, and is permitted even to share by anticipation in that glory which the ultimate effect shall secure.

I cannot but direct attention to the remarkable analogy which in this respect the mythology of ancient Greece bears to a system which is generally held to be, and which in many respects is, its contrast—the religion of Jesus Christ. If one were asked to put his hand upon that form of belief which of all others is most foreign to Christianity, he would probably select the Hellenic worship of nature. And yet it is in this Hellenic worship of nature that we find the germ of that which in Christianity appears in full development—the glorification of weakness. The sensuous Greek and the self-sacrificing Christian have alike distinguished themselves from other forms of faith by incorporating in their Pantheon the shadows of human life; to the one, as to the other, weakness is a condition of strength. No doubt there is a vast difference in their respective reasons for this. The Greek incorporates weakness in his Pantheon in order that he may lend to him who overcomes it a larger meed of praise. The Christian admits weakness into his Pavilion for precisely the opposite reason—in order that the man who strives may be taught the lesson of his own nothingness. Yet, when we look deeper, it may perhaps be found that these two views are not so discordant as they seem; that there is at least a point in which for a moment they find a meeting-place. The Greek magnifies strength, and the Christian magnifies humility; but does not the Christian magnify humility as an ultimate source of strength? Is it not because he sees in self-forgetfulness the road to self-enlargement, because he recognises in the spirit of sacrifice the promise and potence of life, that he insists before all things on the soul becoming unconscious of itself? Is not weakness here also contemplated as a means of struggle, and crowned as a road to victory? Thus strangely do these two forms of faith, so different in their origin and so divergent in their general aspects, exhibit at one corner an attitude of concord and alliance — an attitude which may have found its ultimate realisation in that singular union of the son of Abraham with the son of Hellas which marked the close of the Jewish Theocracy, and constituted the dawn of the Christian day.

And if the Greek mythology presents a point of union with Christian thought, it presents equally a point of union with that which at first sight seems more pronouncedly its opposite than the religion of Jesus; I mean the speculations of modern science. If there are two things which at the outset appear irreconcilable, they are the dreams of the ancient Greek and the conclusions of the modern evolutionist. The one stands at the beginning, and the other at the close of human development. And yet in the optimism of ancient Greece, there is something which finds an analogy with the speculations of modern evolution. As the morning is more like the evening than any other part of the day, so the earliest phase of humanity resembles its latest manifestation more than its intermediate phases. Modern science is on the whole optimistic. It believes that the development of man is an upward development, and that when the creature is fully adjusted to his environment he will find peace. But this ultimate optimism of modern science implies much more; it implies that every step of the process has been a step in the right direction — in the direction of the goal. If ever the time should come in which the millennial age of the modern scientist shall be reached, he himself will be the first to proclaim that it has been reached by the accumulation and combination of all the events which have preceded it—prosperous and adverse, good and bad. He will tell the world of his day that the prosperity to which men have attained has been simply the last result of the whole foregoing panorama, the ultimate issue of that long train of circumstances which is called the course of time. He will make no distinction in his retrospective survey between the defects and the symmetries of nature. The defects will themselves appear in the light of symmetries, because to the eye of the scientist they shall appear as workers in the building. Every step of the preceding evolution shall be found to have been a necessary step to the production of the actual goal. The absence of aught which seemed a blemish, the leaving out of anything which was called a defect, shall be regarded by him as an impossible conception. He will be constrained to say in scientific retrospect what an apostle said in religious faith—that all things have worked together for good. If modern science is optimistic at all, it must be optimistic all through. It cannot be hopeful about the whole without being sanguine about the part, for the very marrow of its doctrine is the belief that the whole is involved in the part. It cannot be optimistic regarding the future without being optimistic in relation to the passing hour, for it is itself based on the principle that the future sleeps in the present, and that the passing hour enfolds the germ of the completed day.[1]

And, to tell this was the message of Greece. That she told it in rough language is true; that she expressed herself very badly is undoubted; but beneath the grotesqueness of the form there abides the spirit of that truth which she meant to convey. It is a truth unique amongst the messages of religions.

[1] All this is conceded even by such a negative writer as Lange in his 'History of Materialism.'

Hitherto the creeds of men had deified the objects of life after having lifted them out of life; they first idealised them and then crowned them. But here the objects of life are crowned without being idealised; they are crowned as they are—in all their present forms, and with all their present imperfections. The Greek has put his hand upon the world as it is—struggling, commonplace, unfinished. He has uncovered his head before the aspect of nature which meets him every day, before the events which befall him every hour, and he has not scrupled to assign divinity to the images of creation as they actually float before him. In so doing, he has supplied a desideratum in the objects of religious worship. Religious worship had deified everything but the common day. It had deified the past in China; it had deified the future in Persia; it had deified even the hour of death in the Buddhism of India; but it had put no crown upon the objects and the events of the living hour. It was reserved for Greece to supply the want in the temple of humanity, and by this she, being dead, yet speaketh.

CHAPTER X.

THE MESSAGE OF ROME.

I REGARD the Roman religion as the earliest attempt at religious union. Its distinctive message to the world was to proclaim the possibility of *destroying* the distinctive, of erasing those lines of demarcation which tend to divide the faiths of men. From the very beginning, from the very constitution of her nature, Rome sought a principle of eclecticism— a principle which should unite and rivet the lives of the multitude. In every department of her history she pursued the same end; her religious instinct only moved in unison with her national reason. As surely as on the life of the bee there is imprinted the necessity to construct an incorporative hive, there was from the outset imprinted on the Roman constitution the necessity to construct an incorporative empire—an empire which in its extent and its vastness might yet leave room for the action of many powers within it. The unity at which Rome aimed was not a uniformity. She did not seek merely to compress the nations by conquest under her own sceptre. She was perfectly willing—nay, earnestly desirous—that the nations should not be compressed, that her conquests should be of such a nature as to leave them in a measure free. She wanted an empire whose glory should consist in holding other empires within it, as a drop of water holds within it a multitude of separate lives. Her political aim was unity, and unity is ever the combination, not the destruction, of the many. Her whole history, with all its changes, is an effort to conserve in the new the elements of the old. When Augustus aimed at undivided empire, he aimed at it in the Roman method; he did not break with the institutions of the past, but gathered them around his own person.[1] It is but an instance in miniature of what Rome sought to do in the gross. She was willing to permit the institutions of the world to remain; she only asked that they would assume her own name.

Now, the Roman religion follows the plan of the Roman politics; strictly speaking, it is but a part of those politics. It never aspires to originality; it would scarcely be too much to say that it aspires to be not original. Originality would have destroyed the Roman design. The Roman design in every sphere was incorporation. Incorporation demands

---

[1] See this point very clearly stated in Dean Merivale's article "Augustus," 'Encyclopædia Britannica,' ninth edition.

eclecticism—the selecting of that which is best in surrounding systems. Rome's eagerness to incorporate made her unwilling to be originative. She was too anxious to gather in the old to be a founder of the new. Her aim was to find a meeting-place for the creeds of the nations. Books on popular Church history have often been misled as to her character by her attitude to Christianity. Viewing her in that attitude, they have represented her as a persecuting power. The truth is, it was the nature of Christianity and not the nature of Rome which gave rise to persecutions. Rome would have tolerated any religion which would consent to nestle under her banner. But this Christianity would not consent to do. Christianity claimed exactly what Rome claimed—to be the wide-spreading tree upon whose branches all other faiths might rest. She claimed to be the principle of union which formed a possible nucleus for the reconciliation of rival beliefs. She claimed to have been herself the unconscious source of all other aspirations—the light which had lighted the worship of every man. Christianity, therefore, could never have accepted the terms of the Roman Pantheon, could never have consented to serve in a house where she asserted the right to rule. Her distinctive characteristic was that she refused to be tolerated, insisted to be recognised alone and supreme. She brooked no rival, and she would admit no second; she demanded, like Rome herself, the suffrages of all other faiths. It is unfair, therefore, to regard Rome's attitude towards Christianity as an exception to her usual policy. She was as willing to extend her toleration to Christianity as to any other creed, and she only exchanged her toleration for hostility because Christianity refused to tolerate *her*.

The result of this eclecticism is that the religion of Rome exhibits not one but many elements. Just as within her body politic there repose side by side the characteristics of many lands, so within the membership of her religious system there sleep the phases of many faiths. Rome brings no new message into the world; her mission is to collect, and, if possible, to combine, those messages which the world has already received. Accordingly, the faith of Rome is a many-sided faith; it would have been universally sided if every aspect of religion had in its day been represented. It took whatever it found. It gathered stones from all surrounding temples, and out of these it built a temple of its own—a temple not very symmetrical indeed, not very harmoniously welded nor aptly adjusted, yet exhibiting a faithful and honest attempt to find in one Pantheon a place for many minds. Let us look at one or two of the different sides of this religion

It has one aspect in which it bears a resemblance to the faith of Judea. Whence that resemblance originates we cannot tell, but it is highly probable that the far-travelling and eagerly incorporating spirit of Rome came at an early date into contact with Judaic forms of thought.[1] Be this as it may, it is certain that in Rome, as in Judea, we find the union of two tendencies which, so far as I know, are in no other faith found combined — the tendency to dwell in the past, and the impulse to push forward into the future. China has exhibited the one, and Parsism has revealed the other; but it has been reserved for Judea and Rome alone to find a meeting-place for both. In Rome, as in Judea, we see hands stretched out in opposite directions — one pointing backward to the gates of a golden paradise, the other pointing forward to the gates of a future kingdom. In the one, as in the other, we behold the spectacle of a mind divided between the pride of a high origin and the expectation of a lofty destiny, vibrating between a glory which has been and a splendour which is coming. If Judea goes back to her Eden, Rome goes back to her Troy; if Judea looks forward to her Messiah, Rome looks forward to her universal dominion. The actual life of each is bounded by two paradises —the glory of a lofty ancestry and the glory of an omnipotent posterity. And in the life of each

[1] Renan says that it is probable Judaic thought would reach Rome earlier than even nearer parts of the empire. See his 'Influence of the Institutions, Thought, and Culture of Rome on Christianity and the Development of the Catholic Church,' Hibbert Lecture, 1880.

the power which mediates between the one and the other is the power of law. In Judea and in Rome alike, the minds of men are developed from the paradise of the past into the paradise of the future by a colossal system of jurisprudence, by which the will of each man is subjugated, and the will of each adjusted to the will of all—a jurisprudence which in both cases has left upon the ages an everlasting impress, and has exerted a permanent influence upon institutions and civilisations foreign to its own.

It will be seen from this that at the root of the Roman religion there lies an element not commonly found in the faiths of the pre-Christian world—the element of morality. In Rome, as in Judea, the conception of law is an ethical conception; it is founded on the reciprocal duties of man to man, and on the duties of all to the body politic. The result is that in the early stages of her history the religion of Rome exhibits, as Mommsen remarks, an aspect of great seriousness.[1] It is unlike other systems of Polytheism in the solemnity with which it approaches the problems of life. If it deifies the powers of nature, it does so not on the ground of their contribution to sensuous joy, but on the ground of their possible service to humanity. The object of the Roman's reverence, like the object of the Jew's

---

[1] Mommsen, indeed, shows how, afterwards, the corruption of the Roman mind destroyed this primitive reverence. See his 'Rome,' book iii. chap. xiii.

reverence, is that collection of individuals comprehended under the name of the State. Everything which is worshipped by him is worshipped by reason of, and in proportion to, its service to the commonwealth. The conceptions of Church and State are not two conceptions, but one; the life of politics is identified with the life of piety. The good citizen and the good man are synonymous terms. There is no difference between treason and sacrilege, no separation between sin and crime. The man who violates the law of his country has violated thereby the divine law, and his expiation to the law of his country is accepted as an expiation to the law of heaven. And because the Roman reverenced the State, he reverenced also the family; here again emerges his resemblance to the Jew. Every family was viewed as a state in miniature, an image or simulacrum of that great commonwealth of which it was a part, and whose laws it was bound to mirror. The word piety, which receives its origin from him, means originally the affection of a son for a father, the devotion of a member to the head of a family. The derivation is significant. It shows that in the mind of the Roman the idea not only of religion but of morality was inseparable from the State, inseparable from the relation of the subordinate to the superior. And it is highly significant of this fact that the word "patriotism," which is also derived from him, means by etymology the love of country viewed as a family and a home. It was because the Roman and the Jew reverenced equally the origin and the climax of things, that they each found a place in their system both for the family and for the nation. The family represented the small beginning, the stream out of which the nation rose; the nation represented the family completed, the perfect development of the individual household.

But if Rome had one aspect turned towards Judea, she had another side turned towards the natural opposite of Judea — Greece. From Greece Rome borrowed wholesale. She conquered Greece by arms, but she allowed Greece to conquer her by peace. She took the Hellenic gods into her Pantheon and bowed down before them. She changed their names, indeed; she called Zeus Jupiter, and Poseidon Neptune, and Ares Mars, and Athene Minerva. Along with their names she changed also much of their garments; she stripped them of their beautiful and poetic dress, and clothed them in commonplace and prosaic attire. But when all was said and done, they were still the old gods; they were reduced in personality, but they preserved their original function. Now, this is one of the heterogenous things in the Roman system. We should have expected that a religion which started from the basis of morality and reverenced the abstraction of law, would have lifted up its eyes to an abstract and invisible Lawgiver. This was what Judea did, and in this Judea was consistent. But Rome was content to be inconsistent. What she wanted was union —a principle of co-operation amongst the nations, of which she herself would be the centre. To secure this she was willing to pay any price—to sacrifice logic, consistency, symmetry. If the stones of other temples were content to be incorporated in her Pantheon, she on her part was willing to receive them without perfect cement. Accordingly, she took the gods of Greece as they were—the personifications of the forces of a world existing in a state of struggle. It was for a state of struggle that she wanted them. Her problem was not how to reach a higher life, but how to make the best of this life. She did not desire the minds of her citizens to be centred on the things above; she wished them to be fixed on the things below. She desired that they should reverence the empire itself, that their religion should be bounded by the length and the breadth, the height and the depth of its possibilities. She sought the aid of no gods with any other end than this. If they did not minister to the needs of the empire, there was no other need to which she wished them to minister. Her very morality was a utilitarian morality. Lofty as it was in its aspirings, and severe as it was in its requirements, it was, still, ever contemplated as a means and not an end. If the Roman was to be courageous, it was because he belonged to a military nation. If he was to be just, it was because he was only one member of a vast empire where vastness could not be preserved without the perfect adjustment of all its parts. The empire itself was the real object of his reverence, and nothing else was reverenced except in so far as it ministered to this. In incorporating the gods of Greece, he was mainly influenced by the fact that the gods of Greece were no transcendental product. He was attracted by their earthliness. He was impelled to receive them, because he saw that they did not set up a high standard, did not profess to represent perfection. He perceived that their worship would not lift the national mind out of its nationality, would not draw it away from the contemplation of mundane things, specially from the contemplation of imperial interests. Himself of an unpoetic nature, and more prone to reverence the strong than the beautiful, he was willing to recognise these forms of æsthetic beauty, provided they would consent to favour the growth of his power.

But here there arises a third aspect of the Roman religion, and one in which it differs essentially from either of the two foregoing. I have said that the main end of Roman morality was the service of the empire. In this service, however, there was demanded, when occasion required, a readiness for the sacrifice of life which can nowhere else be found out of India. Materialistic and utilitarian as is the Roman genius, there is blended with it an element which originally had its source in that which is the reverse of materialism and the opposite of utilitarian—the element of Buddhism. Living, as he does, for this world in its most external aspect and its most mundane interests, the Roman, in the earlier stages of his history, is prepared, in the defence of these interests, to exhibit a sacrifice which is purely unworldly, and a self-surrender which is distinctly spiritual. One has only to read the pages of his opening story in order to be impressed with the fact that, from whatever source it has come, there has entered into his religion a breath of Indian worship. Mythical as in most of its parts that early story is, its very mythology reveals the presence and the influence of this thought of self-abnegation. Again and again we are confronted by the spectacle of a man sacrificing himself for his country, offering up his own life to appease that wrath of the gods which is supposed to have brought calamity upon the fortunes of his native land. Such stories would not be told if the ideal of heroism which they teach did not exist in the national mind. The very word religion, which is a word derived from Rome, implies in its most probable etymology[1] that a man's primary duty is self-sacrifice. It signifies a binding back, a re-

---

[1] The etymology I refer to is that which derives it from *religare*. See Augustin, De Civitate Dei, x. 3, edit. of Benedictines, Paris, 1838; and Lactantius, Insti. Div., iv. 28. Cicero, however, derives it from *religere* (Nat. Deor., ii. 28).

straint of the individual life. Each man is viewed as a victim bound to an altar of sacrifice. His being is offered up not really to the gods but to the State; the office of the gods is simply to approve and to reward. The man is at all times called upon to regard himself as a possible sacrifice to his country's good, as one who may at any moment be required to become an expiation for some national sin. It is highly significant that when a great Christian teacher wanted to exhibit Christianity as an atonement of the one for the guilt of the many, he embodied his view in an epistle to the *Romans*. He could not have sent it to a better quarter, nor to a quarter more likely to appreciate it. The Jew had no adequate sense of what was required from the individual man; he offered animal sacrifices for the wellbeing of the theocratic kingdom. The Roman in this respect saw deeper. He saw that if a kingdom of heaven was to be reached on earth, it must be reached through the surrender of each for all, through the willingness of every individual to give himself up for the whole. This was not Jewish, but it was Indian. It was a practical manifestation of Buddhism with the old intensity but with a new motive. It was no longer a sacrifice for the sake of death; its aim was the conservation and intensification of the national life. Yet it sought its end by the old means—the Buddhist means. It called upon the individual to surrender at the outset all individual desires, to give up his own personality, to resign his own interests. It called upon him to view himself only as one member of a vast body, and a member which ought to be amputated if the wants of the body required it. It incorporated with Western civilisation a breath of the Eastern day, and united to the activity of Europe the passive sacrificialness of Asia.

Nor in this wondrous Pantheon which thus sought to collect the varied thoughts of men, was there altogether wanting a place for Parsism. It is the last form of thought which we should have expected to have had a place there. Parsism started originally from exactly the opposite basis. The earliest vision of Rome was a vision of unity; the earliest vision of Persia was a vision of duality. Rome from the outset beheld the prospect of a world gathered around one centre; Persia began by seeing the impossibility of a common centre. One would have thought that a form of faith which saw in this world an empire divided between two, could never have been incorporated in a creed which proclaimed an empire governed by one only. Yet in the creed of Rome there is found such an incorporation. It comes out with great prominence in its doctrine of good and evil geniuses—in the belief that families and individuals may be advanced or retarded by the patronage or by the opposition of some spiritual power. Just as in the Persian hierarchy there were angels that fought for Ormuzd and angels that strove for

Ahriman, so in the popular mythology of Rome there were spirits which aided the life and there were spirits which impeded its progress. The medieval doctrine of guardian angels on the one hand and of besetting demons on the other, has its parentage in classic and pagan soil; it is a survival of that Roman culture in the midst of which Western Christianity has its cradle. That Rome took it from Persia I do not believe; but she took it from a phase of human nature which Persia made her own. She adopted it through her eclectic tendency to give a place to everything, to find room in her constitution for all forms of man. Nor was there wanting an element in her nature which made even this phase of faith in some sense congenial. Rome from the outset felt that her mission was conquest, that the unity to which she aspired could only be purchased by struggle. It was not wholly inappropriate that the struggle which she experienced in politics should be accepted also in the realm of spirit, and that the battle between strength and weakness should be accompanied by the strife between the powers of good and evil.

I have given these illustrations merely as specimens, as representative instances of that great principle on which the Roman constitution acted. That principle was one of incorporative union. The message of Rome to the religious world was essentially a message of peace. It sought to put an end to all clashings by allowing room for the co-existence of contrary tendencies, whether these tendencies belonged to the world of politics or to the sphere of religion. As in the world of politics it gave permission to the existence of empires within the empire, in the sphere of religion it gave permission to the existence of faiths within the faith. The one great faith of Rome was the belief in her own destiny, the maintaining and enlarging of herself. She was willing to incorporate within her temple every shrine that would favour such an end. The bond of unity which she sought between the different religions of men was the bond of a common devotion to the political interests of the empire. Hers is the earliest attempt to reach an evangelical alliance in the etymological sense of that expression,—to promulgate a message which shall furnish a meeting-place for the messages of other faiths. This is the true significance of the Roman religion, the secret of its protracted stability, and the cause of its long success. Yet it has not been ultimately successful; its attempt at union has eventually proved a failure. With the destruction of Rome's political fabric, the shrines incorporated within her temple have again been severed. The unity of faith which she has sought to secure has melted as utterly as the unity of empire which she actually established, and the fall of the one has been contemporaneous with the fall of the other. The question is, Why? What is the reason that the earliest attempt at religious union, based as it was on such a broad foundation, and conducted on such a princely scale, has proved in the long-run so entirely abortive? Why is it that an effort so persistently planned, and for a time so brilliantly achieved, has left behind it even fewer traces of its influence than those which survive of the effort at *political* unity? The answer to a question so suggestive and so practical demands the consideration of a separate chapter.

CHAPTER XI.

THE SUBJECT CONTINUED.

THE peculiarity of the Roman religion does not lie in its identification with State interests; this is an attribute which it shares in general with the whole ancient world.[1] What distinguishes the religion of Rome from surrounding and from past religions, is its effort to construct a universal Church by the formation of a universal State. Of course, in the old *régime*, the former was inevitably involved in the latter; if State and Church were one, the securing of a universal dominion was the securing of a universal Church. The peculiarity of the Roman worship lies in the fact that it did secure an absolute dominion by becoming the worship of an absolute State. And it is out of this fact that the great problem arises, Why has it failed? If it had not succeeded in its aim, there would be no

---

[1] Canon Westcott points out that the history of the Gentile world exhibits a gradual process of the secularising of religion ('Gospel of the Resurrection,' 2d edit , chap. i., xxxiv.).

room for wonder; but having succeeded, why has it proved abortive? The idea at which Rome aimed is by no means an obsolete idea; on the contrary, it is one of the most modern things in ancient history. The conception of a civic Church, of a Church which shall regulate its membership not by creed but by character, not by services done for the sanctuary but by duties done for man, is one that, with the advance of civilisation, has more and more been coming to the front. In countries holding the Protestant principle, it has been especially and increasingly powerful, and it finds in modern England a growing number of advocates.[1] It is distinctively a Western conception, and it had its home and origin in the West — in that great empire which sought to embrace the world. What is the reason that, as devised and promulgated by this empire, the scheme has proved so illusory? Why has the most gigantic effort to promote it been the most conspicuous for its failure?

In inquiring into a subject of this kind, the first question ought to be a consideration of the formula under which it is proposed to compass religious union. All religious union must be on the ground of some formula. Rome's formula I would express

---

[1] I find, for example, this view advocated by Mr W. T. Stead in an article entitled "The Civic Church," in a periodical styled 'Help,' supplement to the 'Review of Reviews,' March 1892, vol. ii., No. 3.

thus, "Whatever gods exist, exist for the sake of the Roman State." It mattered not whether they actually existed, provided that those who believed in them would recognise them as patrons of the government. Now, I concede at the outset that this formula has an advantage over most other formulas, both ancient and modern; it is based not on the recognition of a fact but on the expression of a desire. The Roman creed is virtually a prayer; it unites men by the subscription to one article—the obligation to aspire towards the wellbeing of the republic. I have always felt that if ever a creed shall be formed which shall obtain universal suffrage, it shall be on such a basis—the basis of a common prayer. I have sometimes imagined that a subscription to the Lord's Prayer would constitute a point of union not only for all Christians, but for some who are popularly regarded as outside the pale of Christianity. It seems to me that the Roman formula constitutes the only deliberate attempt which has been made in the direction of a creed based on aspiration, and it is probably to this that it owes what measure of success it has attained. The question remains why it has not been successful throughout. The principle of the formula is good and makes for union; why has it not achieved union? Clearly there must be something defective in the formula itself, something which has nullified or weakened the force of the aspiration. A moment's consideration will show us that it is here where the vitiating element lies.

The object contemplated by Roman religion is the identification of the Church with the State. It aspires to make the religious duty of man coincident with his political duty. The question is, If such a union were perfected in all the members of the body politic, would it amount to a religion of humanity? And the answer must be, No; it is exactly here that the religion of Rome has failed in its design. It would have been a very different matter if Rome had contemplated the identification of the State with the Church,—if she had said that every man, by reason of the act of worship, was entitled to political privileges. But when she said that the Church was to be identified with the State, she really limited the Church. The State as understood by Rome was not coextensive with the Church as understood by Christianity. The Church as understood by Christianity comprehends every man who is willing to recognise his own weakness; the State as understood by Rome comprehended only those men who were able to exercise certain political powers. Accordingly, when Rome made the Church identical with the State, she really cut off from religious membership a vast section of humanity. There were in the Roman empire, there are in every empire under heaven, a multitude of human beings who have no relation to the State except that of hindrance—who are simply a blot and a barrier upon the constitution and the progress of the body politic. In modern life it is generally conceded that it is the duty of the State to care for these; but the very statement implies that they are a drag upon the wheels of the social fabric, that they constitute one of the elements which prevent any State from being a perfect government. There are those who are so defective in body as to be incapable of bearing their part in the conflict of life. There are those who are so defective in intellect as to be incapable of realising what it is to be in conflict. There are those who are so defective in morality that they are led to the commission of crime with an instinct seemingly as unerring as that by which the bee is led to the construction of its hive. No one will maintain that these are members of a State as such; no one will contend that they are anything less than a retardation of the political mechanism. If, therefore, the Church be identified with the State, it logically follows that the Church is to be barricaded from a large section, and that the most needy section, of humanity.

Rome saw the logical consequence, and she did not shrink from it. It was in her power to have altered or relaxed her formula; she preferred to abide by it, and to accept the inevitable conclusion. That conclusion was the sternest imaginable; it practically consigned to oblivion some millions of the human race. The mentally and bodily defective were no aid to the movement of State mechanism. Rome said, "Let them be taken out of the way." She not only said it, but up to her power she did it. She laboured by every means to suppress incompetents. She had not found the secret of suppressing their *incompetency;* the shortest and easiest method she knew was to annihilate them. She sought to lay the axe to the root of the tree. She recommended infanticide in cases of deformity, desertion of infants in cases of hopeless destitution. She exposed the life of the slave to the sword of the gladiator. She inculcated as a doctrine of moral heroism the practice of suicide when any life was too hard to bear. She left unprovided those forms of mental alienation which, because they are not seen on the surface and not recognised in the first stage of development, were allowed to escape the remedy of infanticide.

These blots on the Roman constitution are popularly regarded as a sign of the low religious life to which the old world had sunk, a sign of how little power the religion of the empire really possessed to influence the lives of its members. And yet a moment's reflection should convince us that this is not the legitimate conclusion. It certainly proves that the religion of the empire was a form of faith very defective in theory and very inadequate in scope; but it does not prove that it was a form of faith which had lost its practical influence. The conclusion is exactly the contrary. It was not by a fall from its religious principle that Rome became neglectful of the maimed masses of society; it was precisely by the *carrying out* of its religious principle. Rome neglected the maimed bodies in the State because her principle of religion taught her to regard these as no part of the State. She was never more religious than in the cold eye she turned towards the halt and the blind. It was no impulse of impiety which prompted her to pass these by on the other side, which induced her to seek for their elimination and extermination. It would hardly be too much to say that in her neglect, and even in her seeming cruelty, she acted under the impulse of religion, under the impulse of that faith which she had made her own. Her ideal was empire; her worship was the reverence of empire; her religion was the service of empire. To her the good citizen and the pious devotee were one. The religious duty of every man was to support those influences which made for the welfare of the State; it was equally his duty to discourage and to suppress those influences which impeded the welfare of the State. In his efforts to eliminate hindrances, in his attempts to extinguish incompetents, in his measures to repress the multiplication of those noxious or useless growths which interfered with the life of the collective body, he might well on his principles believe that he was doing piety good service. The error of Rome must be sought, not in her unfaithfulness to her religious ideal, but in the defectiveness of that ideal itself. The object of her reverence was not being but force, not existence but energy, not thought but action. She valued everything for what it could do, measured everything by its dynamical result. She had no place in her Pantheon for that which had no arithmetical significance. She rated every man by what he could bring, valued every man by the amount of strength he could add to the republic. If he could bring nothing—if, instead of contributing to the State, he required the State to contribute to him—he was there and then regarded as a blot on the political constitution, and a hindrance which ought to be got rid of.

The effect of this appeared in the sequel. Rome ended by reverencing an incarnation or embodiment of that political power which had always in the abstract been the object of her adoration; she ultimately worshipped her own emperor. Let us understand the significance of this act: it has been often misunderstood, and it has frequently been misinterpreted. In books written with a view to show the downward tendency of Paganism, it has been often said that the heathen world reached the lowest depth of its abasement in the Roman deification of the human. There is a famous antithetical sentence which has expressed the thought thus:

"The living God became man at the time when a living man was worshipped as God." And yet nothing is more certain than the fact that the antithesis between the religion of Christ and the religion of Rome does not lie here. So far is the deification of the human from being the last stage of a downward development, there is no stage of religious development which is not founded upon this article. I have already exhibited the principle that not only the root but the very presupposition of all religion is the belief in incarnation, the belief that the human is in the image of the divine. Without this presupposition the only alternative is agnosticism, and agnosticism without end. If the divine be different in essence from the human, there is no possible communion in any world between the human and the divine. It speaks volumes for the discernment of Judaism that, although by nature prone to emphasise to the uttermost the distance between God and man, it asserted from the very foundation that man was made in the image of God. In recognising in man the stamp of divinity, Rome was in strictest alliance with the whole development of religion.

But the point of divergence lay in her ideal of man himself. It is not too much to say that, in conferring divine honours upon her emperor, Rome erred not by deifying man too much but by deifying him too little. Her doctrine of incarnation, instead of going too far, did not go far enough. Her error consisted in putting the crown of divinity on only a part of humanity, and in leaving uncanonised the other part. When Rome put the divine crown upon the head of her emperor, she deified the incarnation of power. She selected from all the attributes of humanity this one attribute, and impressed it with the stamp of divinity. She said that the one element in man worthy to be reverenced and fit to be consecrated was his capacity to put in motion the physical forces of the universe. She deified him in his power to move masses, in his ability to wield the sword, in his strength to construct empires, in his force to exact and maintain obedience. She recognised, in short, the incarnation of humanity in so far as humanity was capable of becoming a State-power. The defect of this ideal was its narrowness. It lay, not as some think, in the presumption of the creature, but in the creature failing to aspire sufficiently high. It did not exalt a large enough number of the elements of man. In crowning his capacity for the exercise of physical power, it left in the background other and more glorious capacities. It forgot to note that there were attributes in the human spirit which exhibited a divine strength precisely in their incapacity to exercise physical power. It omitted to observe that there is a force which consists not in doing but in bearing, a strength which lies not in acting but in lying passive. It was oblivious of the fact that in the display of this strength there might be manifested a height of heroism and a depth of human resources compared with which all the past achievements of the empire were but the exhibitions of child's-play. Rome failed to realise the union of humanity because she failed to perceive the many-sidedness of man.

Now, it is here that there emerges the real contrast between the latest growth of the Roman religion and the manifestation of that faith which arose in the very midst of the empire—the gospel of Jesus Christ. The difference between them lay not in the idea that the one glorified the creature and the other did not. Strictly speaking, they both glorified the creature—both took hold of a human life and lifted it into the presence of the divine. The difference lay in the fact that the life which Christianity lifted into the presence of the divine was a life of larger and fuller humanity than that which Rome exalted. Rome crowned humanity only in one of its aspects—the aspect of physical power. Christianity crowned man all round, in every sphere of his nature, in every promise and potence of his life. It deified him as the prophet, the priest, and the king, and in so doing it exhausted all the possible fields of his action. When it deified him as the king, it was, so far, in unison with the Roman empire; it recognised the truth that there is indeed something godlike in man's power over the physical forces. When it worshipped him as the prophet, it was in unison both with the Greek and with the Jew; it recognised the truth that in the revelations of human thought and in the glimpses of poetic genius there are seen the flashes of a light divine. But when it adored him as the priest, it was in unison neither with Roman nor Greek nor Jew; it transcended all, or rather, it went down beneath all. It took up a part of humanity which had always been regarded as its contemptible part — the susceptibility to pain. It put a crown upon the head of that in man which had hitherto been despised by man himself. It proclaimed a doctrine which to the old world was certainly a paradox. It said that the kingdom of God recognised amongst the trophies of its glory a multitude of souls whom the kingdoms of this world regarded as State hindrances. It declared that man might be as great in his weakness as in his strength, as heroic in his pain as in his power. The priest had, even with the Jew, existed as a representative of human nothingness; with Christianity he stood forth as a representative of something which in man was divine — the power to be touched with the feeling of infirmities.

Hence it is that the incarnation taught by Christianity has been more thorough and fearless than the incarnation taught by Rome. The religion of

Christ has prevailed over the religion of Rome, simply from the fact that it has been less afraid to exalt the human soul. Rome only canonised man as an emperor; Christianity proclaimed the essential sacredness of humanity in all its attributes. There arose in the heart of the Roman empire the conception of another empire called the kingdom of heaven. It partook somewhat of the soil in which it grew. It aimed at finding a meeting-place for all things—a brotherhood amongst the nations and a point of union with the divine. But it aimed at more than that. It was not content to establish a brotherhood of nations; it wanted a brotherhood of souls. It was not satisfied to find a point of union with the divine; it desired the divine and the human to be united along the whole line. It called itself the kingdom of heaven, not to separate itself from the kingdoms of earth, but to indicate its wider comprehensiveness than any earthly kingdom. It proposed to found a State which should embrace amidst its members not only the active but the passive units. It proclaimed for the first time to the world what has since become a commonplace —that they also serve who only stand and wait. In that aphorism there is at once involved an enlargement of the whole idea of empire. The conception of the kingdom of heaven was itself a revelation to the old world. It told men that they had made an inadequate census of the population, that they had failed to enrol in the State the full complement of its members. It told them that they had not sufficiently estimated the actual strength of any community, that in limiting their view to the labourers and ignoring the heavy-laden, they had left out of account the strongest proof of national resources, the highest evidence of imperial power. When it included within its borders the heavy-laden as well as the labouring, it for the first time reached the idea of a State coextensive with the Church, because coextensive with the needs of humanity.

It was fated, then, that the message of Rome should be actually fulfilled within its own dominions and within its own era. It was to be fulfilled, however, not by Rome herself, but by another and a humbler power. The office of Rome was, after all, only that of John the Baptist; she prepared the way. Her relation to Christianity was, indeed, no merely negative one. She did not simply, as church historians affirm, help to create a longing for the light by increasing the power of darkness. Her contribution to the world was a contribution of light, and of light in the direction of Christianity. She aimed at the construction of a universal kingdom, and in so doing she was on the lines of the coming faith. Her error was that her universal kingdom did not embrace a universal humanity. She gained all that she sought, but she sought too little. The Roman empire was less comprehensive than the kingdom of heaven, and it was less comprehensive because it was less microscopic. It measured forces too much by the extensiveness of their range, and too little by the intensiveness of their pressure. It incorporated the length and the breadth, but not the depth of humanity. The kingdom of heaven went down to the roots of human nature—to its wants, to its sins. If I were allowed to express the difference epigrammatically, I would say that the religion of Rome and the religion of Jesus were united in the first three petitions of that Christian aspiration called the Lord's Prayer. Rome said with Christianity, "Hallowed be Thy name"; she was prepared to assert and to maintain the dignity and the solemnity of that imperial structure which she reverenced. She said with Christianity, "Thy kingdom come"; her perpetual prayer was for the establishment of her ideal kingdom. She said with Christianity, "Thy will be done"; she undertook no enterprise until she had first inquired whether that enterprise should be favoured by heaven. But there the concord ended and the difference began. When Rome passed from the divine to the human, she proceeded to halt in her petitions. She had no prayer for the pure and simple forgiveness of moral debts; she could only ask what atonement would be accepted by the gods. She had no prayer to be led out of the way of temptation; she depreciated the danger on this side of life. She had not even an unqualified prayer for the distribution of daily bread; she had not learned the full sense of the word "*our*." Rome had a distinct mission, but it was not a mission of finality; she must be content to occupy the place and to bear the reputation of a forerunner. Her crowning glory must rest in the fact that she devised a scheme of religious union the largest and the most comprehensive which the ancient world had ever seen, that she made an honest and earnest attempt to carry out that scheme into practical realisation, and that she succeeded in the attempt in a measure far beyond what could have been anticipated from a mechanism which, after all, was constructed of such inadequate materials.

CHAPTER XII.

THE MESSAGE OF THE TEUTON.

THE name "Teuton" is the term under which are comprehended the Scandinavian and German races. Between both the speech and the mythology of these races there exists a very close affinity.[1] The result is that, notwithstanding the varieties of detail which distinguish the worship of their different nations, there is one common spirit pervading the whole. The contrariety indeed seems to exist in another direction. It does not strike us so much when we survey the aspect of the ancient Teuton nations, as when we compare the ancient aspect with the modern. It seems strange at first sight that the religion of the ancient Teutons should be so different from the spirit of the modern Germans. Between the earliest and the latest forms of most faiths we can detect a strong analogy. China, through all the changes of the centuries, has retained her original

[1] See Jacob Grimm's 'Teutonic Mythology,' of which there is an excellent English translation.

bias. India, through the circles of the suns, has preserved her native spirit. Even Rome, amid the complete transformation of her Pagan into her Christian life, has retained certain marked resemblances which indicate to the eye of the observer that he is looking on the same fabric. But when we turn to modern Germany, we seem to find an utter contrast between the past and the present. The lapse of time which intervenes between the life of the ancient and the life of the modern Teuton is not so great as the lapse of time which intervenes between the life of ancient and the life of modern Rome. And yet, in the former case, the gulf is far wider and the hiatus far more marked than in the latter. There is an analogy between the saints of the Roman calendar and the gods of the Roman Pantheon; but where shall we find an analogy between the speculations of the modern German and the faith of the primitive Teuton? The one is the ancestor of the other, yet the chasm betwixt them appears impassable. Modern Germany is confessedly the sphere of the highest theological culture and of the most abstruse religious thinking; primitive Teutonism is on the surface the most crude of all beliefs and the most childish of all worships. Is there anywhere to be found a bridge that connects them, anywhere a point of union between the dawn and the meridian day?

I think there is. If we look closely and beneath

the surface, we shall see that there are features in the Teuton mythology which reveal something behind them. We shall see, above all things, that this mythology does not exhibit a *uniform* surface; that, however crude it may be, it is at least decreasingly crude. Every mythology exhibits variety; the Teuton mythology reveals progress in its variety. It is here that, I think, the real bridge is to be found between the old faith and the new, between the religion of the primitive Teuton and the religion of the modern German. If we take the Teuton mythology as a whole, and confine ourselves to its distinctive elements, we shall find that its message to the world is summed up in a single word— development. It is here that, in my opinion, the point of difference lies between this mythology and earlier mythologies. It has features in common with the earliest creed of India, with the primitive worship of Greece, and with the original faith of Rome; but it differs from these in the fact that here we have features of *development*. If it be so, we are ushered into immediate contact with the modern spirit of the Teuton race. The spirit of modern Germany is essentially that of evolution. Even from medieval days it has been the pioneer of human progress, and in the nineteenth century it has led the van. To the German races, in whatever land they have been called to dwell, has been committed the task of revealing the development of humanity.

The philosophy of Hegel has traced back that development on the lines of spirit; the philosophy of Darwin has traced it back on the lines of matter; but both have equally had one aim—to exhibit the connection between the future and the past. If the Teuton mythology can be proved, even amidst its crudeness and rudeness, to have evinced a glimmering sense of the unity of history, we shall plant our feet upon the bridge that identifies the old spirit with the new.

Now, there is one element in this Teuton mythology which deserves careful attention. It is the fact that, notwithstanding the fantastic nature of its materials, these materials, when taken together, blend themselves into a system. I waive altogether any reference to its cosmogony, although even there, I think, it would be possible to trace a plan of progressive development. But, dealing as I am with the element of religion itself, I shall here as elsewhere confine myself to the view taken of the heavenly powers. It would not be at all remarkable that the Teuton mythology should describe a progress in the acts of *creation*. But what strikes me as very remarkable is that this mythology, when taken as a whole, describes a progressive development in the life of the gods themselves. Nowhere does the ancient Teuton mind approach so near to the modern Teuton mind as in the fact here indicated. The peculiarity of German philosophy has not been its attempt to trace a development in history; that has been done by many systems. Its peculiarity lies in its endeavour to show that the development of human history is the development of the divine mind. It is this which constitutes at once its boldness and its originality. But if it should be found that this tendency exists in the Teuton races from the beginning, if it should be seen that it belongs to the earliest as well as to the latest phase of German thought, it will furnish a strong presumption that the message of the Teuton has been one distinctive to himself, and one which by nature he of all others has been best qualified to give.

Now, we find that the history of the gods embraced in this Teuton mythology consists of three ages. The first age is a period of peace; it is a time in which the heavens are silent, free from war, undisturbed by commotion—a time in which the industrial arts flourish, and the value of life is measured by the amount of its beneficial resources. This, in the Teuton mythology, is represented as the golden age. It is rather curious that it should be so. A man's conception of heaven is in general only a transference into the air of the state in which he lives on earth. But the state in which the Teuton lived on earth was a state of war. The beings whom he deifies are representatives of those powers of nature which are distinguished for their strength—a fact which proves conclusively that in the world of his day the power most needed was the capacity for conflict. At the head of the Pantheon stands Woden, a name symbolic of all physical majesty and all warlike strength. On a step beneath him is Thor, the god of cloud, rain, and thunder, enormously strong, and wielding a hammer that can split the mountains. Next comes Tiu— professedly the god of battle, the source of martial honour, the inspirer of military prowess. At a considerably lower remove stands Loki, the being who presides over the element of fire, and who is in future to develop into the great adversary of goodness. But the strange thing is that he is not yet become Satan; he has at the outset his place amongst the angels. Should we not have expected that a race like the early Teutons, living amidst perpetual war, and feeling every day the necessity for a strong protective hand, would have invested the adversary from the beginning with his aspect of Satanic terror, and represented the fields of heaven as from the outset fields of incessant battle?

Yet the first stage of the Teuton mythology is peace. The natural conclusion is that the first stage of his *history* had been peace, that originally he had lived in a state of primitive simplicity, the memory of which still lingered. I do not think he would have assigned this to the gods if he had not experienced it and enjoyed it in himself, for our ideals of heaven were first our ideals of earth. There are traces, too, in this early Pantheon of the existence of such a time. Side by side with the gods of muscular strength, there are seats for female divinities. Wherever the divinity of woman is recognised, it may be assumed that in the national life there has once been an element of culture. When I learn from the hymns of ancient India that she had a place in her early Pantheon for the female side by side with the male, I know assuredly that in the early life of the race there was no place for the zenanas; women could never have been admitted to the fellowship of the gods above, if they had been secluded from the fellowship of men below. Even so, when in the mythology of the ancient Teuton I read of female divinities dwelling beside the sons of thunder—when I hear of Frigga, the goddess of the inhabited earth, free, beautiful, lovable; when I am told of Freyja, the Venus of the Teutons, representing the softer emotions of the heart,[1] I am led to the inevitable conclusion that there was a time in which peace and not war was both the practice and the ideal. I am constrained to believe that the first age of the Teuton was an age of more culture than the second, and that it

---

[1] It is true that in the elder Edda, Freyja is represented as dividing the slain with Woden, but this is probably the result of the corruption of first ideals. Edda is the name given to two collections of national myths—the elder compiled in the twelfth, the younger in the thirteenth century.

was through the lingering memory of that culture that he made the beginning of heaven a scene of calm.

By-and-by the curtain falls upon this scene, and when it rises again there is a complete change. The calm is broken and the storm has begun. If the first age is a day of peace, the second is a night of war. The heavens of the new period are no longer in calm but in commotion. Loki has revealed himself in his true colours. He has ceased to be the servant; he has become the adversary, the Satan. He has set himself in deliberate antagonism to the powers of heaven, and has become the origin of evil. In so doing, he has become at the same time the origin of good, for the one cannot be known without the other. Hitherto the life of the gods had been neither good nor evil; it had been simply natural. They had dwelt in peace, merely because there was no place for war, no opposition to the original current of the stream. But with the rebellion of Loki the opposition began, and along with it came the revelation of the tree of knowledge. The appearance of war for the first time revealed peace. Before this time peace had been an unconscious possession; war made it a realised possession. Accordingly, it is significant that, with the emergence of Loki upon the scene, there emerges also another being on the other side—Balder. If Loki is the principle of evil, Balder is the first conscious and deliberate principle of good. The legends that surround his name constitute some of the most beautiful portions of the Edda. He is the personification of all possible virtues. He is transcendently beautiful, possessing a form of radiant light He is immaculately pure, and into his heavenly mansion nothing unclean can enter. In him are united the attributes at once of the male and the female. Like Thor, he is also the son of Woden, and therefore in him there are found the traces of martial firmness. His judgments are irreversible and beyond repeal; in this appear the qualities of the male. But the female is represented in the mode of execution. The outward *régime* is one of conspicuous mildness; force has given place to persuasion, and the influence of mind has succeeded to the rod of authority. Balder, in short, seems to me to represent the effort to find a union between the gold of the ideal past and the iron of the actual present. He unites in his own person the calm of the one and the strength of the other. He stands as a symbol of the truth that gentleness needs not be weakness, that silence is not incompatible with power, and that the intuitions of a feminine nature may express a decision of character which is unmatched by any exhibition of merely muscular force.

Let us pursue the narrative. The powers of good and evil are now for the first time face to face with one another. A conflict is inevitable, and we stand breathlessly expecting the issue. Balder also stands in expectation, and his expectation is of the most gloomy character. His forebodings are of the worst. He is tormented by horrible dreams, in which he sees himself extinguished by the powers of evil. It is a fine and subtle indication of the fact that the burden of sin falls upon the sinless, and that the shadow forecast by wickedness obscures most the path of the good. To assuage the dreams of Balder, his mother, Frigga, takes an oath of allegiance from all creation. She exacts a promise from every object in the universe that it will do her son no hurt,—from every object but one. She forgets the mistletoe; she probably thought it too contemptible a thing to be dangerous, too parasitic a thing to have any independent efficacy. She ignored it by reason of its smallness, and because its life was so closely attached to other lives. That one act of negligence becomes the death of Balder. The gods, by way of experiment, throw missiles at him composed of darts, stones, and all things supposed to be of greatest natural danger, and when he remains unhurt by these, they are comforted as to his safety. But the real danger lies in the apparently soft and inoffensive thing. The danger of sin is not its openness but its subtleness, its resemblance to that which is good and pure. That this is the thought of the myth is to my mind beyond all question. The missile that destroys Balder is not only the seemingly harmless mistletoe, but it is the mistletoe thrown by the hand of one who is blind. Loki, the principle of evil, does not discharge the dart himself; he guides to the enterprise the hand of a sightless being—the war-god, Other. Will any one say that such a conception is accidental? Can it be thought for a moment that a convergence of circumstances so unlikely and so inappropriate could have been dictated by anything but the deliberate design of establishing a particular idea? And is it not as clear as daylight that the idea designed to be established is the subtlety of the power of sin? Is it not manifest, almost on the surface, that the Teuton is struggling to embody the truth that the danger of temptation to a human soul is not its ugliness but its plausibleness? He wishes to give expression to his belief that the snare which besets the heart of youth lies not in the attraction to any form of sin revealed as sin, but in the fact that sin prefers every form to its own, and habitually clothes itself in the disguise of purity. In rude figures, in coarse emblems, in imperfect metaphors, the mind of the Teuton has given utterance to a truth as old as creation and as modern as the latest day—that the serpent is more subtle than any beast of the field.

Let us still pursue the narrative. Balder is slain by the mistletoe; goodness is blotted out from the world by the subtlety of evil. When it is blotted out its power begins to be felt. Balder is never so greatly reverenced as when he is gone; the strength of his presence is for the first time realised by the blank of his absence. There is a universal weeping amongst the gods, and a deputation is sent to the goddess of the grave supplicating his return. It is answered that the prayer will be granted, provided that all things living and dead shall mourn his loss. The condition is almost universally fulfilled. Every object in creation, whether in heaven or on earth, mourns for Balder, with one solitary exception—an emissary of the Power of evil. It is a striking allegory of the permeating influence of goodness. It represents the truth that every department of nature is in some sense indebted to morality. For is it not true that the loss of Balder is a loss to all things, even to things which originally seemed to occupy a foreign soil? Is it not true that poetry owes half its beauty to the moral sentiment, that art is largely indebted to the sacrificial instincts of the soul, that eloquence receives its point and force from the promptings of right and wrong, that warlike prowess has its root as much in the conscience as in the arm, that success in life is powerfully influenced by the concentration of moral purpose, and that the political ties which bind a nation are closely or feebly riveted in proportion to the social ties that bind the family? All this was felt by the Teuton mind, and all this is expressed in the fact that creation weeps for Balder. Living amid the sinews of war, the hardy Norseman had discernment enough to perceive that the sinews of war could never form the body of a State. He perceived that the root of all strength was something behind it—that very element of morality which is popularly thought to be the source of softness. He saw that to loose the mind from its ethical moorings was to dissolve the whole fabric, social and political, and to reduce to a collection of atoms that structure of imperial power which he believed to dwell in the region of the heavens.

Accordingly, we are not surprised to find that to the mind of the Norseman the death of Balder becomes the beginning of all calamities. The demand for his return has been almost universal, but not altogether; it has been resisted by the Power of evil. By that one act of resistance his return is rendered as impossible as if the whole world had opposed it. And the loss is total. We must remember that in the conception of the Norseman, the death of Balder is not merely the loss of an individual; it is the extinction of an ideal. I have often been struck with the words of St Paul in 1st Corinthians ii. 8, where he says that if the princes of the Roman empire had only known the secret of their national strength "they would not have crucified the Lord of Glory." He is clearly speaking of a moral and not a physical crucifixion. He feels that what the princes of this world wanted to do was not simply to put a *man* to death, but to put an idea to death; that what they desired to crucify was not the outward life of Jesus, but the thought of Him, the spirit of Him, the ideal of Him. And it is just because the death of Christ was to them the death of an ideal that Paul holds them to have made a mistake. He tells them that, by taking away from the young men of their empire the portrait of moral heroism exhibited in the Man of Nazareth, they have deprived the spirit of youth of its greatest and noblest stimulus, have deprived them of that very physical courage on whose foundation they have mainly sought to build. Such, in more extended form, I conceive to have been the thought expressed in the Teuton's grief for Balder. It is the cry not over a man but over an ideal, the tears for the departure of one who is not simply an individual but the embodiment and incarnation of moral purity itself. Hence in his loss the Teuton sees the loss of all things. He forecasts his mythology into the future, and it is a forecast of gloom. He sees a deepening of the conflict between the Powers of hell and heaven, and, ever increasingly, hell prevails. It is in vain that Loki is chained to the subterranean sulphur spring; he bursts his bonds and is free. There is seen approaching a time of unheard-of tribulation—a time which the Eddas signalise as "the twilight of the gods." It is a time of cutting frost, of piercing winds, of sunless air, of winter without spring. It is a time of war and bloodshed, when nation shall rise against nation, and when, above all, a man's foes shall be those of his own household. The father shall be at variance with the child, the brother shall lift his hand against the brother, the ties of the household shall be rent in twain. At last the crisis shall come; the Powers of good and evil shall gather themselves together for a final conflict — the Armageddon of the Teuton mythology. On the plain of Vigrid shall be fought the great battle that is to decide the fate of the universe. It is to be a battle of unexampled fury, of protracted tenacity, and of mutual destructiveness. The two contending hosts are alike to be annihilated. Loki, the Power of evil, is to fall, but Woden and Thor are also to perish. At last the heat of battle is to set fire to the universe. In the warmth of conflict there is to be kindled a spark which shall dissolve both friends and foes, and, like a mimic scene, this whole vast creation shall disappear in lurid flame. The earth shall be burned up, the elements shall melt with fervent heat, the powers of the heavens shall be shaken, and, over the spot where raged the roar of battle, universal silence shall reign.

And here the curtain falls upon the second great epoch of the Teuton mythology. Neither of the two epochs has attained perfection. The first was the age of innocence, when there was virtue in heaven, simply from the fact that there was no war;

it was sinlessness in the absence of temptation. The second was the age of conflict, when the existing state of things was resisted by the Power of evil, and Balder appeared as the antagonist of Loki; it was no longer the age of innocence but the age of law. Yet very sublimely is it said that, even in this time of comparative advancement, the days for Balder had not come. Balder was the personification of holiness, and holiness is just as incompatible with conflict as with innocence. He cannot live in a world where there is a struggle of the will; he demands a surrendered will. The reign of law cannot exist side by side with the reign of grace, for law is virtue by restraint, grace is virtue by nature. Accordingly, Balder had to go away until the times of conflict were completed. The beauties of holiness could only exist in spontaneity, and the presence of contending hosts was the absence of spontaneity. If Balder should come back, it must be by the annihilation of the hosts that contended, and by the destruction of that age of restraint which is incompatible with spontaneous love.

But now this second age has been destroyed, and on both sides the contending hosts are still. The age of conflict has followed the age of innocence; it has ceased to be. Out from the universal silence there comes a new voice of creation. From the under-world, from the world of the dead below the sea, Balder returns. In the place where the old paradise stood there rises a new abode for the good, —an abode of perfect beauty and of waveless peace. Here is to begin afresh the life of humanity, on a larger scale and with higher possibilities. Yet, very significantly, it is suggested that there is to be a thread of continuity between the old life and the new. The inhabitants of the revived world are to find the golden tablets which their race had possessed at the beginning of time. It is a striking metaphor of the belief that the state to which they have finally attained had its germ in the state from which they originally came. The abode of the gods had been originally the home of spontaneous virtue. It was a spontaneity which came, indeed, only from ignorance; none the less was it the natural and normal state of man. By-and-by the spontaneity was broken by the conflict on the Mount of Temptation, and innocence fled away, never to return. But though the innocence could never return, the spontaneity could. There are two ways in which a life may become spontaneous; it may be so by ignorance of conflict, or it may be so by overcoming conflict. The former method was past, and past for ever, but the latter method was to come. There was to open an age like the first, yet different, an age in which virtue was again to become natural to man, but in which the naturalness was to spring not from ignorance but from habit. It was to be an age in which the life of the universe was once more to become a life of peace, no longer merely because there were no materials for war, but because the materials for war had been seen and discarded. The third state of the Teuton, in short, was to be a new paradise, exhibiting all the appearances of the Garden of Eden, but exhibiting them on a totally opposite ground—on the ground of a virtue which had met and conquered the tempter, and become by that conquest the undisputed master of the field.

Will it be said that the view I have here taken attributes to the Teuton an amount of subtlety beyond the reach of a primitive age? I answer that conscious mythology is necessarily subtle. Mythology, as I take it, cannot belong to a primitive age; it marks rather the twilight than the dawn of early religious belief. It indicates the stage in which the forms of nature are no longer sufficient of themselves, and can only preserve their reverence by receiving the clothing of the mind. Mythology is in every instance an effort of the poetic imagination—an effort to make one thing wear the attributes of another, and, as such, it demands and involves a long course of thought and a considerable power of culture. Subtlety, therefore, is inseparable from conscious mythology, and the only question is whether the explanation I have given is, in the circumstances, the most natural. It is only fair to state that mine is but one attempt out of many. The explanations of the myth of Balder have been beyond measure numerous.[1] It has been a favourite practice to see in it an allegorical exposition of the outward processes of nature. Max Müller, for example, regards it as designed to describe the conflict between the winter and the summer — the temporary submergence of nature beneath frost and snow, and its ultimate rising in the spring. I do not deny it. It seems to me beyond all question that the Teuton perceived the conflict of his life in the struggles of the orb of day. But why did he perceive them there? Simply because he had first felt them in himself. We are so familiar with the metaphor of the sun struggling through clouds as to be in danger of forgetting that it *is* a metaphor. There is nothing in the fact of the sun making its way gradually through clouds that could ever suggest the idea of struggle, if that idea were not already in the mind. The idea of struggle is a purely mental conception; it is derived from consciousness alone. It is received by our experience of a sense of resistance, by our meeting with some impediment to the exercise of the will. When, therefore, I look up to the heavens and figure there the battle between light and darkness, I attribute to the heavens something which exists in myself alone. I paint upon the walls of the universe a thought which belongs

[1] For a review of this subject see Weinhold, "Die sagen von Loki," in Haupt's 'Zeitschrift für Deutsches Alterthum' (Leip., 1849).

only to my own spirit, and which never could have
been known at all except through the movements of
that spirit. I write upon the doors of the outward
world an inscription which belongs to my inner
nature, and seem to receive from without an impression which has really been imported from
within.

It is in vain, therefore, to say that the Teuton
derived his conception of Balder from beholding the
phenomena of the heavens; it is true, but it is
irrelevant. If he derived his conception from the
heavens, it was because he had first given it to the
heavens. The alternations of the outward light had
been to him simply a mirror in which he had seen
reflected the movements of his own soul. When he
constructed the idea of Balder from looking on the
struggles of the summer sun, he merely took back
from that sun the thought which he himself had
originally lent to it. The ultimate explanation of
the myth must lie in the region of the mind. Balder
himself is a personification, and so is the sun in the
heavens; the one as much as the other requires to
be explained on mental grounds. If so, the explanation ought to be very simple, and can be nothing
else than what has here been indicated. Balder in
the field of history, and the sun in the field of the
heavens, are alike and equally the embodiment of a
great thought—the thought that the life of man proceeds from peace to conflict, and from conflict back

to peace. But if it be so, it follows beyond all controversy that the message of the Teuton is the message of development. To him distinctively amongst the votaries of the religious world there has fallen the task of exhibiting the progressive nature of the divine life. The votaries of other faiths have been concerned with other elements. The Brahman has seen the God above the world, and the Greek has seen the God *in* the world; to the Teuton has been assigned the part of describing the divine life above the world and the divine life in the world, as separate stages of one and the same existence, as steps of progressive development in the unfolding of the universal plan.

And let it be remembered that to the playing of this part the Teuton has been true. The message of the primitive race has been the message of the race in its phase of highest culture. At the beginning of this century there appeared in Germany a form of thought which has revolutionised all previous philosophies, and exerted an influence even over unsympathetic schools; I allude, of course, to that system called Hegelianism. It is supposed to be a system defying the understanding of ordinary mortals. Yet, when looked at dispassionately, and divested of abstruse language, it will be found to be simply a refined reproduction by the Teuton mind in maturity of that which in primitive days it conceived in germ. Hegel says that in the universe as a whole, and in every part of the universe, there are three successive movements. The first is one of unimpeded motion—of motion without opposition, and therefore without *recognition*. A man running at full speed on a seemingly boundless plain, and with no memory of having ever occupied any other attitude, would never say even to himself that he was free. The idea of freedom could only be reached by an interruption to the seeming boundlessness, could only be realised in the meeting with a barred gate. Accordingly the barred gate appears, and marks the second stage of the universal life. The unimpeded movement is interrupted, the unqualified affirmation is contradicted, and the day of spontaneous growth is succeeded by the day of conflict. It is an hour of apparent decline, but of real progress, the spirit of life has lost its first riches, but in the act of losing, it has learned for the first time what it is to be rich. Then comes the final stage, in which the contradiction itself is reconciled, and the spirit for the second time is actually, for the first time consciously, free. The barred gate is found to have, itself, an opening; it yields to the pressure of the arm, and the struggling soul is again unimpeded on its way. Yet the last stage is by no means a repetition of the first. It is freedom, but it is freedom won. It is no longer the mere rushing over a plain that is boundless; it is the emancipation from a gate that is barred. It is not only the first state restored; it is the first state restored and revealed. Originally it was unrevealed; it was too near to the consciousness to be itself an object of knowledge; it was unopposed, and therefore it was unfelt. The barred gate has restrained it, and therefore manifested it, and in passing through the gate the life has for the first time passed into the consciousness of its own possession.

And what is this modern Hegelianism but a cultured reprint of the primitive Teutonic view? Is it not the same rhythm that is the object of search in the myths of the ancient Eddas? Here also we see the three successive ages. We see the age of spontaneous power, in which Woden and Thor reign supreme, the period when there is peace in heaven because there is as yet no admixture of the earth. We see the age when the spontaneous power is broken, and when, in the arena of deadly conflict, good and evil stand face to face. At last we behold the battle ended and the combatants swept away. The days of spontaneity again return, but they are no longer the spontaneity of ignorance. They are the days in which the power of action has become unconscious of itself through long-continued consciousness, in which virtue has become the native atmosphere of the life by the persistent habit of living within it. The peace of the last stage is not the peace of paradise lost but of paradise regained.

It is no longer simply a state into which the soul is born; it is a state which the soul has chosen, and which by an act of will it has marked out for its own.

And if the Teuton mythology has thus its significance in the field of philosophic development, it is not without a voice also in the field of scientific thought. It has been the office of the Teuton to trace the development of the world not only from within but from without; he has had his Darwin as well as his Hegel. And in the sphere of Darwinism, as in the sphere of Hegelianism, the moral has been the same—peace through conflict, unity through contradiction. Darwinism has sought to trace the process by which the fittest have survived, and it has found that process to have been one of struggle. Here again the Teuton mind has been true to itself, true to its primitive myths and its primitive instincts. What is the mythology of the Eddas but a history of the survival of the fittest, and a delineation of how that survival has been effected through struggle? There is, indeed, in the centre of this mythology a thought which has a deep bearing upon the whole question of scientific survival. It emphasises beyond all other points the fact that the thing which in the long-run is most fitted to survive is, on that very account, the thing which in intermediate periods is least adapted to live. Balder is the personification of all goodness and of all beauty; he is the ideal of completed excellence, and therefore the goal of universal being. To him, accordingly, as a matter of course belongs the final gift of immortality, the right and the necessity to survive at the end of the days. But for that very reason he is unable to live in the middle of the days. His goodness and his beauty fit him for an age of completed excellence, but not for an age of struggling excellence, not for a time when the average mind is intent only upon the things of the outer life. There is an epoch of history in which Balder is bound to die, bound by his very greatness to succumb to other forces. That which makes him great is at the outset that which makes him solitary. He is at the beginning unlike surrounding objects, and therefore he is at the beginning alone. Being alone, he is one against a thousand, and he falls beneath the weight of the thousand. It is the primitive Adam in the centre of the beasts of the field—greater than the serpent in point of right, but inferior in point of fact. It is the Grecian Socrates in the midst of the Athenians —living before his time, and therefore compelled to die ere his work is done. It is the universal Christ in the midst of the men of Judah—proclaiming a gospel for all nations, and therefore crucified by a race which has recognised a gospel only for one. Balder, by reason of his excellence, is always for a time delivered unto death.

Now, why is this? How does it happen that the thing which by its nature is fitted to be the ultimate survivor, and which as a matter of fact proves the ultimate survivor, is yet compelled at the outset to pass through a stage of death, to succumb to lesser things? Science does not escape the problem any more than the Teuton mythology. It is a truth which must be recognised as much by the Darwinian as by the primitive man. We all see as a matter of daily experience that the last are made first and the first last; that the men and systems which are despised and rejected by one age are precisely the men and systems which are lauded and magnified by another. The question is, Why? Does it not involve a principle above and beyond mere evolution, a principle which evolution in itself is not adequate to explain? Evolution can account for the survival of the fittest, but it does not tell me why that which is killed to-day should have its resurrection to-morrow. Balder is always overcome at the beginning, because he is physically less strong than his opponents; but he is not a bit physically stronger at the end than he was at the beginning, nor are his opponents one whit more physically weak. Why, then, is the result so different? It is because the world has changed its ideal of what constitutes beauty. It is because the physically strong is no longer reckoned the highest type of power, and the restraint of passion no longer deemed the natural mark of weakness. Here, it seems to me, there enters an element beyond the merely mechanical—

an element with which evolution may indeed co-operate, but which of itself it cannot comprehend. There is not even any necessity that an evolution should be progressive at all. Huxley says it is equally consistent either with going on, going back, or standing still.[1] If it has consistently gone on even amidst its moments of regress, if it has taken up Balder after he has been slain, and has laid in the dust his once omnipotent foes, it can only be because there is in the universe a principle of selection beyond the natural, and a law of growth superior to the force of mechanism. I think, therefore, that the primitive Teuton has judged well in placing the secret of development not in the earth but in the heavens. It is no accident in his system that the new world rises from the positive annihilation of the old. It is from the blank space of an extinguished firmament and an utterly obliterated earth that there is made to come forth a land wherein dwelleth righteousness. Nowhere has the myth more thoroughly transcended its mythicism than in such a thought as that. It has parted with the material image in search of something that is not material. It has abandoned the metaphors of human analogy in pursuit of an agency whose mode of working is beyond all description of language, and whose process of action is incalculable by human

---

[1] See article "Evolution," 'Encyclopædia Britannica,' ninth edition.

intelligence. It has here again been true to itself, consistent with that instinct which always and everywhere has followed the Teuton race—an instinct which even in physical researches has never paused at the gates of the physical, and which at the back of the scientific universe has found a force that is inscrutable and unknowable.

CHAPTER XIII.

THE MESSAGE OF EGYPT.

It is a long cry from the Teuton to the Egyptian. It is the passage from a living to a dead sea. The Teuton is very much alive; the Egyptian has passed away. The one is an active force, present and potent; the other is a historical memory, venerable and outgrown. They belong, besides, to two different lines of thought. The Teuton is the last of the Aryans; the Egyptian is the first of the Semitics. The distinction is by no means a merely geographical one; it indicates a change of standpoint. The Semitic begins where the Aryan ends. The Aryan starts from nature, from life, from history, and thence rises to the conception of a Power beyond them all; the Semitic starts with the recognition of a transcendent Power, and thence descends to the study of nature, life, and history. The former begins with the seen and temporal, and ends with the unseen and eternal; the latter begins with the unseen and eternal, and ends with the seen and temporal. The result is in each case the same, but the method is different; the one approaches God through the world, the other finds the world through God.

In the Aryan religions we saw the human mind climbing from the temporal into the eternal. India grappled with the problem of *life;* Persia strove with the fact of sin; Greece wrestled with the aspect of things as they are; Rome sought to establish a unity on earth. The Teuton aspired higher still, and aimed to find the unity both of earth and heaven. And we saw how, in the closing scene of all, the Teuton expressed his consciousness that there was something more than all these material things put together, how, even after both the heavens and the earth had passed away, he beheld an unknown and inscrutable Force fashioning a grander and a more enduring universe. Now, the Teuton's ending was the Egyptian's beginning. What the Norseman proclaimed as a last result was from the outset the faith of the dweller on the Nile. To him the root of all religion was the unknowableness of God. He started from the conception that there is a Power man cannot comprehend — a Power whose ultimate essence is beyond human scrutiny. His message to the world was primarily the announcement of mystery, the proclamation that there were more things in heaven and earth than men had yet dreamed of. This is distinctively his message. He has other aspects for other lines of thought — for the historian, for the antiquarian, for the student of the Old Testament. But for the religious life his significance lies in this, that he has striven to worship a God who, in the completeness of His being, has no distinct, definite, or exhaustive image, who cannot in Himself be represented to the sense, who in every object and in every sphere defies computation and eludes scrutiny.[1]

And this is all the more noteworthy from the fact that, on a superficial view, it appears to be the reverse of the truth. So far back as the beginning of the second Christian century, the Egyptian creed was charged with inconsistency by Clement of Alexandria.[2] He makes merry over searching for the veiled god, and finding him at last in such common forms as the cat or the crocodile. But Clement is wrong. The cat and the crocodile, and all other forms whatsoever, are, in the eyes of the Egyptian, themselves only veils—coverings of something which is greater than they. There are two ways in which a man may express his sense that God is incapable of being imaged; he may symbolise Him nowhere, or he may symbolise Him everywhere.

[1] The unity of this primal force in the Egyptian worship is strongly asserted by M. Emmanuel de Rougé, "Conférence sur la religion des anciens Egyptiens," in the 'Annales de la Philosophie Chrétienne,' tome xx. p. 327.

[2] 'Pædagog.,' iii. c. 2.

The latter is as effectual as the former, and it is the method of the Egyptian. He wanted to show that no single image could represent God, and so he made all things image Him. He saw Him in the heavens and in the earth, in the land and in the water, in the male and in the female, in the animal and in the man. He associated with the rites of religion nearly every living thing and wellnigh every human pursuit.[1] He made no difference between the high and the low. He consecrated the palace of the Pharaohs, but he consecrated equally their tombs. He adored the sun in its course, but he adored also the worm in its earthward movement. What annihilated to his mind the distance between great and small was the idea of religion, the sense that always and everywhere the inscrutable Power was abiding. It was this which made one thing not grander than another thing. A common majesty belonged to all—the majesty encircling the fact that every form had in it a life beyond its own, and that each was the receptacle of an unfathomed and unfathomable mystery.

And, in point of fact, I think it will appear that, while the Egyptian reverences all creation, he attaches the greatest reverence to those aspects

---

[1] This universality of religious association in Egypt is pointed out by Renouf, 'Hibbert Lectures (1879) on the Origin and Growth of Religion, as illustrated by the Religion of Ancient Egypt,' p. 26.

of creation which carry with them the idea of concealment. He worships the sun under the name of Osiris. Very significantly, however, it is the setting and not the rising that rivets his eye. It is from the spectacle of the *death* of Osiris that he draws his highest inspiration. In the desolation of the earth under the pall of night, he sees the grief of Isis for her murdered husband, and pays his tribute of adoration to a hidden glory. In the animal world, again, what is that which has evoked his worship? It is the presence of a mystery. He beholds in it something which he cannot understand. Instinct is a hidden life to the man of reason. Its modes of action are unintelligible to calculation. Man must say of the animal as he says of the divine, " I am an agnostic; I cannot comprehend it." It is this which has made the Egyptian reverence the beast of the field—a vision of something which is inscrutable. I know as little of that which is beneath me as of that which is above me; both are to me alike mysterious. Is it surprising that I should revere the one as much as the other, and for precisely the same reason—because both belong to an intelligence that transcends my own?

Nor will this Egyptian tendency be less conspicuously evident, if we turn to that product of the national art whose very name has become synonymous with mystery—the Sphinx. It is a hieroglyphic figure whose lower part is the form of a lion, whose higher is the shape of some other creature—sometimes of an animal, frequently of a man, occasionally, though rarely, of a woman.[1] What is the meaning of this riddle? Various conjectures have been formed, but it seems to me that it lies on the surface. Is it not intended to be conveyed that there is an unseen bond uniting the different lives of creation? We are familiar in modern times with what is called the transmutation of species. The ancient Egyptian was not, nor did he think of it. Yet to his reflective mind—a mind that had already enjoyed a long term of civilisation—it appeared that there was an invisible something which joined together the different parts of creation—a subtle and impalpable element which constituted the unity of life in reptile, bird, beast, and man. Nay, I would add, "in the gods also." I believe the idea of the Sphinx to be at the root of Egyptian theology as well as of Egyptian science. The gods of Egypt are innumerable by name; but are they innumerable in fact? On the contrary, every new research has tended more and more to confirm the impression that in the view of the worshipper the many are but various aspects of the one. Osiris, Isis, Horus, Rā, Set, Anubis, are but the special forms of one Presence which constitutes the boundary of each, and veils the secret of its being. The universe is itself a divine figure, enclosing many shapes, and embodying

---

[1] See Dean Stanley, 'Sinai and Palestine,' p. lvii.

many degrees of intelligence. Each is regarded with reverence, but only on the ground that each is other than itself. It is worshipped not for what it reveals, but for what it keeps hid. It is worshipped because it conceals from the eye and ear of the beholder a life more potent than its own—a life without which its own could not live, and which yet it is powerless to comprehend.

If I were asked to define the religion of Egypt in a single sentence, I should say, it is the faith which apologises for what is called an idolatrous worship. It denies that idolatry is what it is said to be. It is said to be image-worship. To the Egyptian it is the worship of everything *but* the image. It is the reverence of the thing which is hidden, covered, unrepresented. The image is not a revealer but a veil. It provokes curiosity; it tells the bystander that there is something underneath. And in this the Egyptian is true not only to what is technically called idolatry, but to all forms of adoration, all forms of admiration, all forms of love. It may be said as a matter of experience, and without fear of contradiction, that our devotion to any object is founded on more than actually *appears*. What do we mean by saying that such an object is our *ideal?* We mean that it is more than meets the eye, more than meets the ear, more than meets the sense, more than is ever manifested anywhere—that we have attached to it a life other than its own.

I may illustrate this from three different sides of man's nature—the retrospective, the prospective, and the introspective. In order to give all possible force to the illustration, I shall take an example of each of these influences from a physical rather than from a moral ideal. And first: Many a landscape is indebted for half its charm to memory; perhaps every landscape is indebted to memory for *some* of its charm. Mr Herbert Spencer says that all cognition is *recognition*. If it be so, it follows that every perception of beauty is, like the vision of the Sphinx, a sight of two lives in one. It is a perception in which there is a transmutation of to-day into yesterday, in which the present only lives by going back into the past, and the day which has dawned subsists by the day that is dead. You stand in the Bay of Naples and pronounce it beautiful. But is the Bay of Naples at this moment the only object in your mind's eye? Have you not seen in it a real or fancied resemblance to Loch Lomond? If you have, and if you are a native of Britain, you are not an idolater of the Bay of Naples. It is not really or essentially a foreign scene that you are beholding; the figure of the foreign has passed into the figure of home. There are more things than men dream of which are bearing a vicarious merit, which owe their attractiveness to something outside of themselves. The actual image is little more than a veil which conceals from the view the real object of admiration, and claims for the present hour a tribute which is meant for the past.

I shall take the second illustration not from memory but from hope. How many odes have been written to the spring? It is associated with all bright things. It is the symbol of joy, the emblem of good fortune, the synonym for the close of dark days. And yet, let us reflect how much of this belongs not to the spring at all. How much of it is the voice of full-blown summer. We have given the ripeness to the germ; we have assigned to the acorn what only pertains to the oak. Measured by its actual self, the spring effects little. It retains much of the survival of old culture—of the past winter's cold. It gives only a promise and a very small earnest. If the world were to be arrested in its stage of spring and forced to stay there, the lovers of the season would soon desert her. What they love about her is an imputed righteousness. She wears an anticipated glory—the glory of the summer. She has been transmuted in imagination into that which is still in advance of her; she is only what she is by being another. It is the story of the Sphinx repeated. The present and the future lie on one stem, and neither can live apart from the other; neither can say to the other, "I have no need of thee." It is not the image which is worshipped, but its possibility of, one day, imaging greater things.

The third of the influences which exemplify the

Egyptian tendency is what I have called introspective. We may take an instance from one of the most common acts of perception—looking on an expanse of sea. Let us say that it is a very limited expanse. Let it be the place where the waters are only beginning to widen, and where the land is yet visible on every side. Even in these narrow circumstances the impression produced upon the sense will be one of boundlessness. We shall have a feeling of unimpeded freedom, a sense of unqualified enlargement, an experience of complete emancipation from earthly restraints and limits. Now, how are we to explain this phenomenon? We are venerating an arm of the sea for the possession of a quality which does not even belong to all the united oceans of the world. There is not a boundless sea on the globe, nor does the spectator for a moment believe that there is. What, then, does he behold? Not the image, but something beneath the image—the aspirations of his own soul. He looks into the transparent waters to contemplate the trembling of the waves, and he sees there another figure which he cannot distinguish from the waters, which seems to have transformed the waters into its own likeness; it is the spirit of man. The riddle of the Sphinx has its parallel in the things of the common day; it is still equally present and still equally unsolved.

These illustrations may help us, I think, to understand the nature of Egyptian worship. The object of Egyptian reverence seems to me to be in every case that mysterious boundary-line which at once divides and unites the creatures of the world. It is the place where one being separates from another being, to be blended with him again in some unaccountable way. I do not know whether it has been put in this form before, but it will be found, I think, to be in harmony with all modern research and consistent with the facts already known. The message of Egypt is, in short, the message of the Sphinx — the relation between the many and the one. Whatever tends to exhibit this relation, either on the side of separation or on the side of union, is hailed by the ancient Egyptian, and consecrated as an object of adoration. It is adored for its mysteriousness, for its impalpableness, for its subtle power of eluding explanation and baffling scrutiny. And the influence of this tendency will be found to have been most potent, to have made Egypt distinctively what she is. I might show this in many directions, but I confine myself to one, that which is opened up by her oldest and most important document—the Book of the Dead.[1] It is significant that this *should* be her most important document, significant that even in the days of her infancy her eyes should have first rested with fascination on

[1] Detailed information regarding this work will be found in Bunsen's 'Egypt's Place in Universal History.' See also Renouf, p. 172, 'Hibbert Lecture.'

that awful presence of death from which the eyes of others are habitually repelled. A fact so strange and so unique must have some connection with the religious system which contains it, and therefore it demands a special consideration.

From the very dawn of her existence Egypt has consecrated the idea of death. Her position in so doing has been, so far as I know, abnormal. In Christianity alone do we find anything which approaches to similarity. China never consecrated death; it had no place and no provision within her system. India did not consecrate death; she looked upon both life and death as illusions, and so she spurned them both. Persia did not consecrate death; she believed in the immortality of the spirit, and for that very reason she resisted the trappings of the grave. The touch of a dead body was, to her, defiling, and therefore she hastened to consume the unconscious clay. And, although standing at opposite angles from one another, and acting from opposite motives, neither Judea nor Greece consecrated death. Judea saw in it the penalty for a violated law; Greece bewailed in it the interruption of a self-satisfied life; both equally averted their eyes from it. Amid great dissonance of opinion on other points, amid evidences of mental diversity and indications of contrary ideals, there remains on this one head a voice of general unanimity; all alike recoil from the symbols of the grave.

All but one. In the face of the old world, Egypt stands out as a remarkable exception. Here we have not only an absence of the usual recoil from death, but we have substituted for it a positive attraction towards the elsewhere loathed object. If she were a pessimistic nation, we might to some extent understand it; but, as Renouf points out, she was not. She had in her much of the Greek's love of pleasure, and much of his temptation to seize the present hour. Yet, unlike the Greek, the Egyptian haunted the sepulchre. Most nations have been kept alive by preserving their treasures from the tomb; it would hardly be too much to say that Egypt has been kept alive by putting her treasures *in* the tomb. That by which her greatness to-day is known is her Pyramids and her books, and both are memorials of death. Her Pyramids are her testimony to the fact that death has not robbed her kings of their majesty. Her books are more. They are the aspirations of the living after communion with the dead. The Egyptian is not afraid to plant these aspirations in the coffin. When we of modern times write a panegyric on the departed, we do so in order to give it publicity. We design that it shall find its way to the eyes of men. But when an Egyptian wrote a panegyric on one departed, he did so in order that he might put it in the grave; he laid it where he had laid his heart —in the coffin with Cæsar. The reason was that to his mind the symbols of death did not suggest associations contrary to life and immortality. They did not even suggest what they did to Jews and early Christians—the sleep of the soul. To the Egyptian death was not a sleep; it would not be too much to say that it was a waking. In the view of this early faith the blessed dead, so far from having a diminished being, have entered into a larger power. They have entered into a life of three progressive stages. In the first they have to stand before the judgment-seat. In the second they reach the power of transformation—become able at will to take the shape of everything in the universe.[1] In the third they take the likeness of the Supreme God Himself, and become united to the source of all being. Not in spite of death, but by reason of death, does the Egyptian cherish this hope. Others have cherished that hope as well as he, but they have entertained it in defiance of the king of terrors. Egypt has entertained it through a mystic reverence for that king and his kingdom, and has found her portal to immortality in the shadows of the grave.

The question is, Why? What is that which to the Egyptian has robbed death of its terror? As I have said, it is not a pessimistic view of life; the Egyptian loves the world and the things of the world. Why, then, is he so attracted towards that which most

[1] Renouf, ibid., p. 181.

worldly people are desirous to forget? It is by reason not of his life but of his doctrine. He reveres beyond all things the boundary-line, and death is the great boundary-line. The boundary-line is to him that which leads from one stage of being into another stage of being—that which explains the riddle of the Sphinx. So completely has the Egyptian mind been moulded by the Sphinx problem, that, as we have seen, it regards the glory of the higher heaven as consisting in the soul's power to transform itself. Death is looked upon as a possible source of transformation. In the mind of a primitive race there is hardly a step from possibility to certainty. The infant intelligence proverbially leaps to conclusions, and hope passes at a bound into conviction. So was it with the Egyptian. Death was a boundary-line; being a boundary-line, it was a mystery; being a mystery, it was full of all possibilities; being full of possibilities, it was to the world's youth radiant with certainties. Therefore he invested it with a romantic interest, that interest with which the child regards not only the entrance upon a journey but any peculiar vehicle through which the journey is to be accomplished. The locomotive and the steamboat may be new to the child, and they are accompanied by elements which are calculated to excite its fear. Yet both of these facts enhance its attractiveness to the juvenile mind, and the fear itself is transmuted into a joy—that joy of indefinite possibility which, alike to child and man, is ever wrapt up in a sense of unfathomable mystery.

And now let us ask, Is this a permanent message? Has it contributed anything to the spirit of absolute religion? The ancient Egyptian is in a different position from the ancient Indian, the ancient Chinaman, the ancient Jew, the ancient Greek, or even the ancient Teuton. These are the ancestors of races yet alive. But the Egyptian is dead. He is as obsolete as his Pyramids; the place that knew him knows him no more. Nor can it be said that his influence has been great in moulding the faith of other nations. Renouf will not admit that he has influenced either the Greek or the Jew,[1] and, if he has not affected these, he has touched no one. But, conceding all this, there is a question which remains. Does any part of the faith of Egypt belong to the Church universal? She may be dead as a nation, she may be inoperative as a historic power, and yet her experience may be the experience of all the world. And so it is. This message, distinctive of the creed of Egypt, is universal to the thought of mankind. There are two things which are declared in the religious message of Egypt— that the beginning of all faith is mystery, and that the beginning of all mystery is the boundary-line. In neither of these points has Egypt become superannuated.

[1] Renouf, ibid., p. 243.

And first. The Egyptian is right in holding that faith begins with mystery. It would perhaps be more correct to say that the sense of mystery is the essence of faith. One would be apt at first sight to suppose that faith would have its origin in revelation —in the seeing of all things clear. In truth it is not so. Faith demands beyond everything a hazy atmosphere. It cannot sing in the full light; it must at most have no more than the dawn. The root of all worship is wonder, and wonder comes from a sense of baffled reason. It originates in the conviction that we have come to a door for which we cannot find the key, and whose other side is incomprehensible. It is the concealed spots of nature that we worship; it is the veil and not the revelation that we reverence. Nor let it be said that such a view makes religion a thing of childhood. As a matter of fact, the sense of mystery is not deepest in the child; it grows with our growth and expands with our reason. Mr Herbert Spencer does not scruple to say that its highest development is the age of science. He tells us that the scheme of evolution propounded by himself, which has certainly been accepted as the scheme of modern science, is fitted to awaken far deeper wonder than the popular theories of the olden time. In this all will agree with him, whatever they may think of his theory itself; and the concession on his part is remarkable. It amounts to a statement that wonder increases in proportion to the degree of intelligence, and that the measure of human knowledge is the measure of man's sense of mystery.

The first position, therefore, of Egypt is uncontroverted even in the most modern times. Agnosticism is a more religious belief than Atheism, and why? Because it admits that there is something about the universe which compels it to say, "I do not know." In this it is at one with all religion; it finds at the core of things a background of mystery. The psalmist of Israel asks that his eyes may be open to behold " wonderful things out of the law." In old days men only conceived wonder in the violation of law, or, in other words, in the spirit of lawlessness. But the psalmist's prayer has been answered, and the commonplace has been glorified. If the belief in miracle has faded, it is not because the sense of wonder has passed away; it is rather because wonder has been found where miracle is not, because order has been discovered to yield that mystery which was once thought to belong to disorder alone. Thus, at the beginning and at the end of the process, we have perfect unity — the changeless amid the mutable. Between ancient Egypt and modern England there is externally and intellectually a wide gulf; there is all the difference of the meridian and the dawn. Yet as there is something in the dawn which exists in the meridian, so there is something in ancient Egypt which exists in modern England. The spirit of mystery has persisted through all changes. Amid an opposite culture, amid an enlarged universe, amid a new heaven and a new earth, there has remained in the sphere of law that which operated in the sphere of miracle, and the last state, like the first, has been a sense of wonder.

We pass to the second point in the message of Egypt. It is the belief that all mystery lies in the vision of a boundary-line—in that which divides one life from another life. And here again it will be found that the experience of modern times is the same. Take the mystery of modern Agnosticism. What is that which makes the scientist of our day say "I do not know"? It is the fact that he has discovered a boundary-line which he cannot pass. In every department the mystery is felt to be this boundary-line. Each thing is manifestly connected with every other thing; yet between any two objects the manner of connection is veiled. Take the simplest act of perception. What is the reason that a little thing like my eye can hold such a vast field as the visible universe? Why is it that a very small picture like the retina can take in such a wide expanse as the starry firmament with its countless worlds and its interstellar spaces? That is a question which no man can answer. It is an ultimate fact of knowledge, undisputed and indisputable, but perfectly inexplicable. It is the boundary-line between two creations—the human and the physical.

There they stand, parallel to one another and connected with one another, but connected by the riddle of the Sphinx—joined by a bond which no man has seen, and intertwined by a marriage that no man has witnessed. The first act of infancy, the most external act of all life, is as unintelligible to sense as any part of the universe, as profound a mystery as the problem of creation itself.

If we take any other sphere of thought, we shall find the same experience—that mystery lies in the boundary-line. There is a missing link between matter and force, between plant and animal, between animal and man, between one man and another man. It is these missing links which constitute the four great mysteries of earth — the mystery of life, the mystery of consciousness, the mystery of intelligence and the mystery of personality. Before these the scientist bows. They are the margin left for faith, or for what to him stands for faith—Agnosticism. He believes in the riddle of the Sphinx—in the fact that the lives of all creation are somehow united. But that "somehow" is the consecrated spot. It is consecrated by its mystery, by its inscrutability, by its unknowableness. It is a sea which ship has never sailed, a depth which line has never sounded. The ancient Egyptian and the modern scientist stand alike upon the shore and hear the play of incomprehensible waters. The past and the present are reconciled in the vision of the fathomless, and the evening and the morning are one day.

And, if Egypt added yet another boundary-line in the great fact of death, she surely erred not by defect of logic. If she regarded it hypothetically as a transition field, and reverenced it as a hope, she had at least analogy on her side; she was consistent with herself, and consistent with the facts already known. In all departments of life she had found the presence of the Sphinx, found that the close of one form of being was but the entrance into another. She had discovered in each case that the process of transition was perfectly inexplicable. If matter became spirit, it did so by surrendering its own life; if the animal became the man, it did so by losing itself in an existence foreign and destructive to its own. Is it surprising that she should have gone one step further, and claimed a corresponding egress for the valley of the shadow of death? Is it surprising that in this terminus of the individual life she should have seen only a new beginning and a possible entrance into a higher sphere? At all events she has done so, and in doing so she has been guilty of no anachronism. Upon the shore of death the mass of humanity still stands with hope. Even the Positivism of a J. S. Mill did not seek to extinguish hope's trembling star. Agnosticism itself is a form of hope; if it objects to affirm, it refuses to deny. Its attitude is that of the uncovered head acknowledging the presence of a mystery. The mystery which it acknowledges is the same as that before which Egypt bowed six thousand years ago— the recognition of an invisible boundary-line between a world which is seen and temporal, and a state which no man can define.

CHAPTER XIV.

THE MESSAGE OF JUDEA.

IT seems at first sight as if this were a message which needed no chapter. We of the Christian persuasion have read from childhood the books in which it professes to be delivered. We are familiar with their every phrase; we are conversant with their every sentiment. They have become to us as household words. They are a species of literature known alike to the cot and the palace, prized alike by the peasant and the sage. One would certainly imagine that their purport would by this time be read, marked, learned, and inwardly digested. And yet, if we put to ourselves the question, What *is* the message of Judea? we shall probably be struck with the difficulty of giving a defensible answer. Of course it is very easy to tell a hundred things that are taught in the Old Testament; but the question is, Are they taught there alone? If not, then they cannot be regarded as the distinctive message of Judea; they must be looked upon as parts of the religious life itself. Let us consider one or two of the answers which are popularly given to this question; we shall find that they by no means exhaust the problem.

And first. A very common answer is that the mission of Judea was to tell the unity of God. That ultimately it did tell the unity of God is beyond dispute; whether originally it did so is very doubtful. But waiving this, is the unity of God at any time a doctrine peculiar to Judaism? I have pointed out in the introduction to this book that it is at all times more natural to the human mind than Polytheism. We have seen, moreover, that some of the earliest forms of thought have, either at their base or at their apex, held the existence of one central principle. India culminates in this belief, alike in the system called Brahmanism, and in that Nirvana of the future in which the Buddhist sees the goal of all things. Egypt, according to the best interpreters, recognises this thought from the outset, and more distinctly still. The many here are but various forms of the one, and the worship of the many is but the reverence of the manifold wisdom of God. I do not for a moment imagine that Judea got her notion of divine unity from dwelling in Egypt, any more than Egypt received hers by associating with Judea. But I think it very likely that they may have been brought together, and for a time kept together, by the experience common to them both. Neither the one nor the other can claim the unity of God as a distinctive possession; it belongs to both, and therefore it is the property of neither. Judaism never professes to have a special revelation of God; it begins by *assuming* God. Instead of saying that He *is*, it says that He created the heavens and the earth. Why so? Clearly because the discovery of God's being was not appropriated as a part of the national consciousness. The Jew felt that he had come into it as into an inheritance derived from some other source. It had been his from the dawn of his being, and therefore it was not his by conquest. It was a possession which he shared with the race of humanity, a foundation on which he might indeed build a special temple, but which was at the same time the foundation for independent houses, and one on which the Caananite might also build.

A second view of the mission of Judaism is that which regards it as having had its function in the proclaiming of moral law. That it did proclaim moral law is certain; but this was by no means its distinctive message. If the record of Genesis bears witness to the fact that the knowledge of God was earlier than the national existence, the record of Exodus equally attests that the knowledge of morality preceded the national law. At whatever time the thunders of Sinai proclaimed "Thou shalt not kill, thou shalt not steal, thou shalt not bear false witness against thy neighbour," they appealed to an already existing culture. Laws have no meaning except on the supposition that the subjects of them are responsible beings. A moral code never founded morality; it is itself the evidence of the previous existence of morality. Judea only got from Sinai what she brought to Sinai—a conscience. Whence did she derive it? From Egypt? No; from human nature. But undoubtedly she recognised it in Egypt before she recognised it in Sinai. Egypt was her first looking-glass, the earliest mirror in which she beheld herself. Here she saw a morality in many respects kindred to her own. Renouf has not scrupled to say that the morality of Egypt contains every Christian virtue.[1] It is true, there is a leaning rather to the negative than to the positive side; there is more stress laid on what we are *not*, than on what we *are* to do. The man who at the day of judgment is able to disclaim the commission of forty-two sins is permitted to pass into glory. But it must be confessed that Judea herself leans to this tendency; her decalogue is mainly negative, whether as regards man or as regards God. To acknowledge none equal to the God of Israel, to abstain from bowing down to graven images, to avoid irreverence in the use of the holy name, to keep from secular thoughts at sacred times, and, in general, to restrain the heart

---

[1] 'Hibbert Lectures (1879) on the Origin and Growth of Religion, as illustrated by the Religion of Egypt,' p. 71.

and the hand from doing injury to a brother man,—these are main tenets of her moral law. And neither in her case nor in the case of Egypt is the explanation far to seek. It lies in an ultimate law of the mind of man. Conscience only begins with an act of prohibition; it does not exist until we do wrong. I know nothing of good health till I have felt my first physical pain; before that time good health is my nature, and no man recognises his nature. To be recognised, it must be broken, sickness must come, disease must come, the vision of death must come. So is it with holiness; it is only revealed in the breaking. That is why Egypt, that is why Judea, has seen the power of morality rather in that which forbids than in that which impels; they have sought her on the threshold, and the threshold is an act of prohibition. Yet the threshold is neither in Egypt nor in Judea, but in the heart of man. It is older than Egypt, it is older than Judea, for it belongs to the life of the soul, and is therefore distinctive of no land.

A third view is that which regards Judaism as having had for its mission to reveal the ways of Providence. Now, it cannot be denied that the life of Judea is a marvellous illustration of the existence of a Power that makes for righteousness. Whatever be the order of that life, whether it be the old traditional order recognised by our fathers or the new sequence proposed by the light of modern criticism, the result is the same. It matters not to the question in hand whether we say that the law preceded the prophets, or that the prophets preceded the law; on either view the central fact remains unaffected. We see a nation, of very insignificant extent, of very circumscribed position, of very limited natural resources, assuming a commanding, and ultimately a dominant, attitude on the earth. Without large armies, without much wealth, without a knowledge of secular philosophy, without those arts of polish and *finesse* which constitute the astute statesman, this little nation has aimed at and virtually received universal dominion. She has set up an ideal of world-conquest most powerfully asserted in the days of her deepest calamity; and, in a way she never dreamed of, she has carried it through. As a matter of fact, she has given to the world a life which has ruled all civilised nations —a life after whose pattern and model all other lives have sought to mould themselves. Nor is it less remarkable that the life by which she has conquered has not been her own ideal of greatness, has been in direct antagonism to that ideal. She has repudiated the crown which has made her despotic, she has abjured the weapon which has proved her victorious. All this seems to denote a force beyond herself. It seems to indicate the presence and the superintendence of a divine instinct which, as with the bee, has led, by a series of undesigned acts, to the construction of a kingdom of consummate order.

But when all has been said, we must still ask, Is this the message of the nation? Is it not rather its completed result, its exit, its terminus? When this result came, did not the nation as a nation cease to be? Can we say that its function was only to come with its death, that its use was only to be discovered in the hour of its dissolution? Had it no value for its time, no meaning for the thousand years during which it had a local habitation as well as a name? Did it differ from all other lands in being without an influence on its contemporaries? Had it, in short, no place in history as long as its own history lasted, and only the office of giving a lesson to posterity when the curtain had fallen over its own career? This we cannot believe. It is contrary to nature; it is contrary to analogy. It is contradicted even by the continued life of the people without a country—a people who have refused to accept the conclusion derived from their national drama, and have denied its final act to be a part of their destiny. We must look elsewhere for a solution of the problem, What is the message of the Jewish nation?

If we would find that solution, we must look for the most pervading element in the records of the Hebrew race. What is that which from beginning to end permeates its literature most persistently and most unwaveringly? Clearly it must be something of a Semitic caste. I said in the previous chapter that the Semite is distinguished from the Aryan by the predominance of the sense of mystery. We saw that the mystery of Egypt was virtually the mystery of evolution—the process by which one thing passes into another thing. What is the mystery of Judea? Let us listen to one of the latest voices of the nation, and I think we shall find the clue for which we are searching. In the first Epistle to Timothy we read, "Great is the mystery of godliness." The words bore a different meaning then to what they do now, and they must be paraphrased, not translated. A mystery then meant something invisible—something which could not be detected by the sense. The mystery of godliness, therefore, is equivalent to the *unseenness* of godliness; it really amounts to the statement that the path by which we approach the throne of God is the path of the internal. According to this writer, the great message of Judea is the power of inwardness in the religious life. Now, if we fall backward and examine the earlier voices, we shall find that they present a wonderful consistency. We shall find that the power of the internal is the thought on which the Old Testament rings its changes from morn to noon, from noon to dewy eve. It is the moral of all its history, the secret of all its poetry, the burden of all its song. It covers the whole area of its teaching; it permeates the entire course of its development; it runs in a continuous refrain through its endless variations. Other messages may vary with the hour, other thoughts may be modified with the place; but this is independent of time and impervious to locality; it is the same yesterday and to-day and for ever.

Perhaps at the outset one is disposed to be struck with the paradox of such a statement. We have been in the habit of regarding the message of Judea as antagonistic to the message of Christianity. We hear the first Christian teachers distinguishing between the flesh and the spirit, and calling men to abandon the mean and beggarly elements of the letter. We naturally conclude that Judaism must have been a most external faith, and her message a most sensuous hope. But we forget altogether that the men who thus denounce the letter are themselves Jews. The voice of the New Testament is not one nation calling against another; it is a nation summoning *itself*. The disciple of Christ is crying to his countryman, Be true to yourselves, true to your message, true to your national ideal. It is no new voice; it is the cry of all the prophets. What is Jewish prophecy but a great protest in favour of return to the national ideal? It reminds the men of Israel that, in seeking the flesh in preference to the spirit, they are deserting their own standard and abandoning their own landmarks; that is the reason why their watchword is so constantly "return." It is a going back to the primitive type which the prophets of Israel desired; and that primitive type is believed to have its root in a recognition of the things that are unseen.

The only question is, Were they right in their belief? Does an examination of the Hebrew writings lead to the conviction that they are based on a preference for the internal? There are four distinct departments under which the life of the Jew may be considered—his history, his theology, his poetry, and his morality. Let us look at these one by one. And first. By the history, I mean of course the recorded history. I have here nothing to do with the putting right of the Hebrew annals; I leave that to the latest criticism. We have only to consider the account these annals give of themselves, and thence to determine the message which they design to convey. Now on their very threshold there is a remarkable narrative, popularly called the story of the Fall. We are familiar with it theologically; but what is it artistically,—in other words, what is the actual picture which it presents? In plain language, it is simply the vision of a man who gets his choice between the internal and the external, and who prefers the latter. We see a tree of knowledge desired, not because it was a tree of knowledge, but because it was pleasant to the sight and good for food, and eligible for the reputation it conferred of being wise. As a form of life knowledge itself is not prized; it is only prized as a form of display. The tree of life — the other central growth of the garden—is never forbidden, but it is never coveted. It is uncoveted simply because it is inward. With the primitive man, as with his descendants, the effect is a greater object of interest than the cause, and the thing which is produced more valuable than that which produced it. In this fine allegory there is no anachronism; the essence of human nature is revealed once for all. The Hebrew race in this story has put its hand on its own imperfection and the imperfection of humanity; but the power to discover one's imperfection is already a sign that we have passed beyond it. The Hebrew has admitted his own failure, but in the very act he has revealed the strength of his ideal; his narrative of the Fall is his first protest in favour of the inner life.

The second remarkable narrative in the Hebrew annals brings out the same principle in a different form; it is the call of Abraham. Here again we have an act of choice. True, it is no longer the direct choice between the outward and the inward; it is rather the alternative between two kinds of physical good. There stand before the eyes of Abraham two prospects—a land in present possession, and a land which can only be possessed in the future, and as the result of much toil. Yet the choice of Abraham is indirectly the same as the choice of the primitive Adam. However outward the coming land may have been, it was to him as yet a thing of imagination alone. The approach to it was compassed by seeming impossibilities. He could only begin to journey towards it by closing his eyes to everything around him, by shutting out from his sight all that was present or palpable. He had to leave his country, his kindred, his home, to part from the associations of his youth, to abandon the worship of his ancestors, and to travel into a region to him utterly unknown, and presenting to his view not a single avenue of approach. The writer to the Hebrews has caught the true moral of the story when he places this man among the heroes of faith; he feels that such a choice was essentially a choice of the internal. The faith of Abraham has become a proverbial phrase; why so? Because faith is the sight of the internal. Abraham had other qualities on which tradition might well have fastened; he had courage, and chivalry, and generosity, and fidelity, and, above all, the spirit of sacrificial love. But in the mind of the world all these fall into the background before the radiant fact that he followed an aim which was invisible. They are overshadowed in the presence of a life which abandons to-day for to-morrow, and leaves the bread of the hour for something which can yield its interest only in an age to come.

Now, let us observe, this type of character is preserved throughout the history of the Jewish nation —preserved consciously and deliberately as the distinctive feature of the national mind. How often are the words repeated, " I am the God of Abraham "?

And what do they mean but simply this, that the rise or fall of the nation is to be estimated by the height of its faith? Luther said that justification by faith was the doctrine of a standing or of a falling Church; the Jewish scriptures say that justification by faith is the doctrine of a standing or of a falling State. The Old Testament measures all its heroes by their power to resist the external; to postpone the impression of the hour. Take Jacob and Esau. Why is the former preferred to the latter? The bold hunter had many qualities which were not shared by the sleek shepherd. But the shepherd excelled him in one thing—the power to withstand the influence of the moment. Esau sells his birthright for a mess of pottage; he prefers the visible to the invisible. Jacob sells the pottage for the birthright; he prefers the bird in the bush to that in the hand. What was that birthright? It was the heirship to an uncertainty, so far as human knowledge was concerned. It was the right to search for gold in an undiscovered country, to assume a title for which the world as yet had no place; the man who could do this was a man of faith. Or, take Moses. His was a life of great eventfulness. It began in the burning aspirations of Midian, and it ended in the shadowless retrospect of Nebo. It was a life of thunders and lightnings, such as poet and painter would have longed to portray. Yet, to the writer of the Epistle to the Hebrews, its moral is all summed up in one word—inwardness.

To him the glory of Moses is that "he esteemed the reproach of Christ greater riches than all the treasures of Egypt." It is by his meekness that this man has inherited the earth; it is his gentleness that makes him great. He follows the long instead of the short road to the land of Canaan, and he endures "as seeing Him who is invisible." Or, take Solomon—the type of the national wealth and magnificence. In the most brilliant period of the country's annals, in the age when the appetite for war had been stimulated by conquest, and the lust for money had been quickened by luxury, he is represented as making his choice in favour of the inward riches. It is the one element which connects the meridian of Jewish history with its dawn. Between the patriarchal and the regal age there is little sympathy; the king that has risen knows not Joseph. But amid all the changes in government and polity and life, amid the passing away of the old and the emerging of the new, one thing remains constant, unwavering, ever green; it is that which constituted the distinctiveness of the nation's youth, and continues to constitute the distinctiveness of its manhood,—the search for gold below the surface, the choice of the internal.

Here I take leave of the historical aspect of the nation. I have given only a few specimens, but they are specimens not of a part but of the whole. They are representative of the Jewish commonwealth, and I know not a single exception to their message. The moral of all Jewish history is that the elder should serve the younger—that the natural man, who comes first, should be superseded by the spiritual man, who comes last. This is the burden of all its teaching from the beginning to the end. Cain and Abel, Isaac and Ishmael, Joseph and Reuben, Saul and David, are only landmarks of a tendency that runs along the whole line of the national life. There are evidences that it was not unopposed by the nation, there are traces that it had to be taught by stern experience. Eve says of her firstborn, Cain, "I have gotten a *man* from the Lord;" and Abraham prays for the more warlike of his sons, "O that *Ishmael* might live before Thee." But none the less, nay, all the more, is it the message of the children of Israel. If it is not the result of estheticism, if it is not the fruit of inborn admiration, if it has persisted through opposition and survived in spite of prejudice, it furnishes only an additional proof that Judea was impelled by a destiny higher than her own will.

CHAPTER XV.

THE SUBJECT CONTINUED.

The second point of interest in the life of Judea is its theology. And in its theology as in its history, the central article is inwardness. That article is expressed in the second commandment of the Jewish law, "Thou shalt not make unto thee any graven image, nor any likeness of anything that is in heaven above nor in the earth beneath nor in the waters under the earth; thou shalt not bow down thyself to them nor serve them." The command is more comprehensive than is popularly supposed. It includes two parts. On the one hand, the Jew is forbidden to make a reverential likeness of any object of creation; on the other, he is forbidden to make any object of creation a likeness of God Himself. The design is therefore to prevent both idolatry and nature-worship — in other words, to exclude from the true faith all symbolism whatsoever. You will observe at once the analogy and the difference between this and Egypt. Egypt, like

Judea, has no special symbol of God, but why? Just that the whole universe may be His symbol. To the Egyptian the important part of every object is the point where it fades into another object; the image of God must to him be the world as a whole. But to the Jew not even this was to be God's image; God was to have no image.[1] The heaven of heavens could not contain Him; He charged His very angels with folly. To the eye of the lawgiver, as to the eye of the psalmist, the aspect of united nature was but one of the changes in the vesture of the Eternal; he would say of a thousand universes, "They perish, but Thou remainest; they all wax old as doth a garment, and as a vesture shalt Thou fold them up, and they shall be changed; but Thou art the same, and Thy years shall have no end."

I would not have it thought, however, that the Hebrew notion of God was one of impersonality; this is one of the points in which, I think, Mr Matthew Arnold has erred. The creed of Judaism is a protest in favour of an inward God; but to the Jew inward meant human. Let us never forget that the act forbidden to him was not the conceiving of God after a likeness, but the conceiving of God after the likeness of a *thing*. The root of Jewish religion is placed in the belief that man was made in the image of God. If man is not to image God, it is because he is not to stoop below himself.

[1] Compare Isaiah xl. 18.

He contains within himself the inward principle, and that principle is not only God-given but God-breathed; it is itself an integral part of the life of the Eternal. Judaism is not so far from Christianity as is commonly supposed. It is founded on the identity of the human and the divine. The distance is one of miles, not of nature. If the Creator is placed beyond the direct reach of the creature, it is in the same sense that a king is beyond the direct reach of a peasant. There is never such a distance as would make mind one thing in God and another thing in man. To the son of Israel the mind of man was the miniature of the mind of God. To him the divinest thing in the universe was will— the innermost force, the force behind nature, the force that can say "Thou shalt; thou shalt not." The image of God in man was the power of choice. When the soul received its first alternative, it received its first likeness to the divine; for that which unites the human to the divine is the voice of personality—the power to say "I will." Hence to the son of Israel the voice and not the form becomes the likeness of God.[1] "The Lord saith" is the formula which expresses the Jewish sense of the nature of God. The Greek would have clothed Him in all the glories of the morning; but to the Hebrew the glories of the morning were nothing to the glory of personality. What the Jew magnified in God

[1] See specially Psalm xxix.

was His law. It was not merely that it was a moral law, but that it *was* a law—an expression of will, a voice of command. The prerogative of God was to reign, and the majesty of reigning lay in its manifestation of a will. Hence to the Jew the most glorious of all things became the possession of a kingdom. His most secular life had its root in his most religious, in his most *internal* life. He sought a kingdom not from ambition but from veneration —to be like God. If his God had been a representative of beauty, he would have carved statues in His praise; but his God is a representative of will, and therefore he carves for Him a kingdom. His search for universal empire is in its root an act of worship—the worship of the innermost thing in human nature, contemplated as the likeness of the divine Life.

I cannot quit this part of the subject without pointing out that nowhere has Judaism been so little superannuated as in this worship of the will. It is the one point in which modern science can still unite itself with theological study. This science is in its essence a recognition of Force as the supreme entity. Force is a mental conception. It is an idea derived from the exercise of will, and derivable from no other source. If there be an ultimate force in the universe, so far as our present knowledge extends, it can only be a will force. When I speak of the power of gravity, the power of cohesion—nay, even the power of motion — what do I mean? Have I not simply transferred a mental thought to a physical object? I know nothing of power in nature except as suggested by my own consciousness. The very idea of cause is a mental idea. Mr Mill is quite right when he says that from the sight of nature alone we get nothing but antecedents and consequents. If I put my hand to the light of a taper, it is burned; but if I say that the taper had power to burn my hand, I have gone beyond the facts of mere nature. I have put into the taper the analogy of my own spirit, and have conceived it after the likeness of man. So is it with the conception of force. It is a conception rather of theology than of science. It is a clothing of the universe in the likeness of the human soul. It is a regress towards that creed of the man of Israel which placed in the centre of all things the movements of a personal will.

The third distinctive element in the life of the Jewish nation is its poetry. In the introduction to this volume, I have defined poetry to be the incarnation of truth — the clothing of one thing in the vesture of another thing. In Judaism the thing which is clothed is the innermost force of life — the nation's religious faith. Do not imagine that when I speak of the poetic character of the Hebrew mind, I limit the phrase to the works of an Isaiah or a Jeremiah. To me the poetry of the Old Testament is interwoven with its history. On any view, even on the most orthodox view, the facts are not the revelation; they are only the symbols of the revelation. The poetry lies in the thought beneath the form, or rather in the symmetry with which the thought *expresses* the form. Where lies the charm, the unique charm, of the narratives of the Old Testament? What is that which has made them delightful to the Sabbath-school child and interesting to the grave philosopher? It is that in them which lurks below the colouring. It is not their local or national element; it is the fact that the garb of the nation conceals something which is not local, not limited, not geographical,—something which has enshrined itself in a temporary form, but which is itself contemporaneous with all time and independent of any space, the possession of the world, and the property of man as man.

A moment's glance at one or two of these narratives will make this abundantly clear. What, for example, is the poetic beauty of the story of the Fall? Is it the statement that the sin of the human race began with a trivial act on the surface? On the contrary, it is the statement that this trivial act was not a beginning at all but an ending, that when the sin came to the commonplace surface of life it came to its climax. This is the thought which has been incarnated in the old story of Eden, and it is a thought as modern to the Englishman as to the

Jew. We are made to feel that the overt act is the least culpable part of the process, that it is only the last result of a long series of mental errors. We are made to see, in the most subtle manner, that ere ever the human soul disobeyed it had learnt to distrust; that before it violated the existing law it had come to think of the Lawgiver as one who was jealous of His creatures. Mr Browning could have expressed no better a very abstruse thought. It is indeed a thought which belongs essentially to his line of poetry, and even its expression has somewhat of his ring. It is a keen analysis of human nature, given in the form of allegory. The figures move before us in the simplest garb, and use very few words. If you would understand their meaning, you must read between the lines. If you would penetrate the depth of the dramatic situation, you must come to the scene with an already rich human nature, amply stored with worldly experience. The narrative is poetic and childlike, but it is the reverse of childish. It is the artlessness which conceals art. It is the poetry of reflection, not of spontaneous impulse. On what professes to be the threshold of the national history, it asserts once for all the message of the nation. It is a song not for the sake of singing, but for the sake of morals. It is sung with a purpose, and, though it decks itself in all the leaves of the garden, that purpose is not beauty. It is a song whose object is not sense but soul, not charm but chastity, not radiance but righteousness. It has survived the scene, even the imagination of the scene, in which it had its birth; it has been eternal because it has been *in*ternal.

Again. The sacrifice of Abraham is one of the most picturesque narratives which have ever been written. It has appealed to all nations, to all ages, to all circumstances. Yet where lies the poetry of that narrative? Clearly in the fact that the sacrifice was an internal one. If Abraham had really offered his son, the picture would have been revoltingly unpoetical. The beauty lies in the knowledge that the offering was never outwardly accepted, that the will was taken for the deed. Here we have a heroism of a singular kind—a man who has the merit of doing everything without actually doing anything. It is a heroism in which the combatant wrestles not against flesh and blood, but against the solicitations of his own mind. The battle-field is inward, the weapons are inward, the warfare is inward. It is a conflict that has no spectators, and for whose decision there can be no wreath. On every side the poetry of the narrative depends on the shifting of the scene from the world without to the world within. Heaven must receive the offering from earth only in a figure;[1] reality would make the record worse than prosaic. Man must be taught the lesson that there may be a divine sacrifice which

[1] Compare Hebrews xi. 19.

gives no material gift, and that the deepest surrender of the soul is in that moment when its love can find no expression. It is a point of high significance that the clothing of this thought in symbolism should have been reserved for the inspiration of a race whose message was the power of the internal.

Take one instance more—the vision which Moses beheld of a bush that burned and was not consumed. Where lies the poetry of this symbol? Is it in the fact of its marvellousness? Certainly not. The appeal which it makes is not to the eye but to the heart. The poetry consists in its being a symbol not of that which is rare, but of that which is constant and abiding. It points to a law of the inner life. It tells Moses that the best preservative from being consumed is that very fire which he dreads; that the soul is kept alive by its own burning. This, and not the wonder, is the poetry of the scene. It is a call to the future leader to enter into the enthusiasm of love, with a promise that this enthusiasm will rob the cares of life of the power to make him old. And the promise is declared to have been most wonderfully fulfilled in that last hour of the lawgiver's pilgrimage, in which, amid the shadows of age, he stood on the heights of Pisgah and surveyed the coming land with an eye that was not dim and a natural strength that was not abated. The vision of Mount Pisgah and the vision of the burning bush are one. They both sing the same song—the triumph of the inward over the outward, the conquest of the fires of earth by the fire of the soul. They tell of a fiery furnace which, if only sufficiently heated, will preserve without hurt those that are cast therein, and which, so far from adding to the chains of life, will cause many for the first time to walk cumberless and free.

I regard, therefore, the poetry of the Bible as something which is inextricably bound up in its history, and which teaches the same lesson as its history—the subservience of the form to the spirit. If we look at those Old Testament writings which in a special sense are called poetic, we shall find precisely the same experience. If I were asked to lay my hand on the thing which above all others characterises these writings, I would say "inwardness." It may seem a bold statement, but I do not at present know a single passage in these writings which deals with outward nature for its own sake. There is a sacred poetry which begins with nature and then rises to nature's God; but Judea is not content with that. She begins with God, continues with God, and ends with God. I look in vain for any instance in which the eye of her poet rests on beauty for itself alone. He considers the heavens, but it is as the work of God's hands; he views the earth, but it is as God's footstool; he contemplates the winds, but it is as God's ministers; he studies the stars, but it is as God's host; he hears the thunder, but it is as

God's voice. There are passages in the book of Job as majestically descriptive of nature as anything in literature; but none of them is introduced for its own sake. They are hung upon the fringe of an argument whose decision belongs to another region, and whose interest conceals from the reader's view the form and the beauty of all earthly things. It has often been said that the Hebrew had a very limited notion of the size of the universe. I would ask, Of what universe? If the visible universe be meant, the saying is true; but the same is true even of the modern telescope. What *we* mean by the universe is, after all, very much what the Jew meant —a vast, unseen something of which we only behold the edges. The modern calls the unseen thing "Nature," the Jew called it "God." But both are alike agreed that, in the presence of its vast and incomprehensible expanse, the universe comprised by the human eye is indeed infinitely small. Therefore it is that in the Hebrew poetry the visible has only a secondary place. The Hebrew worships the unseen side of nature, and the unseen side of nature to him is God. The seeming limitation of his view is itself a proof of his large imagining; his poetry has been inspired by his sense of the internal.

I come now to the fourth department in which the message of Judea is illustrated—its morality. What is the difference between the morality of Egypt and the morality of Judea? I would not say that the latter is higher than the former; I think that in form they are very much alike. But the difference lies here. The morality of Egypt is stimulated by the rewards and punishments of a life beyond the grave; the morality of Judea has no motive beyond the day and hour. And to say this is to say a great deal more. It is to say that, for the large amount of his moral actions, the Jew had no motive even *in* the day and hour. It is true that in the state of Israel, as in other states, there were penalties attached to the commission of crime. But crime is a very small part of sin. The root of moral evil is in the heart, and the heart can have no magistrate over it; to itself it stands or falls. If the future be not seen, the visible present has little power. The outward law may say, "Thou shalt not kill," "thou shalt not steal," "thou shalt not bear false witness"; but what outward law can say, "Thou shalt be holy," "thou shalt be just," "thou shalt be good"? Who can penetrate into the secret places of a man's soul and read his silent moments? And if, in spite of this absence of outward law, there were men in Israel who *were* holy and just and good, if, notwithstanding the silence from without, there were those that could walk through the mire and keep their garments unspotted, it furnishes an indisputable proof that the force which impelled them was the power of the internal.

To my mind, indeed, the spectacle of Jewish morality is the grandest thing in the world. We see a nation living in order to *be* a nation—influenced in its deepest life by no other motive than the love of country and the transmission of a pure name. It is highly significant of its character, that among the statutes of its moral life there is said to be only one " commandment with promise," only one precept to which there is attached an outward reward,—" Honour thy father and thy mother, that thy days may be long in the land which the Lord thy God giveth thee." Is even this a command with individual promise? No. It is not the man but the nation that is addressed as *thou*. The length of days to which the Israelite looks forward is a duration not for himself, but for his kingdom—a duration in which his family shall be perpetuated from age to age, and his institutions extended from shore to shore. Such a motive as this had nothing of self in it; it had patriotism, it had family affection, but it had no self. The man who had accepted it had relinquished the thought of his own being, had ceased to view himself as anything more than the member of another life. He had entered into one of the sublimest self-surrenders, into one of the completest sacrifices conceivable by human nature or expressible in human history—a sacrifice of which Christianity itself is the climax, and of which Christian aspiration is the mirror. The most spiritual and the most sacrificial of all systems has justly found its root in the life of a nation where the part has been impelled to surrender itself to the whole.

And what is the power by which this surrender has been made? It is the power of morality itself, without extraneous aid. It is this which constitutes the distinctive feature of the Jewish ethics. The son of Israel neither looked forward nor looked backward; he looked *in*. The Parsee had his hope of a consummated glory; the Buddhist had his Nirvana of coming rest; but the Jew was influenced by the hope neither of immortality nor of forgetfulness. He was impelled by the strength of an inward present. The voice of conscience had to him no voice to compete with it; it ruled without a rival and without a second. It issued its absolute mandates, "thou shalt"; "thou shalt not"; from its law there could be no swerving, and from its verdict there could be no appeal. In that attitude Judea stands unique and alone, a spectacle to all ages and an example to all times. She is the one witness in the world to the inherent majesty of moral law. She tells the human race that, beneath the thunder and the earthquake and the fire, there is a still small voice which is more potent than all, a voice that can neither strive nor cry, but is mighty in its calm, clear decidedness. The voice is still speaking in the wilderness. Driven from her home, stripped of her glory, denuded of her kingdom, spoiled of her priestly robes, deprived of her place among the nations, Judea still lives by the echoes of her voice, still exercises authority by the mandate of that inner conscience which, amid the dearth of stars and systems, says from within the veil, "Let there be light."

CHAPTER XVI.

CONCLUSION: CHRISTIANITY AND THE MESSAGES OF THE PAST.

I HAVE not given a separate chapter to the message of Christianity, because by the title of this book I limited myself to the religions older than it. All the phases of faith I have taken up have their origin in a much remoter past, with the exception perhaps of the Teuton; but even the Teuton has long since passed away, and Christianity is still green. I have therefore excluded from formal treatment the bit of ground on which I stand, and have made it rather the pivot of observation than itself a thing to be observed. Now, however, that we have completed our survey, it is not inexpedient to ask what is the Christian message as distinguished from these other messages. That is a point on which we are not left in doubt. In all other cases we have to search the records for their purpose; but here the purpose is revealed by the religion itself. Christianity declares that its mission to the world is one of *reconciliation*.

No religion has ever before claimed to be the bearer of such a message. Neither Brahman, nor Buddhist, nor Parsee, nor Jew, nor Greek, ever aspired to such a destiny. The nearest approach to the aspiration came from the Roman, who aimed, as we have seen, at the incorporation of all things within his own state. But incorporation is not reconciliation. The problem of the Roman could be solved by geography; it placed heterogeneous things side by side, and left them heterogeneous still. But the religion of Christ is not anxious to put things locally together, nor even to make them similar in appearance. It seeks to reconcile them *in* their differences, — to make them, in the very midst of their diversity, work out one common end. It is not eager for uniformity, not solicitous for the recognition of one mode of government, not desirous that all should think on the same plane; it desires that the air may run through the variations, that the diversity of gifts may enfold a unity of the spirit.

Is it possible that the religions of the past may themselves be included in this message of reconciliation? Is it conceivable that Christianity has furnished a ground for peace not only within but without its own fold? Paul says that in Christ "all things stand together"; and it is a most remarkable statement. It seems to suggest that the angles of opposing faiths are rubbed off when they stand in the Christian temple, and that ideas once mutually conflicting can there rest side by side. Do not misunderstand me. I do not for a moment imagine that the first Christians said to themselves, "We shall found a religion which shall embrace the faiths of the world." I do not suppose that any one of these disciples had ever heard of Brahmanism, or Buddhism, or Parsism. But this does not even touch the question. These religions are representative of certain ideas which belong to human nature. If a religion appears which professes to be a universal faith, it must show its universality by uniting these ideas. It must be a ladder reaching from earth unto heaven, each of whose ascending steps shall find a place for one of the systems of the past. Instead of being manifested to reveal the falsity of former views, it must, for the first time, vindicate the truth of all, —must discover a point in which beliefs hitherto deemed at variance may lie down together in unity, and receive from the heart of man a common justification. Let us see whether the religion of Christ will furnish such a meeting-place for the messages of the nations.

In the order of nature the starting-point is the land of Egypt. The message of Egypt, it will be remembered, was the mystery of the boundary-line—the reverence for the spot where one life passes into another. Is there anything in the Christian doctrine which corresponds to this thought? There is. What do we mean by the word "aspiration"? Neither more nor less than the Egyptian meant. Aspiration is simply the effort of one life to pass over into another, to be something other than itself. Christian aspiration is just the soul looking over the boundary-line,—contemplating a life beyond the limits of its own personality, and longing to be like it. Man sees in the glass a figure besides himself, and feels himself passing toward that figure. It has more attraction for him than the form which he actually wears, more control over his movements, more influence over his mind. "I live, yet not I," are the words in which Paul expresses the sense of Christian aspiration. It is the riddle of the Sphinx in the sphere of the gospel. Two lives shoot out from one stem—the one popularly called the real, the other the ideal. One is animal, the other human; one natural, the other spiritual; one at the beginning, the other at the end. While the man yet dwells in the one, he can look out at the window and gaze at the other. He has the power to pass beyond his boundary, to open the casement that encloses him, and rejoice in the anticipation of a life that is not yet come. There is a place for ancient Egypt in the Pantheon of modern Christianity.

But let us go a step further. This desire after another life could not have existed unless by nature that life had been already ours. No man can aspire to anything that has not at some time been his. His longing may be only the result of ancestral descent; but ancestral descent is itself a form of possession.

And so, on the steps of the Christian ladder, we pass from Egypt into India, from the vision of the Sphinx to the creed of the Brahman. The message of Brahmanism, as we found, was the soul's life in God, the proclamation of the truth that the highest reality of things lay above the forms that are seen and temporal. Now, this is precisely the doctrine of Christianity. It proclaims that aspiration is itself God in the soul. Why is it that in the system of Christ such peculiar value is attached to the act of prayer? It is because the desire of God is the memory of God. In any spiritual sphere no man can seek more than he was born to. If he asks for God, it is a proof that he has come from God; his want is itself his birthright, his weakness is his strength. It is here that the gospel of Christ meets with the creed of the Brahman. It declares that in his very destitution, by reason of the very *sense* of his destitution, man is proved to be divine, on a level with that for which he prays; so that the Founder of Christianity Himself has not scrupled to say, "Whatsoever things ye have need of, believe that ye receive them, and ye *have* received them." The Christian has excelled the Brahman in the boldness of his claims. He has declared that his life is already hid with God, that he is even now risen from the grave, that he has passed from death unto life, that he is a citizen of the upper world, that he is seated at God's right hand in the heavenly places, that the divine Life is at this moment dwelling within him. And so vivid is this consciousness, that to him, as to the Brahman, there are times in which every other life is felt to be a shadow, in which this world appears to be but a vain show, but a blaze of stage-scenery, with no present reality and not even a lengthened semblance of reality. What is it that prevents him from going straight to the Brahman's conclusion, and regarding this earthly state as an idle dream?

It is because Christianity here passes from Brahmanism into Parsism. You remember the message of Parsism. It told the world that the shadows which dim the vision of eternity are no dreams, that they are the result of an intense reality—something which has gone wrong in the mechanism of the moral universe. And here Christianity takes up the Parsee's story. It tells me that I dare not regard this scene of time as a series of delusions, dare not persuade myself that I have entered into rest. I have not entered into rest. However much I wish it, however strongly I aspire after it, there is something which holds me back and impedes the movement of my wing. I call it sin, but it matters not much what we call it; it is there, and it is no dream. In this the ancient Parsee[1] and the Christian are at one. They both emphasise the tremendous reality of the

---

[1] I use the expression "*ancient* Parsee" advisedly; modern Parsism has entirely deserted the distinctive tenet of the old religion—its recognition of two Powers.

hindrance to the moral life of man. They both recognise the fact that there is a twofold nature in the human soul—a law in the members warring against the law of the mind, an antagonism of the spirit to the flesh, and of the flesh to the spirit. They both, in accents equally piercing, reveal the same great burden and utter the same great cry, " Oh wretched man that I am! who shall deliver me from this body of death ?"

But with the utterance of that cry Parsism and Christianity part company. With neither is the cry one of despair; yet their ground of hope is different. Parsism looks forward; its hope is for a golden future. But Christianity's first glance is turned backward. The darkest cloud it sees is not in the future but in the past. It feels that, before it can advance into anything golden, it must retrace its steps to undo something in the bygone years. It is here that, as I have pointed out in an earlier chapter of this book, the religion of Christ finds a place for another and a very different religion — the faith of the Chinese empire. We have seen how that empire, spite of its materialism, and notwithstanding its utilitarianism, has been unable to rest in the hour. We have seen how it has been unable even to rest in the prospect of a coming hour. It has sought redemption not so much by the advent of something new as by the clearing away of something old. It aims to get back to the morning that is past, not forward to the morning that is coming. Corruptions have gathered during the day; abuses have accumulated in the circling of the suns. No future morning will avail to wipe these out; each brighter sun will make them only more evident. The shadow itself must be rolled backward on the dial; the past must be unspoken, the word must be unsaid. Here, as I have indicated, is the place in the Christian Pantheon in which the Chinese empire can stand. She is unlike everything else in Asia; but she is justified by Christ. Her place in history is vindicated by the creed of the Son of man. She loses her absurdity, her grotesqueness, her peculiarity, when she stands on the steps of the only ladder which professes to find a foothold for all sorts and conditions of men. The idea which she has ventilated has received a part to play in Christ's message of reconciliation.

And the next place is one for Buddhism. After redemption from the past comes surrender to human brotherhood. Christ, in the system of St Paul, is not an individual; he is the Head of a body— the body of humanity. To surrender myself to Christ, therefore, is to do exactly what the Buddhist does—to yield myself to the service of man. The difference is one not of act but of spirit. It mainly lies in the fact that the Buddhist begins his sacrifice while the past is still pressing on him; the

Christian waits till the burden has been removed. The effect of this is the difference between a sacrifice of despair and a sacrifice of hope. Buddhism, as it appears in Christianity, is not a different star, but the old star in a new position. It shines with the same brightness, but it shines from an opposite locality. It was once lit by grief; it is now illuminated by joy. It was once fired by despondency; it is now inspired by hope. It is no longer prompted by the belief that life is not worth living, and that the essence of existence is pain. It arises rather from the consciousness that life has revealed undreamt-of possibilities of expansion, and from a conviction that the most seemingly hopeless soul may yet be partaker of unclouded joy. The Buddhism of Christianity is impelled to the Cross by the crown.

And, the result of this surrender is the reappearance on the Christian ladder of that faith which it superseded—Judaism. "Love is the fulfilling of the law," are the words in which Christianity itself proclaims the possibility that, in a new order of things, Moses may live again. Judaism failed to keep a perfect morality, because the keeping of a perfect morality was its aim; the obstruction of self-consciousness was created by the thought of self-righteousness. But the religion of Christ declares that, if love came first, there would be no fear of failure. It declares that, if a man, instead of seeking his own perfection, could begin by fixing his affections on a perfect ideal, he would be borne into law through love. The message of Judaism was the power of the internal—the proclamation that all strength came from within. But Judaism herself never got far enough in to have much power. It did not reach the centre—the heart. Christianity found the mine for which Judaism was seeking. It touched the most subterranean spring in human nature, and unsealed the deepest well from which the waters of the life can flow—the impulse of the affections. It made the yoke of morality easy and its burden light. It enabled men to leap at a bound over paths which hitherto had taxed their utmost energy. It outran the commandments contained in ordinances; it went beyond the letter; it did more than was expected of it; it left Moses in the rear. The law of Christ goes further than the law of Sinai, and secures more success in its observance. Sinai forbids to hurt; but Calvary commands to heal. Sinai forbids to impose a yoke; Calvary commands to bear a burden. Sinai forbids to pass the beggar on the highway; Calvary commands to *seek* as well as save. The law of Moses has received in Christ more than it lost in Judaism; it has found in Him its "times for the restitution of all things."

And, in proportion as the moral law increases in the power of its observance, will a place be found in the Christian Pantheon for the ideas of Greece and

Rome. We defined the position of Greece to be the reverence for the present as distinguished from either the past or the future. Such a state of things cannot exist now; but religion is at one with science in hoping for a time when it shall exist. Christianity and modern science profess to differ in many things, but they are agreed in the anticipation of a golden age for man, an age in which the present order of things shall be perfected and glorified. To this time of completed evolution the message of Greece may look forward for its fulfilment. Alike from the scientific and from the Christian stand-point, we may contemplate the coming of a day when the earth itself shall be worthy of reverence, when the passing hour shall be worth preserving, and the present shall be valued for itself alone. What does Paul mean when he says, "The creation itself shall be delivered from the bondage of corruption into the glorious liberty of the sons of God"? Is it not simply a prediction that the time is coming in which the aspirations of Greece shall be fulfilled, when poetry shall speak the language of prose, and beauty shall become itself a teacher of truth? The Roman too has his place in this vision of the glorious liberty of the sons of God. I have shown, in a previous chapter, how the Roman ideal of a son of God was itself but a premature and abortive effort to realise a Christian conception. It was the search for a kingdom which should embrace under its sway all other kingdoms, which, without destroying diversities of nature, should keep the unity of law. We have seen how the ideal of Rome was above her power. Her power was only physical, and therefore it could not rule without crushing. But, as I have already pointed out, Christianity offers to the old Roman religion a realisation of its dream. ' It tells of a dominion which she extends from sea to sea without destroying the sea—without obliterating the boundaries that now divide, or annihilating the diversities that now distinguish. It shows us this kingdom already existing in miniature, already growing in strength, already prophetic of its future fulness; and, by the very presentation of the vision, it connects the modern with the ancient world, and joins the culture of the later age with the civilisation of an age that has passed away.

Nor has the message of the Teuton been omitted in this accumulation of thought which has gathered round the religion of the Cross. It will be remembered that we defined this message to be the association of development with the idea of divinity. I indicated that the novelty lay in the association. Progress was not a new idea as applied to the affairs of *men*. But in the mythology of the Teuton the scene of the progressive drama is laid not in earth but heaven, and the growth through the successive stages is a growth among the gods. Here is a thought sufficiently bold to challenge our attention, and specially striking among a people whose earliest reverence was for the idea of complete and instantaneous power. To say that the Divine Life can itself partake in the changes of the universe, to admit that the Absolute Spirit can be affected by the transmutations of existence, is a less natural thought than in modern times it seems. Brahmanism appears to hold it; but it is only in appearance. The universe of the Brahmin is an illusion; there is no real movement either of the human or of the divine, and nothing reigns but everlasting stillness. But with the Teuton it is all the reverse: the world is a reality; the external world is a special reality. The acts of the gods are no parts of a sleeping consciousness; the changes in the life of the gods are no interludes of a dream. The drama in heaven is a real drama; the progress is a genuine progress. The growth of the Divine Life is distinctively the message of the Teuton.

But, unique as it is among the religions of the world, it is vindicated in that faith which professes to find a place for all. In Christianity, as in the mythology of the Teuton, we meet the same otherwise anomalous doctrine that the Divine Life can grow. Here the kingdom of heaven is compared not to something which is fashioned and finished from the beginning, but to a seed which is cast into the ground, which is at first the least of all seeds, which is long hid from the view of the beholder, which lies for days and nights unnoticed, and which, at last, springs up, he cannot tell how. Paul declares in the boldest language that there is a "law of the Spirit of Life." He means that the Spirit of Life has made itself subject to the progress of humanity, has flowed with man's growth and ebbed with man's arrested development. He tells us that the Christian life—the life of the Eternal—is itself a process of incarnation, by which the stages of humanity are conquered one by one, a process by which the infant becomes a child, the child a youth, and the youth a full-grown man. We see the life born amid trouble, hid in obscurity, reared in subjection, tried by temptation, matured by suffering, ripened by crucifixion, and only reaching its perfect beauty at the end of the days. We see first the blade, then the ear, afterward the full corn in the ear. Yet we are taught to think of the process as divine from the very beginning—divine in its germ, divine in its struggle, divine in its consummation. The message of the Teuton has been redelivered by the Spirit of Christ; it has received its justification from the religion of humanity.

I have thus endeavoured to show that the appearance of Christianity has been accompanied by a resurrection from the dead. It is popularly said to have conquered the faiths of the past. And so it has; but in a very peculiar way. It has conquered as the Roman empire wished to conquer—not by submergence, but by incorporation. It would not be true to say that it has destroyed them; it would be more correct to affirm that it has kept them alive. They had all outgrown their youth, all survived their time, all failed to bring rest to the soul. The form remained; the sensuous life remained; but the spirit had passed away. If Christianity had not appeared, paradoxical as it may seem, I think these religions would have become supremely uninteresting; Christianity has made them vivid by making them living. In its many-sidedness it has a side for each of these. It has let in its light upon them; it has given its breath to them; it has found a place for them in its own system. It has given them a logical order which has dispelled the contradictions of the natural order. Indian and Greek, Roman and Teuton, Buddhist and Parsee, Egyptian and Chinaman, can meet here hand in hand; because in the comprehensive temple of Christian truth there is not only a niche which each may fill, but a niche which, at some stage of its development, must be filled by one and all.

Therefore it is that the religion of Christ ought to have peculiar interest in the faiths of the past. They are not, to her, dead faiths; they are not even modernised. They are preserved inviolable as parts of herself—more inviolable than they would have been if she had never come. Christianity has claimed to be "the manifold wisdom of God." In this ascription she has been candid to the past. She has not denied its wisdom; she has only aspired to enfold it. She has not sought to derogate from the doctrines of antiquity; she has only sought to diminish their antagonisms. China may keep her materialism, and India may retain her mysticism; Rome may grasp her strength, and Greece may nurse her beauty; Persia may tell of the opposition to God's power, and Egypt may sing of His pre-eminence even amid the tombs: but for each and all there is a seat in the Christian Pantheon, and a justification in the light of the manifold wisdom of God.

THE END.

PRINTED BY WILLIAM BLACKWOOD AND SONS.

www.ingramcontent.com/pod-product-compliance
Lightning Source LLC
Chambersburg PA
CBHW032354230426
43672CB00007B/703